Francis Xavier Weninger

Photographic Views

Or, Religious and moral Truths reflected in the Universe. Second Edition

Francis Xavier Weninger

Photographic Views
Or, Religious and moral Truths reflected in the Universe. Second Edition

ISBN/EAN: 9783337128616

Printed in Europe, USA, Canada, Australia, Japan

Cover: Foto ©ninafisch / pixelio.de

More available books at **www.hansebooks.com**

PHOTOGRAPHIC VIEWS;

OR,

RELIGIOUS AND MORAL TRUTHS

REFLECTED IN THE

UNIVERSE.

SECOND EDITION.

By F. X. WENINGER, D.D.,
Of the Society of Jesus.

NEW YORK:
P. O'SHEA, Publisher.
1873.

Entered according to Act of Congress,
In the year one thousand eight hundred and seventy-two,
By F. X. WENINGER,
In the office of the Librarian of Congress, at Washington.

INTRODUCTION.

BEFORE opening this photographic gallery of moral and religious truths, we must premise a few words, in order that the attentive reader may the better understand the bearing of these pictures when presented to his mind. No doubt there exists a deep and mysterious connection between intellectual truth and its reflection in the mind, and even in the exterior world.

The mysterious depth of the Divine Nature itself, through the eternal generation of the Word, the second Person in the Godhead, points to this fact. St. Paul calls the Eternal Word "the figure of the substance" of God the Father.

The nature of the human soul also bears witness to this relation, for, as Holy Writ testifies, it is an image of the Divine Nature.

The most essential operations of the soul partake of this character.

First, our intellectual operations evidently depend on the connection existing between the intellectual truth and its reflection, the word. For, without some interior word, thinking would be impossible. Now, what is a word but the formal reflection of some thought, and consequently of some truth contained therein? Hence, in forming words, when speaking aloud, the use of the figure called *onomatopœia*, to imitate, if possible, even by the sound of the word, the meaning of what we desire to express.

Next to spoken words, signs, and, among civilized nations, writing are used as a means of communicating our ideas.

Now, what is the language of signs but the typical manifestation of what we think? And what is writing but a conventional type representing our thoughts? The Chinese characters, which are the oldest, are purely typical; and in our Western languages, the letters used by the press are very properly called *types*. History proves that, even before the invention of writing, men were instinctively led to clothe their knowledge in the mysterious garb of figurative representations. It was the pride and the boast of Egypt, the birthplace of ancient learning, to convey the truth by hieroglyphics.

Introduction.

To the eyes of the Christian thinker, the whole world appears filled with innumerable symbolical figures—hieroglyphics—expressive of moral and religious truths. To discover these truths by simply glancing at these figures is the object of his most sublime contemplations. In this manner, truth itself is often better and more clearly understood in all its bearings. We have an evident proof of this fact in ascetical matters. Let us suppose a Saint to be speaking of great supernatural favors which he enjoyed in his union with God. Through want of personal experience, many a listener would find his language almost unintelligible. But one comparison will often throw so wonderful a light upon the subject as to make it almost intelligible, even to the uninitiated. Witness the writings of St. Teresa. Those who have not been favored with the experience of the Saint, must find it difficult, nay, impossible, to fathom her meaning when she speaks of "the flight and rapture of the spirit." But as soon as she has recourse to a comparison, her meaning becomes clearer, and even the inexperienced may form at least some idea of it. Concerning this "flight of the spirit" toward God, by means of an interior elevation, the Saint writes as follows: "It seems to me that the soul and the spirit must be one thing. I find no other difference between them than that existing between a brightly burning fire and its flame. The fire remains below, but the flame flashes upward; nevertheless, the fire and the flame are one thing. So, also, when the soul, by the influence of God, is burning with the fire of His love, she sends forth a flame, which is the upward flight of the spirit, not distinguishable from the soul itself, but so subtile and swift that it ascends into the superior regions, wherever God pleases to elevate it."

Every one perceives how this figurative and emblematic representation of St. Teresa assists the reader to understand her meaning.

Another proof of this mysterious connection between truth and its type is found in the vivacity and power of poetry. The figurative expressions of truth furnish our minds with the wings of poetical rapture. The truth, elevation, and dignity of poetical representations depend on the choice, correctness, power, and sublimity of the comparisons employed. The real poet is like a painter; with the vivid colors of his fancy he portrays the truth, and sketches a picture of thought.

In many instances, even the persuasive powers of the orator must be aided and sustained by the use of figurative expressions.

The ingenious application of figurative expressions imparts even to our conversation a great part of that charm and grace called *wit*.

All that has been hitherto said in regard to truth and its expression by the aid of figurative forms, is confirmed by the example and authority of Holy Writ. St. Paul, as we have observed, refers to the typical character of the relations between God the Son and God the Father.

The same Apostle calls the whole economy and institution of the Old Testament "typical and figurative"—a foreshadowing of the New Testament.

The Church militant stands in the same relation to the Church triumphant.

According to the Apostle, the end of all the manifestations of Divine wisdom and mercy is to renew in us the likeness of God. *Coloss. III.* 10.

The very language of the Bible is eminently figurative. If it were for no other reason, the correctness, the grandeur and sublimity of the comparisons would render the Sacred Scriptures, even in a literary point of view, superior to all the efforts of merely human eloquence.

All know how Christ, the Incarnate Word of God, communicated truth to mankind by the aid of typical representations. It had been written of Him long before His coming: "He will open His mouth in parables." (*Ps* 77.) And the Gospel relates: "Without parables He did not speak to them."

Finally, the very manner employed in writing these photographic views became to the author a most striking proof of the correctness of his views on the subject. For neither study nor labor was required in their conception; he had merely to let the manifold objects of the universe pass before him in review, and to note rapidly the flashes of light reflecting the moral and religious truths contained in this volume.

Nature, indeed, seems to be electrified by the truth of faith, so that coming in contact with the contemplative intellect, these relations, like electric sparks, flash upon the mind, to the great delight and surprise of the Christian thinker. Or, to change the figure, it may be affirmed that the exterior or typical manifestation of truth is the pulse of a mysterious life, hidden in nature through its relations to faith, so that we may apply to it the words in which the Church prays: " Regem Cui omnia vivunt Venite adoremus"—Let us adore the King to Whom all things live. In this sense, St. Augustine, according to another reading of the Bible, interprets the words of St. John: " Quod factum est, in Ipso vita erat"—What was made, was life in Him.

So viewed, all nature, inanimate as well as animate, speaks to the heart, and becomes a teacher, as we read in the book of Job: "Ask the beasts, and they shall teach thee; and the birds of the air, and they shall tell thee. Speak to the earth, and it shall answer thee, and the fishes of the sea shall tell."

So, for us, all creatures may become guides pointing to God, our Creator and Redeemer, and to the way of salvation, conducting us by the hand toward heaven, where we shall see God Himself, the Infinite Truth, not dimly, as in a mirror, but face to face.

THE AUTHOR.

Feast of the Transfiguration, a. d. 1872.

INTRODUCTION.

Part I.

THE WORLD.

	PAGES.
Nature in General,	1 – 7
The Firmament,	7 – 9
The Sun,	9 – 20
Stars—Meteors—Comets,	20 – 29
Air, Rain, Storms, Lightning, Rainbow,	29 – 39
Light, Color,	40 – 44
Fire,	44 – 56
The Seasons,	56 – 59
Mountains, Hills and Plains,	60 – 71
Water—Streams—the Ocean,	72 – 79
Fields and Gardens,	80 – 84
Plants and Trees,	85 – 92
Flowers and Fruits,	93 –103
Animals,	104–128
The Interior of the Earth,	129–135

Part II.

MAN.

The Body—its Senses and Members,	136–153
The Soul—its Faculties, Sources of Knowledge,	154–165
Man considered in Society—Language,	166–178
Social Intercourse	179–207
Civilization—the Fine Arts—Painting,	208–217
Music,	218–228
Sculpture—Architecture,	229–233

Part III.

GOD.

	Pages.
Man in relation to God,	235-250
Christ,	251-271
The Word of God,	272-292
Our Life for God,	293-312
Models of Perfection—The Saints,	313-316
The Angels,	317-321
The Way of Perfection,	322-340
Means of Perfection—the Sacraments,	341-345
The Most Holy Eucharist,	346-360
The State of Perfection,	361-372

Part I.

THE WORLD.

NATURE IN GENERAL.

CONTEMPLATING the Universe in its general aspect, we behold a scene of noble, quiet, imposing grandeur, united with an unremitting energy. Our life in the service of God should be marked with the same characteristic qualities. But how different the picture that meets our view when we turn to the children of men! The vast majority of them, instead of reflecting in their conduct the grandeur of the universe, lower themselves to the dust by their groveling desires and vain self-seeking. Instead of imitating its unshaken firmness, they are whirled about by every blast of trial and vanity.

There are in nature especially two powers, which preserve the order and harmony of the visible world: they are *attraction* and *repulsion*. The same may be remarked of the *moral* world. By *attraction*, our free will, to be consistent, consents to what is good; by *repulsion*, it rejects what is evil.

✸

In regard to *social* life, the great principle of order, development, political success, and prosperity is also that of an attractive and repulsive force, by which men, singly or formed into societies. seek to draw to them whatever tends to promote their success, and to repel whatever opposes it. Herein is hidden the mystery of the diplomatic art, and even the happiness of the domestic circle seems to depend on the well-regulated efficiency of this twofold power. Blessed is the family in which all the members are attracted by mutual love and linked together by the golden chain of affection, and where everything that interferes with this blissful union is carefully rejected and repelled.

✸

How happy and united would society in general be, if all men were ever influenced by the attractive power of the love of God and our neighbor, and by the repulsive power of every kind of hatred and aversion. This world would then resemble an earthly paradise.

✸

What would be the consequence of the violation of this great principle of attractive and repulsive power in Nature? The utter destruction of the world. In regard to the family circle, its consequence is misery; in regard to civil life, rebellion; in regard to morality, sin; in regard to eternity, hell.

*

The other great natural principle of order and subsistence is *equilibrium*. This power also has its reflex in human life. Equilibrium is the first thing a child must learn in order to walk. Equilibrium enables us to stand with safety upon the edge of a precipice, and keep our balance upon a slender rope. Equilibrium sends the vessel in the proper direction, and steers it safely through the dangers of the ocean. Equilibrium is the great principle of peace in the social and moral world. Our will must maintain a perfect equilibrium among created things, solicitous only to know and accomplish the holy will of God, our true center of gravity.

*

The universe is, as it were, suspended in the emptiness of space. Nature is deeply absorbed in contemplative quiet; the starry firmament, especially, seems to be immovably balanced in a ravishing and harmonious repose, while our globe gazes in silent admiration toward heaven. Nevertheless, what mighty but deeply hidden causes are constantly acting and producing the most wonderful changes! The return of each successive Spring gives new proof of this universal, harmonious, and powerful activity, by which in perfect silence nature weaves for herself a new garment. So the most contemplative life of the faithful servants of God is, in some degree, always joined to one of the greatest activity, directed, of course, to the glory of God, the welfare of our neighbor, and our own growth in virtue. St. Bernard, St. Francis Xavier, St. Teresa, and many other saints are like mirrors, which reflect this beautiful union of a contemplative with a powerfully active life.

*

The earth seems to be immensely large, while the sun and stars appear comparatively small; yet the size of many of the heavenly bodies far surpasses that of our globe. So, in the eyes of man, the fleeting pleasures of this world are great, while the eternal joys of Heaven pass for mean and insignificant. But, oh! how sad the delusion! How infinitely more precious than aught below are the treasures hidden behind the stars!

*

Behold how Nature exemplifies the truth, that true greatness and excellence are often combined with exterior humiliation. The brilliant orbs that light up the heavens seem to our eyes but little sparks of light. The splendor of the sun may be obscured by a mist or fog, leaving us buried in darkness and gloom. The moon looks modestly down upon the earth, as if she would confess that her light is only borrowed. Jewels and precious metals lie deeply embedded in the ground. The sparkling pearl and gleaming coral are buried in the caverns of the shadowy deep. The best fruit-trees are usually dwarfed and crooked. The most aromatic spices have the appearance of worthless grains. Then, look at the world of flowers! The most fragrant are arrayed in simple though delicate colors. Witness the modest violet! The vanilla, and nearly all aromatics, are lowly, unpretending shrubs. The rich herbage with which the meadows are carpeted, the most sweetly scented flowers with which they are sprinkled, all creep along the ground. Would not the woodland songsters, which warble the sweetest notes, pass unnoticed in an aviary, because they are not decked with gorgeous plumage? The nightingale, the sweetest songster in the world, is also the most plainly attired. Purple is the distinctive color of royalty, and silk the richest material for clothing; yet the one is the juice of a little fish, and the other the production of an insignificant worm.

*

In many cases, the beauties of Nature are hidden from man until, by cultivating and developing her powers, he unvails them to the eye. What wildernesses were Belgium and Italy before their cultivation! So the grace of God imparts to our actions the beauty and value of true virtue. Yet we must co-operate. The strength, efficacy, grandeur, majesty, and sublimity of genuine virtue, and the wonderful grace and beauty of fervent piety, will become more and more visible only in proportion to our personal efforts to co-operate with God.

*

Turn around the most beautiful painting, and on the back you will see nothing—a mere blank. Nature also, though bearing on its face the colors and delineations of Divine Omnipotence, Wisdom, and Goodness, exhibits on the other side a mere blank. For it sprang out of nothingness, and in its own essence could not subsist, but would return to nothing.

Time and space are by their very nature without definite bounds, therefore capable of illimited extension. These two primitive conditions of creative existence beautifully point to eternity. It was an eternal decree of the Divine Will which brought the world from nothing to existence in space, changeable indeed, but never to pass away for all the time to come.

*

The sense of our own nothingness, through true humility, is for the creation of grace in our hearts what the possibility of space was for the creation of the visible world.

*

"God, in whose presence I am." This was the familiar expression of the ancient patriarchs. The universe seems to be ever giving utterance to the same thought by its solemn silence. How wonderfully sublime is the silence of Nature; and how deeply we are impressed by it when alone on the summit of a high mountain, or in the deep shadows of a mighty forest, or on the shore of the quiet ocean! Still more sublime is the awful silence of the starry firmament; and yet this mysterious silence is far more eloquent in the praise of God than myriads of tongues.

*

In contemplative silence, earth seems to listen to the strains of heavenly harmony, which, as Scripture affirms, are incessantly telling the glory of God. And, on the other hand, the stars seem to gaze with undying interest upon the wonders of Divine Grace and Love which are hourly performed upon the surface of the globe, the chosen spot of God's unspeakable mercies, and of His own Incarnation through love.

THE FIRMAMENT.

THE firmament, adorned with millions of stars, radiant with the splendor of the sun, announces, as Holy Writ affirms, the glory of God. No sound is heard, and nevertheless what sublime praise of God is contained in this silent homage! So the lives of the Saints, adorned with millions of illustrious deeds done for the glory of God, and made resplendent by the rays of the Sun of Justice, give praise to God, even after they have entered the silence of death. Their works are speaking, and we hear their praise of God with admiration.

*

The name of the firmament indicates the quality by which it especially announces the glory of God, the Creator. That name expresses the steadfastness of the world's subsistence, the regularity of its movement in free space, and the fidelity with which the laws of Nature are observed. It means order, harmony, and exactness. Order—that every one of the celestial orbs is in its place. Harmony—in accordance with all the others. Exactness—that, in its movement, it keeps its appointed time through thousands of years. These are the three charms by which the firmament is distinguished in creation

The lives of the Saints are distinguished also by these properties among the lives of men. They became Saints by the steadfastness of their resolution to become Saints. Order, harmony, and the most punctual exactness in the service of God are, and were always, the characteristic qualities of the lives of the Saints as true servants of God.

*

God, as Holy Scripture attests, ordered the heavens especially to regulate time—to divide years, and months, and days, hours, minutes, and seconds. Happy, if we listen to that solemn admonition continually addressed to us by the starry firmament, viz: Keep your time! That value of time made men become Saints and remain Saints.

*

The firmament has no apparent support; its firmness is grounded on God's omnipotence alone, whose will is its foundation in the empty space. So we have to repose, in our service of God, only in God, and in the power of His grace, conscious of our nothingness. His most holy will, confidence in His never-failing Divine Providence, has to be the immovable foundation on which our firmness in His Divine service is grounded; a confidence which never can be too great, and which has inspired all the Saints to do the great things they did for the glory of God.

THE SUN.

GOD has set the sun and the moon in the firmament to give us light. To the eye of man, these two orbs appear to be of almost equal dimensions; but, after all, how widely different is their power of giving light! In like manner, God has placed reason and faith in the human mind. At first view, these two enlightening powers seem to be of equal importance, and yet how great a disparity exists between them! Reason by itself is a guide only for our moral and social conduct as citizens of this globe. If ever it places itself between man and faith, intercepting the rays which fall on him from above, the soul can no longer live the supernatural life of the children of light.

*

The sun diffuses light over the face of Nature, and sheds upon everything the splendor of day; the moon gives but a glimmering radiance, and a figure resembling the face of a man peers out of it. The size of the sun always remains the same; that of the moon increases and wanes. So, sincere zeal for the glory of God is ever unchangeable, imparting life and light to our daily actions; while the zeal of self-interest, on the contrary, is extremely variable, and our own likeness may always be observed shining through it.

✻

Though so great and luminous a body, the sun begins his daily course in profound silence, and yet the very first beam which he sends forth is perceived. Real greatness does not need the applause and recommendation of others; it makes itself known and appreciated.

✻

From the very moment of rising, the sun, to our eye at least, is continually advancing toward its setting. Its motion is so gradual that we scarcely notice it, and yet, because its course is constant, it crosses in a few hours the immense expanse of the sky. This admonishes us how much virtue lies in a constant activity, especially in regard to our daily service of God. If the sunlight of a right intention always fell upon our actions; if, strangers to idleness, we hourly pressed forward in the way of Christian perfection, how marked would be our progress from day to day!

✻

The sun continues on its daily course as well through a cloudy as through a clear sky. It moves with the same steadiness amidst the darkness of rising tempests, the lurid glare of lightning, and the roar of rolling thunders, as along the serene canopy of heaven. If we, in like manner, go on in the service of God, no less in the season of adversity and persecution than in the time of consolation and exterior applause, with what marked success shall we move toward our last end! If, on the contrary, we pause on the way to sanctity, who can estimate the loss which we sustain, even in one day! There is no comparison between a single degree of perfection, with its merits and recompense in heaven, and this world's greatest riches.

*

The sun, rising higher and higher, loses none of its heat and invigorating power, but rather becomes more productive and efficacious in proportion as it approaches the zenith. So a real increase in recollection, uniting the soul more and more closely to her Creator, does not render her less active, less capable of good, less fit for her daily duties; on the contrary, it greatly increases her influence for promoting the greater glory of God and the salvation of mankind.

*

Christ is the Eternal "Sun of Justice, that has penetrated the heavens." Seated at the right hand of His Father, He is surely not less powerful and active for the welfare of His Church, and of every soul in it, than when He abode with us on earth. Nay, He now manifests this power of fructifying and producing all the more evidently and gloriously, even as does the sun when elevated to its zenith.

*

True devotion elevates the heart and mind toward heaven. But it would be a great mistake to suppose, that it should therefore divest itself of its influence on our daily life on earth. On the contrary, as the sun from its height gives light, and life, and fertility to the globe, in proportion to its elevation, so a real elevation of devotion by our union with God, according to its height, influences our daily life for a higher degree of sanctification.

*

During the whole day the sun seems to scan, with ever watchful eye, the surface of the world, as if solicitous to do its duty and to see that all is well. We ought, in like manner, to watch over our actions, with the utmost care, and to see that they be performed in the proper spirit.

*

The earth, on the other hand, appears to look continually at the sun and to take advantage of its gifts. In fact, without the light of the sun, there would be no life, no color, no blossoms, no fruits. So should man, in his every action, turn toward heaven and study Christ our Savior, who is called "The Sun of Justice," and who, in regard to grace and merit, is the light of the world, and the source whence are derived the color of virtue and all vital activity for everlasting life.

*

There is only one sun and there is only one God. There is one great source of light that sheds its effulgence over the earth; and there is only one first principle of grace and power, from which every beam of holiness and authority emanates. No matter how fine that beam, it is yet connected with its eternal center, just as, through all the immense distance of space, the farthest point of the sun's ray is connected with the sun in heaven.

*

The light, splendor, and warmth of the sun are beautiful emblems of the three theological virtues. Faith enlightens our souls; Hope makes them resplendent with virtue; Love casts a sweet and genial warmth over our entire being.

*

Christ calls Himself the light of the world. Like it, He diffuses the splendor of His grace and doctrine, with equal power, in all directions. The difference in the effect produced, depends altogether upon the position in which men are exposed to the rays of the uncreated Light.

*

"Christ to-day, yesterday, and forever," all give witness of Him—the past, the present, and the future. We have only to open the eyes of our intellect, to recognize the Divine character of His person, and of the work which He completed on earth, as we have only to open our eyes to see the sun in the blue sky.

*

They, who take a *siesta* during the day, draw curtains before the windows to shut out the dazzling brightness of the sunlight. The devil acts in like manner, when he wishes to keep the soul asleep. How could Christians, with the brilliant radiance of Faith shining upon them, remain in the state of sin? What, then, does the devil do? He draws before their minds the curtains of carelessness, of indifference, of doubt, of prejudice, or of ignorance, as the case may be. These curtains so effectually exclude the light of Faith, and throw such a shadow over the mind, that the sinner reposes upon the couch of his passions with perfect unconcern. If, at times, Reason and Reflection stretch out their hands to draw aside these blinds, awakened passion hastens to interfere; and so the sinner is left undisturbed in his fatal slumber.

*

The arch-enemy is equally solicitous to prevent the infidel from being aroused by the light of Faith. He carefully draws curtains of illusory reasons before his mind, and often succeeds in keeping the conscience in darkness, till the sleeper is buried in the lethargy of utter indifference.

*

Though the sun is so brilliant and luminous a body, its light may be diminished and obscured by clouds that pass before it. After nightfall, darkness is spread over the earth, like a pall, though the sun remains in the firmament on the other side of the globe. Faith is a light more luminous than the sun itself; nevertheless, that light may be diminished, nay, almost entirely hidden, by clouds which rise from the heart and darken the intellect of man. In the tender years of childhood, the clouds of a mind still undeveloped prevent the efficacy of the enlightening gift of Faith. Then alas! with each successive year, the mist of passion rises more densely from the heart, and dims that light, till the love of man is completely turned away from his Creator, and he becomes guilty of mortal sins of habit. Then does that light become lost in darkness, and the sun of Faith refuse its vivifying heat. But it has not left forever; it still shines as if it were upon another hemisphere. The shades of night fall around that heart, till, by a real conversion, it returns again to God.

*

In the polar lands, the sun appears to come upon the horizon before it rises; but this phenomenon is only a cold and lifeless counterfeit of the "King of day." A similar illusion often takes place in those from whose souls divine Faith has departed, and who are in the polar land of infidelity. They fancy that they see the sun of truth in many of their illusory axioms and systems; but they are deceived. It is only a phantasm, but not the sun of truth.

*

The same illusion takes place in every little pool. Though the water is muddy, we see reflected in its depths the orb of the sun, whose position now appears changed, though it still revolves above and not below. So to the sinner it seems that he will find in the muddy water of his passions the gratification of his desires; but he will one day discover that it was a mere illusion, and that he was pursuing a phantom.

*

The very appearance of the sun, from its rising till its setting, seems solemnly to proclaim, "All for the greater glory of God." For, from the dawn of day, the sun sends forth its beams in all directions through the universe to *serve* and to *glorify* Him, who first said: "Let light be: and light was;" and *to enable* us to behold the wonderful works of God and give Him praise.

*

What is more resplendent to the eyes of men than the sun, which appears to surround with a halo every object on earth? Yet how feeble is its radiance compared with the splendor shed over the world by the glorified humanity of Jesus Christ in the Blessed Sacrament! If a million suns were to unite their lustre, what a flood of light would they pour around creation! Upon the many altars of the Catholic Church, there are millions of consecrated Hosts. With what brilliancy, then, must they not shine in the sight of God's angels, who, from their heavenly home, contemplate the universe!

*

To this glory spread over the earth, by the presence of our Lord, we must add the effusion of the Divine light of grace imparted by the administration of the Sacraments of the Holy Church. Most assuredly, in the eyes of the angels, our earth becomes the jewel of creation, reflecting more wonders of Divine Providence than all the rest of the universe. When we consider this perpetual dwelling of the Son of God upon earth, are we not naturally led to look upon the sun as a "lamp of the sanctuary," burning before the tabernacle of the globe?

*

From the moment of rising, the sun appears to look forward, without ceasing, to the West, and, when setting, it seems to cast a glance back to the East, whence it started, as if to examine how it has run its course; its last, as well as its first, beam is sent forth to heaven. There is hidden in this phenomenon another advice for our daily life. On awaking in the morning, we must, first of all, make the good intention of doing everything for the greater glory of God, seeking nothing but the fulfillment of His holy will; just as the sun, from dawn to the last light of day, obeys the laws which the Author of Nature has established. Let us, then, call to mind successively the different events of the day—what we shall have to do before its close, what persons we may meet, into what circumstances we may be thrown. In the evening, a careful examination of conscience should prove, whether we have been faithful to our resolve. Our last act ought to be the renewal of the intention, " All for God," accompanied by affections of thanksgiving and love.

*

If the setting sun does not thus review its path, but, on the contrary, hides its face behind a dark, dull mass of clouds, we look upon it as foreboding bad weather for the coming day. In like manner, if the evening examination of conscience be neglected, it does not argue well for our advancement in perfection on the morrow.

*

The aurora at daybreak, and the evening red at sunset, very beautifully typify the practice of morning and night prayer. As the sun sketches its first and last splendors on the broad canvas of the sky, Nature glows under its magic pencil with a deeper tinge. Just so our morning prayer ought to glow with the desire of loving and glorifying God on the new-born day, and our night prayer with the fervor of gratitude for all the good which, as a pledge of future bliss, He has bestowed upon us.

*

See how modestly the sun begins its daily course, humbly peeping from behind the hills, as if asking leave to rise. The aurora, which heralds its approach, may be likened to the roseate blush of modesty. One who never beheld the king of day, in his noontide glory, could form no idea of the heat, light, and life, which he imparts to the earth, as, in radiant majesty, he rides along the firmament. Again, when evening approaches, and he sinks behind the western hills, he bids farewell with the same charming modesty that marked his rising, yet with more grandeur and solemnity. He who delivers a sermon should learn a lesson from the sun. To begin with an air of too great confidence is altogether improper; unassuming modesty rather should prevail in the opening of an address. The speaker may then develop his matter, and, with due force and the full weight of reasoning, throw all the light possible upon his subject till he reaches the culminating point; and his arguments become unanswerable. At this stage, his hearers will not be displeased at a display of superior intellectual power and logical strength; they will rather expect it and respect it. But, as the discourse draws to its close, the speaker should resume a more quiet bearing, and apply the truths proposed to the end for which we were placed on earth, namely, "To love and serve God in this life, and dwell with Him in a happy eternity." Thus will he color, with a master's touch, the close of his address, as the sinking sun paints with his dying splendors the last hours of the day. Practical applications and appeals to our devotion, after logical arguments, are like gentle breezes that refresh us at the sunset of a sermon; whereas arguments alone would have left us panting in the heat and glare of noonday.

*

A rosy color in the sky betokens wet or murky weather. The same may be said of such as meet everything with careless hilarity, fancying that, because fortune has tinged their horizon with gorgeous hues, no clouds shall rise to dim its glory. Persons who thus trifle with the future are often in a short time thrown into great embarrassments, and, when undeceived, discover the truth of the saying: "All is not gold that glitters." We must view life with manly earnestness, and not glide through it in childlike sport and giddy self-assurance.

*

The concentration of the solar rays increases their power to such a degree that, even in winter, they may be made to ignite tinder. A similar effect is produced, in a moral point of view, by recollection of mind. He who walks in the presence of God may, even in the winter of desolation, concentrate the rays of ordinary graces to such an extent as to kindle in his heart the fire of heavenly love.

*

On the contrary, even in the torrid zone, the rays of the sun, if dispersed, lose their effect. Dissipation of mind renders the most powerful inspirations of grace ineffective.

*

It is not the fault of the sun that a vail as of night enshrouds the eyes of him, who, by his own free will, shuts his eyes and says, There is no sun. Nor is it the fault of God, if the night of infidelity overtakes the man who turns away from Him, and says in his heart, "There is no God."

*

It is not the fault of the sun, if darkness pervades an apartment when the shutters are closed. The person who willfully excludes the light of day is the only one to be taken to task. Apply this comparison to the spiritual life. The sun of mercy and Faith sends forth its light to illumine and bless the infidel and the sinner, as well as the believer and the just man. But if, of their own accord, they close their eyes to its enlightening rays, and prefer the shadows of sophistry, the darkness in which they walk can be attributed to them alone.

STARS—METEORS—COMETS.

EACH successive year finds Nature busily engaged in painting the earth with new and beautiful colors. The seasons come and go, and the chilly hand of Winter annually tears away the garments in which Spring has clothed all things. Only the firmament, with its glittering stars, remains ever the same. So all things below are transitory—only those above remain forever. The means of reaching the latter is perseverance.

*

Even if we bid adieu to our dearest friends, the sun, moon, and stars accompany us to the extremities of the globe. They remind us, that our only true and constant friend is heaven.

*

From the surface of the earth, we behold the milky-way as a mist of light, produced and reflected by myriad clusters of stars. Upon the mountain-tops this misty appearance dissolves, and a brilliant flood of rays is poured upon the sight. By the aid of the telescope, the eye perceives an endless number of blazing worlds swimming in the farthest depths of space. So, in a purely human view, the revealed truths of holy Faith may seem to man dim, and, as it were, covered with a mist; but on the clear heights of pious contemplation they shine in distinct beauty, and brilliantly illuminate the way to heaven.

*

A man who looks into a limpid stream, and sees in it a reflection of the starry firmament, would be sadly disappointed if he hoped to meet that bright expanse by throwing himself into the water. No less bitter will be the disappointment of them who plunge into the shining allurements of this world, and think that by so doing they will enjoy upon earth the bliss of heaven.

*

St. Ignatius used to say, that one act of heroic virtue is often worth a hundred others, which do not demand an equal victory over our feelings. We may compare such an act of extraordinary virtue to the sun, and those "daily virtues" to the stars. The whole firmament seems to pale before the dazzling rays of the sun. In like manner those little practices, which one performs every day, pale and lose their lustre before the rays of one great, generous, and really heroic act of virtue.

*

To continue the comparison. On a clear December night, numberless stars twinkle in the skies, and pour their flickering light upon the snow-covered earth: and yet they leave Nature cold and cheerless, because they have little power upon animate or inanimate creatures.

But as soon as the first bright beam of the rising sun illumines the world below, the whole surface of the globe is changed: everything is presently instinct with life, light, and activity. In the same manner, every-day acts of moral goodness may shine even in the chilly night of a life that is, in many respects, sinful; but no really heroic act of virtue can be performed without increasing in our souls the vigor of sanctifying grace. Very often such an act has proved to be the sunrise of a holy life.

*

If, when God drew the world out of nothing, the angelic hosts rejoiced, how great must be their jubilee, when the creative act of grace works the conversion of a sinner! Before this creation, the soul of the sinner is a mere chaos, over which disorder and gloomy darkness brood. "Let light be," says God in his divine omnipotence to the sinner, and grace sheds its cheering light over the darkened heart. Now the penitent soul perceives at once the foulness of sin and her own danger. Soon, by the exercise of her free will, she opens her heart to the light of grace, and chaos is no more. The stars of the divine promises of mercy and forgiveness appear on the firmament of Revelation. The rays of the sun of Faith warm the softened bosom of the penitent, and prepare him to receive the seeds of grace. He hastens to avail himself of the forgiveness offered, and forthwith piety springs up and buds forth in the sweetest flowerets of fervent resolutions of amendment. Then, from afar, the voice of God is heard, repeating the solemn words: "Let us make man according to our likeness." And sanctifying grace, through the Sacrament of Penance, is communicated to man, and he, in very deed, becomes a child of God.

When Christ entered this world a star of wondrous brightness announced His birth. A brilliant light shone about the shepherds, changing the darkness of night into the dazzling glare of midday. When He was about to leave the world the sun refused its light, and noonday was buried in the gloom and horror of midnight. When He will come again, the Eternal Sun of Justice shall dawn upon the good, to set no more. But for the wicked, the light of day shall be changed into the darkness of hell, which not the faintest gleam from the palest star shall ever relieve. Yes, every star of hope shall have faded and vanished forever!

*

The stars do not shine with a steady, immovable light, but emit continued scintillations, which enhance the beauty of their appearance. We may compare the stars with the revealed truths of holy Faith. These are all accompanied by many different, practical relations, which cause them to look so bright on the firmament of grace.

*

The darker the night, the more brilliantly do the stars shine. So the heavenly promises of our holy Faith never appear more consoling to the heart, than in the night and darkness of earthly trials and miseries.

*

Shooting stars appear to be high in the firmament, and at first pass for real stars; but how quickly they vanish, leaving not a trace behind! They symbolize those high conceptions and resolutions formed by souls in the time of prayer, but never executed. They disappear from the horizon of life, as they appeared, without any practical consequence.

*

These shooting stars are believed by astronomers to be the pieces of some star which has been destroyed. They are a proper emblem of those unfortunate souls, who once shone in the brightness of virtue, and followed a regular life of Christian devotion, but suffered shipwreck by collision with their overpowering passions. Sinking from a great height of piety and devotion, such souls are the most difficult to reconvert. The Apostle calls it almost impossible, especially when it happens that, to drown their remorse of conscience, they give way to temptations of infidelity.

*

Shooting stars are observed to fall in August, during the heats of Summer, and in November, during the chills of Winter. So these souls may have some idea of conversion, when pressed by an extraordinary call of grace, or when haunted by the chilling thought of death. But those feelings pass away, and leave no trace of a real resolution behind.

*

There are also souls, who, by the supernatural life which they lead, look like meteors on the firmament of grace. Their brilliancy, indeed, sometimes surpasses that of other stars. But, like meteors, they often disappear with a sudden flash, and sink in obscurity to the common level of a mere worldly life; and having seemed for some time to be like Seraphim in the eyes of men, they prove themselves very human, and subject to all the weaknesses of the flesh.

※

Comets, generally, excite much wonder, and, from the space which they occupy, seem to be greater than the sun. They shine, but their misty light imparts no heat; and notwithstanding their great extent, they have scarcely any compact center. In the social and scientific world, we may compare with the comets those *savants*, apparently possessed of extraordinary learning and erudition, and drawing after them an immense train of dupes and admirers, who foolishly fancy that these pretended geniuses will, by their wisdom, reform the world. "Come," say these comets to their admiring train, "follow us, and you shall be like unto God—knowing all things." But they soon fade away before the rays of the sun of Faith.

※

There was a time, during the first part of our century, when there appeared, like comets, on the horizon of the social and scientific world, different philosophical systems. They held out promises of unlimited knowledge to their followers, and threatened to destroy every other system, and even Faith itself. But their disappearance was as sudden as their advent, and of many scarcely more than a historical remembrance remains.

※

At the present day, it is the political horizon, especially, which flares with these comets. They promise wealth, perfect freedom, and every bliss of social life, if their views be accepted as leading principles. Sometimes, indeed, they draw after them a large train; and the brighter the hopes which they raise, the longer the train. But their career is generally short-lived. Ere long they pass into oblivion, and are lost in its contemptuous abyss.

*

We may also compare the many different heresiarchs on the horizon of the religious firmament with so many comets. They move in an eccentric orbit around the sun of Faith. They borrow some of its light, and draw in their train many deluded zealots. But they do not possess the solid nucleus of authority, and, erring, they return to the darkness whence they came.

*

But, no matter how many of these comets appear on the scientific, political, or religious horizon, fear not; they can not destroy the firmament of revealed truth, since their orbits, however eccentric, are controlled and influenced by the providence of God. They may destroy each other; they never can destroy the word of revealed truth, which is sustained by the solar system of the infallible authority of holy Church. They may menace, they may terrify the weak in Faith; in the true believer, they meet with calm firmness and scorn. He heeds them not, because he trusts in the promise of Him who said: "Heaven and earth shall pass away, but my words shall not pass away."

*

As often as a soul in the state of grace falls into sin, and consequently incurs the anger of God, we may see in her an emblem of what will happen at the final judgment of this sinful world. The sun of Faith is darkened; the moon of human reason and wisdom loses its brightness; the stars of virtue fall, and the firmament of resolutions, once so strong, gives way; a sea of remorse of conscience rages, and announces the approach of reprobation. The sight of the cross terrifies the soul, because it recalls to her mind the many graces she has lost by indulging in her unbridled passions, and she dreads the coming of the Judge.

AIR. RAIN, STORMS, LIGHTNING, RAINBOW.

PURE air presents to the eye almost the appearance of nothing; nevertheless, it is essential for hearing and breathing, and hides within its depths the wonderful world of tone. It is a beautiful emblem of humility. For this amiable virtue, which makes man feel his own nothingness, is necessary for hearing the softest whispering of divine grace; it is requisite for the breath and life of the soul, which is suffocated by pride; in fine, it is indispensable for the harmony of virtue.

*

We know the power of steam or condensed air; we hear the tremendous roar of distant thunder, as the air rushes into empty space; even the mountains seem to tremble beneath its reverberations. There is in humility —true humility—a strength and force before which the powers of darkness quail.

*

The ocean is very much affected by the atmosphere, the color and temperature of its waters depending almost entirely upon the state of the surrounding air. In the same manner, the great mass of mankind are swayed by the voice of public opinion. Fickle, like a gust of air, this merciless despot is yet for many the guide of their views, the prompter of their actions, the arbiter of their hopes. It dictates their politics, modifies their creed, and decides the most momentous questions for time and eternity.

*

A draught of air is often fatal to a man who is exposed to it, when overheated. To men who work hard in order to please, flattery is just such a draught, and often enough it proves fatal. The consequence of imprudent exposure is usually to take cold. In proportion as man lives to please men, he ceases to desire to please God, and becomes lukewarm and cold.

*

We speak of a dew or a rain of grace. Dew and rain are necessary for the healthy growth of plants and fruits. But, if the earth did not absorb the falling drops, the stagnant water would soon be changed into a swamp, filled with disagreeable insects. So our hearts must, likewise, eagerly drink in the dew of grace with which God blesses them. If they do not avail themselves of this precious boon, and act accordingly and with increasing perfection, they will soon resemble a marsh swarming with the insects of willful imperfections. It were far better for us never to have been favored with those graces than to abuse them by sloth and indifference.

*

Holy Writ records, that, when the Deluge poured its avenging waves over a sinful world, all the fountains of the deep and the flood-gates of heaven were opened, the rain descending in such quantities as to cover the tops of the highest mountains. Thus a true contrition should soften our hardened feelings, and a flood of tears and emotion bury all our iniquities, without excepting the rock of passion or the mountain of self-love. Then will the ark of a new life rest upon the rocky summit of a real change of life, and the sunbeam of grace be reflected in the rainbow of a perfect reconciliation.

*

"May the heavens rain down the Just One!" Such was the prayer in which the patriarchs of old were wont to express their longing desire for the first advent of the Messiah. "May the heavens rain down the Just One!" This is also the wish of the good in the New Covenant, who sigh for the second advent of Jesus glorified.

*

When clouds begin to overcast the sky, nature looks dull and gloomy; yet the rain which follows is one of heaven's greatest blessings. So, when the clouds of dryness and affliction darken the soul, all is dismal and depressing. But these clouds of interior trial often bring a rain of graces and blessings, which render the heart fruitful in merits and heroic virtues.

*

There is a certain sadness, which, far from being injurious to the soul, is a special grace of God. "Blessed are they that mourn, for they shall be comforted." But there is another sadness, which comes from the sinful disposition of the heart, and has very dangerous consequences. Yet the former, as well as the latter, darkens the mind. All clouds obscure the sky, but some, ere long, pour down gentle, refreshing showers; while others bring tempests, storms, and hurricanes, bearing desolation and ruin in their path.

*

Rain-clouds are generally of a neutral tint, and float tranquilly upon the horizon. But thunder-clouds are terrible, dark, and menacing in appearance. They symbolize the sinful sadness, which is destitute of hope and confidence in God, and which accompanies the hurricane of the predominant passion.

*

As long as the clouds hang suspended in the lower regions of the atmosphere, they are constantly borne to and fro by every breath of wind. But, lifted up higher, they cease to be subject to the varying currents of air, and follow the movement of the firmament only. So, men, who content themselves with the practice of ordinary virtue, are easily driven about in various directions by a multitude of temptations; while those, who have reached the summit of perfection, no longer feel any disturbance in the higher regions of the soul. Their wills are united to the will of God, whose good pleasure is the only law according to which they move.

*

The rays of the sun can draw, even from poisonous marshes, vapors, which, when condensed and purified, come down again in the form of refreshing rain. So our Lord can draw, even from the misdeeds of the wicked, salutary effects for the sanctification of the good, and render them holier and purer.

*

The state of a soul, fully and freely yielding to sin, may be justly likened to a thunder-storm. The gathering masses of clouds symbolize the power of increasing temptation; the hurricane which precedes the tempest marks the confusion that reigns in the mind—the vivid lightnings, which, for a moment, illumine the scene of horror, typify the sinful charm that seeks to allure the heart. The last fatal stroke represents the consent of the will, followed by the momentary flash of guilty satisfaction and the thunder of a reproaching conscience.

*

Refreshing showers are sometimes accompanied with ghastly streaks of lightning and fearful peals of thunder, all serving to purify the atmosphere from the malaria with which it is impregnated. Extraordinary graces may also be communicated in the midst of a tempest of temptations and adversities, tending to cleanse our souls from the many imperfections with which they are tainted.

*

We congratulate ourselves on not being exposed to the violence of a tempest raging afar-off. We look with a feeling of mingled awe and security at the distant lightnings, as they course through the sky, or, like spectral figures, chase each other along the clouds. Let us avoid every shadow of sin, and live such a holy life that we may feel so far assured against the dread judgments of God, as to adore and admire the manifestations of Divine Justice, without being alarmingly terrified.

*

We feel the pressure of besetting temptations, but when we have victoriously resisted, oh what a change! The soul breathes the pure air of an approving conscience, and as the lark, after the clouds and rain have passed away, ascends, with joyous song, far into the depths of ether, so the heart, raised toward God, intones a glad canticle of praise to Him who bade the raging storm subside.

*

In some countries, the custom exists of ringing the bells, when a storm is seen rising in the distance. But often the tempest still comes on; the rain falls, the thunder peals, the lightning flashes. It is otherwise with the approaching storm of temptation. As soon as you behold the clouds gathering, ring the bell of prayer; but oh! ring especially the great bell of meditation on the eternal truths. If you continue, the clouds will soon disperse, and the winds be lulled asleep. The thunders of temptation are often terrible to the faithful soul, but the thunders, with which she repels the assaults of hell, are far more terrible to Satan.

*

When tempest-clouds gather slowly, and remain for a long time exposed to the rays of the sun, they announce a most fearful storm. O how fearful, then, will be the storm of the Judgment day, announced by those clouds of Divine vengeance which have been exposed to the Sun of Justice for six thousand years! How appalling will be those flashes from the countenance of the Divine Judge, which will expose the reprobate to the gaze of all; and how terrific the thunders of that voice which will pronounce their eternal doom!

*

To carry off the flash, a lightning-rod must be tipped with gold or platinum, connected with the earth, and perfectly isolated from all surrounding objects. When tempted, instant recollection ought to be to us a lightning-rod, whose gilded point is the thought of heaven, ever connected with the remembrance of the grave, and isolated by a complete detachment from all the things of this world.

*

How many tempests pass over the earth, and yet the fatal flash seldom strikes the ground, and still more seldom human beings. There is a providence which guides the lightning's course. Many more clouds hang in threatening masses over human life, impregnated with the electricity of passion, and ready to hurl down destruction with the lightning of hatred, persecution, and murder. But here, too, Divine Providence is ever watchful, turning many a flash from its original direction, and rendering it perfectly harmless. If God did not thus mercifully interpose, how dreadful would be the consequences!

Lightning often descends in vivid flashes of Divine Justice, which do not strike, but only threaten the guilty, to warn them that, unless they change their evil ways, while it is still in their power, the fatal stroke will lay them low, when they least expect it.

*

A flash of lightning generally descends in a direction quite different from what we would have supposed, often singling out as its victims those who appeared to be least in danger. It is the same with the punishments of Divine Justice. Very often they descend with the swiftness of lightning, and, changing in the most sudden and unexpected manner, pursue those who deem themselves most secure.

*

Lightning seems to take, in its descent, a very irregular, or zigzag course; but the last direction is decisive. So Divine Justice, when meditating the punishment of guilty man, allows its judgments to follow, as it were, an indirect course, and the sinner consoles himself by thinking that he has no immediate cause for fear. The reason of this apparent indecision on the part of God is, that He does not oppose, or rather does not hinder, the exercise of man's free will, which, for a time, may seem to influence the decrees of Providence. But when the hour arrives that God has fixed upon to pour out the vials of His wrath, He visits the wretched sinner in the most awful and striking manner.

*

St. Augustine was once asked, why God so often permitted the lightning flash to strike the tall tree upon the mountain top, while He allows the sinner, living in the valley below, to escape unscathed. "God acts thus," replied the Saint, "prudently, wisely, and mercifully, as a father who, before punishing his refractory son with severity, first strikes the table with the rod, to frighten the culprit and induce him to amend."

*

Since the days of the deluge, the *rainbow* has been the symbol of reconciliation and mercy. Its principal colors should teach us, how our hearts ought to be disposed, and what virtues we ought to practice, in order that our reconciliation may be real, and that the light of grace, reflected by the tear-drops of penance, may encircle our souls with the rainbow of peace.

*

The principal colors of the rainbow are: *violet*, *blue*, *green*, *yellow*, and *red*. They beautifully symbolize those virtues which distinguish a sincere conversion of the heart.

*

Violet is the first of these colors; humility is also the first requisite for conversion. "Whom shall I forgive," says the Lord, "but him that is of a contrite spirit?" *Violet* is followed by *blue;* the second condition of reconciliation is the spirit of penance, according to the words of Jesus Christ himself: "Unless you do penance, you shall all perish." And in another place: "Do penance, for the kingdom of heaven is at hand." And again: "The kingdom of heaven suffereth violence, and the violent bear it away."

*

There is a double *blue* in the rainbow; the spirit of penance must also show itself in a twofold manner, by the practice of interior and of exterior mortification.

*

The next color is *green;* the third condition for reconciliation with God is hope. "Through hope we are saved," says St. Paul. He who does not hope thinks not of reconciliation, but falls into despair. Where there is humility, with a penitential spirit and a readiness to perform acts of mortification, there is also hope. On the contrary, where these three requisites are wanting, there may be presumption, but there can be no hope.

*

Yellow follows the *green*. A person truly converted is not satisfied with merely abstaining from evil, but he is animated with the desire of doing good in future, and of regaining, by redoubled zeal, what he lost. According to the admonition of the Apostle: "Work out your salvation," which means, Do with fervor whatever you can for your own salvation, and for that of your neighbor. There is a double *yellow* in the rainbow, and it typifies this twofold zeal.

*

Red is the last color of the rainbow. It is the symbol of love—our love of God above all things. Love completes the work of reconciliation; without it, there can be no sincere repentance. This ardent love is also the surest pledge of perseverance; without it, our supposed conversion would prove to have been a mere illusion.

*

Happy the soul in which appears the rainbow of true conversion, shining in the full splendor of its seven brilliant colors. Those colors mingled together will produce the dazzling white of justification—that white of the nuptial robe, in which are arrayed all those who have bathed their souls in the Blood of the Lamb.

*

But, though the rainbow is so magnificent, and though it seems to touch the earth, we can never put our hands upon it, to feel that it is certainly there. In the same way, we can never be so sure of our reconciliation with God as, in a manner, to touch it with our hands. Only by a special revelation from above can we have more than a moral evidence. We may hope with confidence, but, after all, we must work out our salvation "in fear and trembling."

LIGHT—COLOR.

LIGHT is very etherial, diffusing itself in every direction. Our conversation should partake of this quality. We need not keep aloof from profound subjects, but we must so treat of them as to make our meaning clear. Thus the rays of truth will be diffused over all who hear us.

*

Light dispels darkness. If the evil spirit persecutes you, place yourself at once in the presence of God. How can the angel of darkness approach you, if you are united to the Lord, who is essentially light?

*

If, with the view of making the light of a candle more visible, you would expose it to the rays of the sun, you would soon discover that precisely the contrary effect would result. The flame would grow dimmer, and the candle itself would melt away; while, in the dark, the candle would have remained uninjured, and the flame continued to burn brilliantly. So the light of talent and grace is far more radiant in modest retirement than when, from a desire of pleasing men rather than God, it is exposed to the rays of applause and vanity. Good qualities then lose much of their lustre, and the Divine gifts upon which they live, as the flame does upon the candle, soon melt away.

*

A surface is black, when it reflects none of the sun's rays; colored, when it reflects a portion of them; and white, when it reflects all. The same holds true of the soul. When it reflects none of the rays of grace, it is black and hideous in the sight of God; when it reflects some of them, it wears a garb checkered with a mixture of imperfections; but when it reflects, through full co-operation, the whole glorious sunlight of grace, it appears clothed in a robe of dazzling whiteness.

*

People generally have a strong liking for a certain color, and that one is called their "favorite color." Persons also have a predilection for particular virtues, of which the colors are often taken as symbols. *Red* is an emblem of love, *blue* of mildness, *rose* of mirth, *green* of hope, *yellow* of zeal, *black* of mourning, and *white*, which is produced by the blending of all the colors, is the symbol of innocence and purity. *All honor to God, who is Himself the Eternal Light!*

*

Green, when viewed through a transparent medium, always seems tinged with red. Green is the color of hope, red the type of love. What a beautiful thought is thus suggested! Christian hope united inseparably with Divine Love!

*

Looking at colors by candle-light, we take blue for green, violet for red, and so on for other shades. What a change is produced by the light of day! It proves that we were mistaken, and that the colors are quite other than we had supposed. So the infidel, viewing things by the feeble glimmer of prejudiced reason, pronounces on many matters with quite an erroneous judgment; as if the most sublime truths were only visionary fables devoid of all reality; whereas, if seen and examined in the true and glorious light of reason and faith, they appear, as they really are, eternal truths.

*

Green and blue are the predominating colors of Nature. Green is the garb of the earth—blue, that of the sky. Green is the emblem of hope—blue, that of desire and penance. Christian soul! may hope, united to the desire of heaven and the spirit of penance, be thy distinctive marks, and God in his mercy will be pleased with thy nuptial garments.

*

Another color is often mingled with the azure of the sky, and that is white, the emblem of innocence. May this remind us, that there are only two ways which surely lead to heaven—that of penance and that of innocence. Happy he who, like St. Aloysius, unites the two. How certain is he of reaching his eternal home!

How magnificent the effect of a brilliant illumination in a hall, whose walls are composed of mirrors! The multiplied reflections of the lights give it the appearance of one blaze of light. Our soul should be like such a hall. It should reflect through co-operation the light of grace from its every faculty, thought, desire, and action.

*

God is described in Holy Writ as Light: "Quoniam Deus lux est." He created light, that "the wonders of His works" might be seen. According to the present economy of Divine Providence, light is essential to every living thing, to its subsistence and activity. What is the whole visible world, the "cosmos," but the effect of that ray of the Divine light, which reflected the eternal decree bidding all things exist? No wonder, then, that light holds so prominent and so glorious a place in the universe.

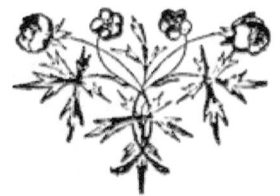

FIRE.

HOW often we complain, when our zeal meets with the slightest opposition! We imagine, that, if we could only have things our own way, we would do wonders for the glory of God. But let us reflect that, in this case, our zeal would resemble a fire burning in open air, and that, after producing a slight degree of heat around, it will be extinguished. When, on the contrary, it meets with opposition, it is like a fire in a close furnace, whose heat is more concentrated and of longer duration.

❉

A fire burning in a brick oven may, at first view, look like a useless consumption of fuel. It is not so, however. For the bricks thus become sufficiently heated to bake bread. In like manner, the fire of zeal may burn in our hearts for some years of preparation, before we engage in the active duties of the holy ministry. Yet the heat of that fire is not wasted. Longing for an occasion to exercise its zeal, it will joyfully embrace it, as soon as it presents itself, and turn it to the best advantage.

How inconsiderate is the conduct of those who, for the sake of keeping alive a spark of indiscreet devotion, hesitate not to enkindle quite a destructive conflagration of domestic troubles.

*

Light, splendor, and warmth, the three properties of fire, are emblematic of the Persons of the Most Holy Trinity, existing in unity of essence. They also typify, most beautifully, the three religious vows, by which we make a holocaust of ourselves in the fire of charity. Obedience affords light to the mind in the way of salvation; Poverty imparts to the soul the most brilliant splendor, chasing away the clouds and mists of covetousness and selfishness; Chastity inflames the heart with the love of God, and the desire of belonging to Him alone.

*

Reason is also a light. Be on your guard, lest you place it in the dark-lantern of self-love, or behind the distorting lens of an excited imagination.

*

Dry wood, when cast into the stove, instantly bursts into a flame. But, before becoming useful as fuel, it must have lain for a long time exposed to the sun. The economy of grace is closely allied to nature. Before making use of His servants for the salvation of mankind, God often allows them, apparently, to lie idle in some obscure corner. Meanwhile, however, the rays of the Eternal Sun of Grace are falling upon them for their glorious mission. And when, in its own good time, Divine Wisdom calls them from this retreat, their zeal suddenly takes fire, diffusing light and heat on all around.

*

Souls, led by God's providence in this manner, may be compared to magazines, in which wood is stored away and preserved in sufficient quantities to kindle a powerful fire, able by its heat to melt stone and metal. The zeal of such souls, if afterward put to the test, is strong enough to overcome the most obstinate difficulties. It is not so with those whose zeal, like the feeble flame of a chip on the hearth, is exhausted in the ordinary duties of daily life.

*

A fire, occasionally stirred, burns with a more cheerful flame. In the same manner, zeal, harassed by trial and vexations, glows with a purer affection.

*

Quartz is fused by the action of an intense fire, and, in its liquid state, is extensively used in the manufacture of glass. Fire, then, can change the hardest rock into the most brittle substance. The fire of strong temptations, if not stifled in time, may decompose the purest virtue, and render it as fragile as glass.

*

But glass, if compressed till it acquires a certain density, regains almost the hardness of quartz, the cause of its fragility, in its ordinary state, being due to its great expansion. In a moral sense, the principal reason of our fragility, when assailed by temptation, is our expansion of mind. We live in too dissipated a manner; we do not strive to center our thoughts upon God, and to lead an interior life, which would impart to our moral weakness a strength capable of withstanding the heaviest blows.

*

Soft wood takes fire very readily, but it is also consumed very quickly; hard wood does not kindle so easily, but it feeds the flame much longer. A similar difference may be noticed between persons of an ardent and those of a cold nature. The former are easily moved to devotion, and, for a time, seem to be all on fire with piety; but their fervor is soon spent. The latter, on the contrary, are not so easily affected, but they glow with the warmth of true piety, long after more sensitive natures have cooled.

*

A fire is not always increased by fresh supplies of fuel; on the contrary, if there is not a strong draught, it is very apt to be extinguished. In like manner, zeal is not always nourished in a person of good will by loading him with labor; frequently it is more likely to be suffocated altogether. Use consideration, and, by allowing time for innocent recreation, fan the smoldering embers into a flame, till the fire of zeal is strong enough to consume everything before it.

*

In order that a fire may burn brightly, it requires frequent stirring during the course of the day. The fire of devotion is stirred by renewing our good intentions and making pious aspirations and ejaculations, from time to time. The fire of Divine Love is also stirred by bearing patiently the trials and vexations with which we may meet.

*

If you were to close a stove completely, so as to leave no draught whatever, the fire would gradually grow less, and at last be wholly extinguished. In like manner, if a person charged with the religious training of others were unwilling to suffer the slightest imperfection in his spiritual children, the fire of their zeal for advancement in perfection would slowly die away and would ere long leave their souls cold and indifferent.

*

As it is the nature of fire to diffuse its heat, a stove, set up in one corner of an apartment, will soon make us feel a cheering warmth all around. Be not obtrusive! If the fire of zeal and of Divine Love is really burning within you, the hearts of others will soon become sensible of its presence, and will, of their own accord, approach you. If, with meddlesome eagerness, you pursue your neighbor, and, regardless of time and place, insist upon giving him the benefit of your zeal, he will, in all likelihood, become angry with you, and seek by all means to avoid your presence.

*

A powerful wind does not extinguish a strong fire, but rather increases its flame and heat. The same holds true of trial and temptations, when the fire of love burns ardently in the heart.

*

"A burned child dreads the fire," and yet the grown man, continually burned by the flames of excited passion, only adds more fuel to them. Even the "ass," as the saw has it, "can be only once got over the breaking ice." The sinner, then, does not bear comparison even with this stupid, dumb animal. Scripture, regardless of the false delicacy that would gloss over everything, plainly calls him a "*fool.*"

*

Who has not looked upon a brightly blazing fire and admired its glowing light? Who has not rejoiced at its cheerful warmth? Yet, in a short time it burns away, and nothing remains but a mass of blackened cinders. Such is not the case with the fire of zeal; indeed, its intensity infinitely exceeds that of material fire. Witness St. Francis Xavier. The vivifying influence of that flame which glowed in his heart was diffused unto the remotest corners of the earth; and its warmth is not yet spent, though three hundred years have slowly ebbed away. Neither the wave of the ocean, nor the icy breath of the north can extinguish that holy fire; neither time nor space can destroy its salutary influence.

*

Put as much wood as you please into a stove; if you do not kindle a fire, the stove, as well as the room in which it stands, will remain as cold as ever. So all amassing of theological science is useless, if we neglect to enkindle, by meditation, the fire of Divine Love. Bare, abstract truths will leave the heart unmoved, and fail to bring about any reformation of our lives. But if science and a profound knowledge of religious truth are combined with the spirit of meditation and prayer, they serve as fuel to feed the flame of Divine Love.

*

When a fire is dying away, it still continues to smoke. Indeed, we do not often see a fire without some smoke. Devotion is a fire; hence, it need not surprise us that it is seldom found without the smoke of willful imperfections. We may, however, be quite content that it burns at all. It is always in danger of dying away. Let us but do our best to keep it alive, the Lord will not fail to bless our untiring efforts.

*

Prayer is like a candle, always keeping alive the flame of devotion. Be careful, therefore, that your candle be not melted down by the particles detached from the wick through willful distractions. How often do a few such particles hinder most of the effect of prayer!

*

If we wish a lamp to burn with a clear and brilliant light, we must from time to time cleanse it of the half-burned particles which fall from the wick. In like manner, we must cleanse the lamps of our hearts daily, or even oftener, of a thousand little imperfections of selfish intention, that may obscure the light of virtue, or perhaps extinguish it altogether.

*

If a small portion of the wick falls upon the candle and takes fire, it may gradually waste the candle. So the slightest particle of self-love, detached from the wick of a pure intention can mar and even destroy the merit of our best actions.

*

When, on entering a room, we find a person carelessly seated at a table, upon which a neglected light is dimly burning, we conclude that he has fallen asleep. That sleeper is a fair emblem of those Christians who fail to purify their good intentions by repeated acts of the love of God, and, heedless about the sanctification of their souls, indulge in the slumber of tepidity.

*

Christ commands us to wait for his coming with burning lamps. For a lamp burns a long time, and with a uniform light; while a candle, on the contrary, is soon melted down by the flickering of the wick. The lamp is an emblem of those fervent Christians, who, constantly supplied with the oil of interior prayer, continue all the days of their lives with a steady devotion to shine like brilliant lights in the house of God. The candle symbolizes, with no less propriety, those worldly-minded souls, whose short-lived fervor is at an end as soon as the motives of self-interest, which fed it, have ceased to exist;

so that after wasting their talents and undermining their strength, they are doomed to meet the bridegroom in utter darkness, and to be forever excluded from the heavenly wedding-feast.

✱

A wick that has not been saturated with oil is soon consumed and reduced to ashes. For some moments its flame is bright and lively, but soon it will die away and leave us in utter darkness. On the contrary, if it is dipped in oil, it will give a steady flame, and last through all the night. We may compare the will to the wick, and grace to the oil. The will alone, heated by enthusiasm, may kindle with the flames of zeal; but they will soon die away, if not kept alive by supernatural motives.

✱

A slight turn of the screws fitted to some of our modern lamps, either increases or diminishes the flame. The pressure of sadness and sorrow may, in like manner, either augment or lessen our piety and hope; all depends upon the direction which we give to that pressure. If, amid the trials that encompass us on every side, we seek aid from God alone, and bless the hand that scourges us, the lamp of our hope will shine with increased lustre; but if we turn down toward creatures and repine at the visitations of Heaven, the faint gleam of our confidence in Providence will, ere long, die away and leave us enveloped in the darkness of despair.

✱

The greatest danger of temptation lies in this, that the devil represents the sinful object as innocent and harmless, and as indispensable, in some respects, to our wellbeing here below. Lured by the bait which he holds out, we are constantly in danger of rushing headlong into his toils, with the hope of securing to ourselves a portion of necessary bliss. Thus the moth flutters around the light, as if attracted by a hidden charm; but woe to the unwary insect if it is decoyed into the flame!

*

We may compare with such a flame the so-called lights of progress, which, in our times, pretend to shed a new splendor upon all sciences and systems. Millions of ignorant, narrow-minded persons swarm like moths around them, and come, at last, to an unhappy end.

*

A light increases in brilliancy in a darkened room. There is a species of false humility, which prompts him who is under its influence so to act as to draw upon himself the especial attention and esteem of others, and thus to be more generally admired.

*

A light intended to be carried out into the open air is placed in a lantern, the glasses of which must be clean and bright. The heart is a lantern; Faith is the light within, kept alive by the oil of grace. But you must have a care to keep this heart clean, in order that the light of Faith may illuminate with splendor the way to heaven.

*

Photographic Views.

The beacon of a light-house gives only a small flame, but how much good is effected by it, and how many disasters prevented! With that light may be compared the various texts of Holy Scripture and the maxims of the Saints. How many dangers shall we avoid if we are always mindful of them!

✱

"Flame does not rise without smoke," says the devout author of the Imitation. If this holds in the physical world, it does so likewise in the spiritual, in which smoke is appropriately made to represent vain-glory. Unless we are very watchful, this smoke will mingle with the flame of our good intention, and dim the lustre of our good actions. How unsubstantial smoke is! Yet even a little almost blinds and suffocates us. It injures whatever comes within its reach, blackening the whitest wall and sullying the most costly furniture. In the moral order, vain-glory produces the same effect.

✱

Matches are so quickly consumed that unless used immediately they may burn the fingers. Creatures pass away with equal rapidity, and should only serve to enkindle in our hearts the love of God. If sought for their own sake they will certainly injure the soul, and place its salvation in jeopardy.

✱

The more lightsome a room, the easier it is to perceive the smallest particle of dust, and whoever has charge of the place is careful to sweep and dust it daily. It is so with a soul when the light of grace dawns upon her. The slightest imperfection becomes visible, and she can not rest till it has been wiped away by regret for the past and new resolutions of amendment for the future.

*

One of the means which we use to purify the air of a room is to burn in it every morning and evening the wood of the juniper tree. If we wish to purify our hearts from the dangerous exhalations of our imperfections, we must, in like manner, by ardent prayer, enkindle in our heart, every morning and evening, the flame of our love for God.

THE SEASONS.

THE four seasons of the year are produced by the different positions of the sun in respect to the earth. In *winter* the sun's influence upon the earth is comparatively slight. So is the effect of God's holy word upon a soul, whose indifference to grace has cooled its fervor. While the inspired accents of the preacher fall upon the sinner's ear, the warmth of the Divine word exercises some influence upon his heart. Sometimes even the icy crust of indifference is thawed, and tears of emotion quiver in his eyes. But how transitory that impression! With the concluding words of the sermon the emotion passes away, the glow of affection fades, and, as the sinner leaves the Church, his tears are again converted into the ice of religious indifference.

*

Let us consider, next, newly-converted souls, who are in their first fervor, or, to keep up the figure, in the *spring-time* of piety. The word of God, addressed to them, calls forth an abundance of buds, exhaling a delightful fragrance. They are easily moved to pious affections, and elevated by the consoling truths of divine faith to the regions of sensible devotion.

But it does not suffice to indulge in these special favors. The operation of the Holy Ghost, whose grace always accompanies the word of God, must convert those buds into the flowers of earnest, practical resolutions, the purpose of advancing by works, and not by affections only, in the way of Christian perfection. The aspirant after Christian virtue still presses onward, and soon enters the *summer* of piety. He becomes active, and begins to put his resolutions into practice, regardless of the difficulties which cross his path. Gradually the fruit begins to ripen. The soul has reached *autumn*, the fourth season of a religious life, whose closing scene will find her with a bounteous harvest of merits, to be forever garnered up in heaven.

*

Summer clothes the forest trees in a graceful foliage; but autumn steals upon her footsteps, and robs them of their verdant glory. So do the modern systems of philosophy pass away: their antiquated volumes are the fading autumnal foliage of human thought, and deserve no better fate than to be shelved in the "house of oblivion."

*

At the return of Fall the earth always loses her luxuriant garb. The trees shed their leaves, and the meadows doff their cloak of green. All the labor of the year seems to be effaced from the book of nature. May we not say that Winter turns a new leaf, upon which to trace, in Spring, further proofs of the loving goodness of our Creator in the bounties of nature!

*

The cold of Winter is never more penetrating, not more keenly felt, than when accompanied by a cutting wind. So, likewise, indifference in matters of religion is never more hurtful than when persons, whose early religious education has been neglected, come in contact with the chilling blast of *public opinion*. Whatever religious feeling may still remain in their hearts, is quickly frozen.

*

Every flower blooms and every fruit ripens in its own season. The same should be true of the heart. According to the returning seasons of the ecclesiastical year, this garden of grace should be fragrant with the varied perfume of prayer, praise, thanksgiving, and penance, and bring forth the fruits of meritorious thoughts and actions.

*

The earth yearly celebrates a Mass, which, like the sacrifice of our altars, consists of four principal parts. In *Winter*, prostrate nature recites the *Confiteor* and *Kyrie*. Stript of the charms which it wore in the garden of Eden, it seems to weep over its present state, and humbly to acknowledge itself incapable of yielding any fruit, except by a special favor of God, who is rich in mercy, and who ever turns a ready ear to the cries of the penitent. *Spring* opens the *Gospel*, and heralds the joyful tidings of a new year of blessings; then, amid the fragrance of flowers, rising like clouds of incense up to the pure vault of nature's temple, it celebrates the *Offertory*, while the mellow voices of a thousand little birds, mingling a sweet concert of praise, invite us to raise our hearts aloft. *Summer* operates a mysterious

Transubstantiation, expanding the nascent bud into the fruit, and tinging every leaf with a deeper hue, while the boundless seas of waving crops, the bending fruit-trees, and the shady forests attest, perhaps more plainly than ever, the presence of an all-pervading divinity. *Autumn* yields its harvest of fruits, and with it gives man an emblem of *holy Communion*, until the heart, overflowing with thanks, pronounces its "Deo Gratias" for the blessings received, and the falling leaves proclaim the "Ite missa est;" a year is gone, the harvest is gathered in.

MOUNTAINS, HILLS, AND PLAINS.

THE elementary substance of the earth typifies the intimate connection of the three theological virtues of Faith, Hope, and Charity. Granite, the chief constituent of the solid crust, is a type of the solidity of Holy Faith. Did not Christ himself say to Simon: "Thou art Peter," that is, a Rock—and "I have prayed for thee, that thy faith fail not"?

The surface of the earth is dressed in green, the favorite color of nature and the emblem of Hope.

The atmosphere that surrounds us is essential for light, sound, and life, and exercises a peculiar influence upon the waters, which cover so large a portion of the globe. Air is, therefore, an emblem of the Holy Ghost, and consequently of Divine Love.

*

High mountains are accompanied by valleys, of which they are the safeguards, and which they fertilize by an abundant supply of water. The abstract dogmatical truths on the heights of holy Faith are always attended by practical applications for the guidance of our daily life; the former are the high mountains, which protect the latter and impart to them the streams of a Divine Faith. In comparison with the Eden-like dales of fervent piety, watered from the heights of revealed truth, mere philosophical speculations on virtue are like a sandy desert or a sterile heath.

*

There is a great difference between the first sight and the close inspection of any object. This is particularly true of scenery. Even from the plain we may have a view of a landscape or city; but let us ascend a hill, and oh, what a difference! The whole scenery now wears a new and more agreeable aspect. So we shall soon be sensible of a change in our judgments on the ordinary occurrences of social life, if, aided by the spirit of prayer and contemplation, we strive to raise ourselves above the common level, and to consider the things of earth from the elevated stand-point of holy Faith.

*

Castles are generally erected on the crest of a mountain, as being there less accessible to any hostile force. Natural talents, education, science, and nobility of character are like a hill, at the summit of which the castle of virtue is more conspicuous, while it is at the same time more strongly fortified.

*

Our life on earth is called a journey toward our heavenly home. Oh, how certain should we be of reaching the place of our destination, were we always moved by an earnest desire of advancing in perfection, and guided by the twofold precept of love toward God and our fellow-man!

When we travel in a new country, our route is not unfrequently broken by precipices or cliffs. But if we climb some prominent peak, and look out over the surrounding plain, we may, perhaps, discover a much shorter and better road than the one which we were following. In the spiritual life, we shall derive equal advantages from the difficulties that beset our course if, instead of being alarmed, we rise superior to them, and use them as means to shorten our way to heaven. For this purpose we shall often find it expedient to make a partial, or even an entire change in our mode of life.

*

It is advisable, and sometimes absolutely necessary, to lock the wheels of a wagon when we drive down a hill. On the way to perfection there are many hills, which meet the level of ordinary life with a very sudden descent; and the heart, with its inordinate affections and earthly tendency, is but too prone to bear us downward at a hurried pace. Christian prudence should, therefore, always have in readiness the chain of mortification and self-denial, to check the impetuosity with which we run in pursuit of whatever flatters our natural inclinations and unruly appetites.

*

Sometimes the hill is so steep that the chain is very liable to break, unless the wagoner uses the greatest precaution. In like manner, we may be thrown into occasions in which our ordinary good resolutions will prove insufficient to curb our wayward passions, unless we carefully watch the first involuntary movements of the heart.

St. Paul says that "the body burdens the soul." We see this remark illustrated in walking up a hill, which is an emblem of striving after exalted virtue.

*

The path toward heaven is strewn with thorns. But what matters it? If we put on the shoes of confidence in God, as the Apostle advises us to do, we may walk fearlessly ahead. So far from being seriously wounded by those thorns, we shall even be delighted with the fragrance of the roses which are mingled with them.

*

The road to hell is often smooth and pleasant, especially for those upon whom the world has chosen to heap riches and honors. Yet even they can not traverse that pleasant road without feeling a sharp, stinging pain, which they can neither prevent nor soothe. And why? Because through the shoes, and into the very feet of the worldly pilgrim, a thorn has found its way. The sinner may wear the stout shoes of indifference and contempt of Divine Justice and its threats. But all in vain. The thorn of a wounded conscience will sting him; and though he may try to forget the pain by plunging headlong down the road to perdition, the cause of his uneasiness will remain. It will penetrate more and more deeply, until at last it extorts from the wretched sinner the heart-rending cry: "I have walked in the way of iniquity, and have grown tired thereof."

*

On rising ground, the prudent teamster drives at a slow but steady pace, and sometimes even adds another span of horses. So, in the time of adversity, we must not act with precipitate haste, trying to force matters into the right direction. We must rather accommodate ourselves to circumstances, and, while we act with prudence, beware of giving way to discouragement and indecision. Let us not desist from our efforts to be virtuous, because, perhaps, we meet some difficulty. On the contrary, let us with renewed fervor pursue our course, till we have reached the summit of perfection. And, as the driver employs relay horses, let us also seek for additional motives, even of temporary and earthly advantage, calculated to strengthen our resolution of securing the rewards, which God holds out to those that persevere unto the end.

*

We make use of a walking-staff in ascending a mountain, and sometimes even stud the heels of our boots with sharp points, in order to be in less danger of sliding. On the road to perfection, our resolutions of improving from day to day may serve us as a staff, while the constant practice of humility and self-denial, combined with the sharp points of fear, will prevent us from being suddenly hurled down into the abyss of sin, when we seem to have almost reached the height of sanctity.

*

After traveling for some time, even on the most level road, we look for an agreeable spot to rest. So, though an exhortation is replete with pleasant truths, it will soon produce, in persons who listen even most attentively, a vivid desire for repose. It would be a relief, if practical applications, comparisons, and historical illustrations were, from time to time, introduced among the abstract arguments of the speaker.

*

How wearisome is the journey across a prairie, when nothing meets the eye but a vast level plain, without even so much as a solitary tree to break the monotony of the view. It were far more pleasant to take the mountain pass, hemmed in on every side by hills and crags, the sight of which continually offers something to divert the eye, and prompts us to visit the yet unexplored region further on, which ever-busy fancy decks with charms of its own creation. So we soon tire of a discourse in which the speaker unfolds everything at once, leaving nothing to excite the curiosity of his hearers.

*

One who is walking on slippery ground, continually turns his eyes downward, and moves his feet with the utmost precaution. This downcast look and unremitting watchfulness typify the sister virtues of humility and discretion, so necessary to us on our perilous passage through this world. What wonder, that, without them so many fall and perish forever!

*

When we pave a walk with granite flags, it is advisable not to dress them too smoothly, but to let them keep some of their natural roughness. A greater polish might, perhaps, give them a better appearance, but it would put us in constant danger of falling. So, though it is quite proper for us to borrow from the world a certain courtesy and ease of manner, yet it is well to retain in our intercourse with others a degree of sternness and reserve. Too great complaisance is apt to degenerate into servility, which panders to every taste, and cringes before the fickle will of fashion and public opinion. Such a polish is highly unbecoming in a follower of Christ, and must ere long lead to sin.

*

This figure contains another very instructive moral. Even in regard to those that are most fervent in the study of Christian perfection, God permits that they retain certain natural defects, which are not less a source of security to them than the unevenness of a stone pavement is to the traveler. For, seeing their deficiency, they feel ashamed and humbled, and the world refrains from lavishing on them injudicious or excessive praise, which might give rise to temptations of vain-glory and self-esteem. Hence it was that St. Francis of Sales used to call those little defects, his "well-beloved imperfections," considering them as the safeguards of his humility.

*

Planks are of no service in enabling us to pass over a river unless they are long enough to reach across. In like manner, in struggling against sin, or in aiming at perfection, half-formed resolutions can not benefit us in the least.

*

The cross-beams of a bridge undoubtedly constitute its main strength; nevertheless we can not walk over it without planks stretching across and binding the whole together. In the same way, grace is the chief support of virtue; still we can not cross over the dangerous abyss of life without making our own resolutions, and keeping them with the grace of God.

*

The more a road is used, the greater need there is of renewing the gravel or stones, in order to fill up the ruts made by wagons. So it is very good, and, in some respects, even necessary, that one who mingles with the world should meet with hardships and contradictions. These are the gravel and stones which fill up the hollows of self-confidence, and level the unevenness of obstinacy and caprice.

*

As long as there is no wind, we walk over the dust quite unconcernedly and almost without noticing how deep it is. But as soon as the wind blows a gust, our eyes, mouth, and nostrils forthwith perceive the presence of the unwelcome substance. Dust is an emblem of worldly inclinations, which are but too apt to underlie our most praiseworthy undertakings. While all is calm, the sinister motives that may prompt a virtuous action are not noticed by others. But let the winds of adversity and contradiction arise, and presently the dust will rise in whirling masses and cloud the air of social life, to the great annoyance of all who come in contact with us. If, therefore, we consult our own quiet of mind, or the peace of our fellow-man, let us strive to be free from this fatal dust. Whatever storm may then arise will only tend to give proof of our hidden virtues, just as the gale that sweeps over a blooming meadow bears on its wings the sweet perfume of a thousand little flowers, which before we passed heedlessly or crushed beneath our feet.

*

Pedestrians often shorten their route by taking another path, generally a little raised above the common highroad. This course may require a little more exertion, but it frequently secures the advantage of a purer air and more pleasant shade. In the way of perfection, these by-paths are the three evangelical counsels. Happy they that follow them!

*

A traveler, whose path lies through a thicket of thorn-bushes, will find it hard to effect a passage without an ax. Our earthly course is overgrown with the thorns of trials and temptations, through which we must cut our way with the ax of self-denial and penance. If we seek to remove them with the delicate hands of a fastidious and effeminate life, we shall only expose ourselves to the danger of being wounded, and of suffering many other evils which we might have escaped by resoluteness and fervor.

*

A person walking upon stilts looks taller than he really is. But his height makes him awkward. He stalks along with an unsteady, shambling step, and all his motions are without grace. In the same manner the proud man who exalts himself, rests his greatness upon a very slender support. He is in an unnatural position, and often renders himself truly ridiculous.

*

The smallest balustrade enables us to pass with safety along a path skirted by yawning precipices, and overhung by craggy heights and beetling cliffs. The consciousness of our own frailty is a similar aid to us while clambering up the dizzy heights of Christian perfection.

*

Every careful driver considers the state of the road upon which he travels, and moves with greater or less speed, according to circumstances. So must we do when we conduct others on the way of Christian perfection. We must reflect whether they walk on the straight and pleasant road of interior peace and heavenly consolation, or, on the contrary, hesitatingly feel their way along the rugged path of desolation, checked at every step of their course by the projecting rocks of interior troubles.

*

It is dangerous, as well as injurious to health, to run up stairs, for by so doing we are liable to stumble and fall. An inconsiderate eagerness in the performance of exterior acts of virtue, is likewise prejudicial to the health of the soul. This should be remembered by those who are still as children learning to climb up the ladder of perfection, and who must be led at every step by the guiding hand of an experienced director. A confessor, who thinks that his penitents can do what he does, and all that promotes his sanctification will promote theirs, is like an imprudent guide, who tries to urge children to run quickly up a steep flight of stairs, before they are well able to walk on level ground.

*

It may be that God has spoken to your heart, and that, like David, you can "run and fly" without losing breath. But after a time you will, perhaps, reach a steep and dangerous road. Then move slowly and carefully, if you wish to avoid a fall, involving all the more serious consequences in proportion to the height which you have attained.

*

A person walking along carelessly is in danger of stumbling when he comes to a trifling declivity, which, with a little vigilance on his part, would have only tended to accelerate his pace. It is thus with the Christian, who does not watch every step which he takes in the pathway of virtue.

*

The Divine hand is extended to lead you; but you must grasp it firmly, and yourself make an effort to walk. Do what you can, and God will do the rest. If the road should grow very rugged, He will even carry you in His arms, as a mother does her child when its feeble steps refuse to bear it further.

*

To accommodate ourselves, in all that is not sinful, to the manners and inclinations of others, and to become all to all with the view of gaining souls, is like traveling *incognito*, in the interest of Jesus and for the promotion of His great work, which is no other than the salvation of souls.

*

A traveler must consider the weather and the seasons. We must do the same on our journey toward our heavenly home. We must adopt one course in time of spiritual dryness—another in the season of consolation. We must take one route during the storm of temptation—another during the sunshine of interior calm. We may also consult, to some advantage, the almanacs of psychology and experience; yet, as their authority is not always reliable, it is well to seek the advice of other experienced travelers. Let us guard against unforeseen accidents. Let us not fail to take with us a cloak to protect us against the cold of disappointment, and an umbrella, as well to shelter us from the showers of reviling and persecution, as to defend us from the sun-stroke of vanity, so fatal during the season of worldly applause.

*

Calendars are got up, in which the weather is calculated for a hundred years in advance. We know that little confidence is to be placed in these pretended oracles of the future, yet they occasionally contain some coincident truth. If we would carefully consult our own past life, each one of us could become, by the aid of experience, his own calendar for twenty, forty, or sixty years, and for a hundred years, if he lived so long.

*

WATER—STREAMS—THE OCEAN.

THE sacred writers, and Christ himself, when treating of the grace of God, often draw comparisons from water. Water is the element which covers the greater portion of the globe, penetrating the immense depths of the earth, gushing from the summits of the highest mountains, and everywhere enriching the soil, that it may yield its harvests and fruits. The want of it causes a torment keener than the pangs of famine; we need not speak of the power and uses of steam, which is produced from water. In regard to our spiritual welfare, this element is the ordinary condition of salvation, being the matter or element of the Sacrament of Baptism.

✱

Holy Writ often compares trials to overwhelming floods. They may terrify and threaten to engulf you, yet, amidst their wildest fury, you have at hand a means of escape. Provided you do spiritually what swimmers do bodily, you shall rise above the waves of tribulation, impatience, diffidence, or despair, and, after such a salutary bath, you shall appear more pure and pleasing than ever in the eyes of God. Swimmers first extend themselves on the water, then they push the water back with their feet, fold their hands, separate them, and finally draw them back again to their breasts. This completes one stroke, after which they repeat the same actions as before, and thus propel themselves gradually. Upon the precision, force, and continuance of these motions, depend the ease and rapidity with which they swim. Those who know the art, safely breast the tide, while others struggle in vain and find a watery grave. Imitate swimmers whenever you are in the midst of tribulations. Throw yourself by an act of great confidence into the hands of God's Providence, without whose permission no trials can come upon you. Push back with the greatest contempt the sinful means which the devil may suggest to deliver you; fold your hands in prayer that thus you may steer your course aright; separate them to implore aid; but, fully resigned whether it come or not, bring your hands back to your breast in childlike submission to the will of Heaven. Renew these pious affections while your troubles last: pray with increased fervor and devotion, and you will glide securely through the swelling tide.

*

While swimming, you must be especially careful to keep your head above water. As long as you do that, you are safe. Following out the comparison begun above, we may therefore say: The head of the soul is the will; as long as that is not overwhelmed by the waves of temptation, you need not be alarmed.

*

A mill is set in motion by a little stream of water falling uninterruptedly from a height. Water is, as we said, an emblem of grace, which descends with an uninterrupted flow from the height of heaven. Need we then wonder, that the power of grace is so great as to enable our wills to perform the most stupendous works of zeal?

*

This comparison beautifully illustrates another effect of grace. If a little falling stream is able to exercise such a power, what would not be the force of a cataract like the Niagara? It is said that if the power of the Niagara Falls could be properly divided and properly applied, it would be sufficient to move all the machinery in the world. Why, then, should we wonder, that the saints have done so much for the glory of God and the salvation of men, considering those cataracts of Divine mercy falling upon their hearts?

*

There is no beauty in a stream which, like a canal, flows along in one unbroken, straight line. But how charming and picturesque is a river that winds along between romantic banks, sometimes lost to the sight, then suddenly flashing with silvery whiteness upon the view! Now it flows by the steep and rocky cliffs which line its sides, and, unmindful of obstacles, pursues its steady course. Now it passes pleasant fields and gardens, and again it washes the foot of a giant mountain thousands of feet high, like Mount Hood in Oregon. Could you only see the magnificent Columbia river! So virtues acquired without effort, and practiced merely because our own inclinations lead us toward them, are neither so agreeable nor so meritorious before God as those acquired at the price of self-sacrifice, and in spite of every opposition and difficulty.

*

All the rivers of the world empty into the ocean. In our life, all our daily thoughts and our affections and exertions should always bear in the same direction, viz: toward the great affair of our salvation should all be absorbed, which will be completed when our life is pouring out into the ocean of eternity.

*

Standing upon the banks of a mighty stream, we may often have remarked the violence with which a boat, breaking loose from its moorings, is carried along by the current, against whose resistless power the strongest cables are as slender threads. In like manner, when the soul has departed, by her own free will, from the landing of virtue and of Divine law, no mere human power is able to arrest her downward course. Hurried along by the current of passion, she heeds not the most earnest and pathetic remonstrances; nay, often treats them with indifference and contempt.

*

A barrier of weak and tender rods may stem the current of a powerful river, and gradually turn it in quite another direction. That slender barrier resembles our good resolutions. They may appear powerless in comparison with the mighty and violent stream of passions and evil inclinations; yet, if faithfully kept, they may prove to be stronger than the violence of temptation, which threatens to break through them and overwhelm us.

*

This comparison may be applied also to our natural temperament. Some are of a gay, others of a melancholy disposition. Some are naturally violent, others calm. It seems almost impossible for us to bring these various temperaments so much under the control of the will as apparently to change them into their opposites. Nevertheless, experience proves that it is possible; and the means by which it is effected is fidelity in controlling every sally of the passions to which we are inclined.

*

Some kinds of wood quickly decay in water; others, on the contrary, can be preserved in it and petrified. For the weak and faint-hearted, adversities are dangerous, because they are apt to affect their good resolutions. For the courageous, on the contrary, they constitute the very element of heroic virtues and endurance.

*

Though a steamboat, impelled by its machinery, glides gracefully along over the water, a jarring sensation is always felt by the passenger, occasioned by the inertia of the boat, or its inability to move itself. So, in the most advanced stages of a spiritual life, our natural reluctance to virtue and our impotence for good, unless aided by the impelling power of grace, are felt by all, even the greatest Saints.

afflicted heart feels confident that, under God's providence, we may overcome the waves of temptation and opposition, and victoriously carry our merits and good works to the port of heaven.

*

Every o e who has had occasion to stand alone on the shore of the ocean, especially every true servant of God, must have felt that the view of those boundless waves, filling the unfathomable depths of the sea, and carrying on their bosom the most precious cargoes of goods, gold, corals, or pearls, excites in our heart sentiments of admiration of God's omnipotence and providence, together with a longing for that heaven, which expands itself over the waves of the ocean of human life.

*

Especially every afflicted heart, oppressed by saddening accidents, and tempted to falter in the execution of great works for the glory of God, perceives this consoling influence at the sight of the ocean enlarging and extending itself without bounds; hope is strengthened, and the

*

In the ocean there are comparatively few rocks, and still many vessels suffer shipwreck. In the sea of life there are innumerable rocks, and people are so careless; no wonder, then, that many souls suffer the most fearful disasters.

*

Breakers are especially dangerous near the shore. This should teach you that it is necessary to be careful, particularly at the beginning and end of a work, if you do not wish to lose the merit of a virtuous action.

*

On the high sea but little is to be feared from storms; the danger is near the coasts. As long as we sail with full confidence in God and His fathomless goodness, our bark is comparatively safe. But dangers beset us when we try to escape the storm, seeking help from shore, accommodating ourselves to the maxims of the children of the world.

*

An experienced sailor sets and spreads his sails according to the direction and strength of the wind. Were he negligent in this respect he would be tossed by every gale and rocked by every breaker, in constant danger of having his canvas torn and his craft swallowed by the raging waters. Learn from this a lesson of prudence for the spiritual life. We should be guarded not to unfold our plans to every one. Indiscretion may expose us to an opposition, which is easily avoided by being less communicative.

*

This comparison has a special reference to those who have been called to the government of a society or congregation. If superiors reveal, without prudence and consideration, all they meditate for the common good, their plans may be wholly unsuccessful, and instead of promoting the glory of God, foster only dissension and ill-will among their subjects.

Why is a tempest-tossed ship in so much danger? Because it has to struggle against the waves of an agitated sea. Hence the whole care of the pilot consists in steering in the direction of the wind and current. Could the vessel follow the course of the waves, it would take but little heed of the fury of the hurricane. Borne along upon the wings of the wind, it would arrive all the sooner at the end of the voyage. Our souls are like weather-beaten crafts, riding upon the tempestuous main of life. If, with an entire conformity to God's holy will, they would commit themselves to the waves of troubles and persecutions, they would not be retarded on their homeward course. The gusts of exterior trials swelling their sails would but bear them, with greater rapidity, to the port of everlasting bliss.

*

The quantity of the cargo which a ship can carry, depends upon the size of the hull. Similarly, the more profound our humility, and the greater our detachment from self and from all that is not God, the more capable also shall we be of bearing a large cargo of merits to the port of eternity.

FIELDS AND GARDENS.

WHAT was Italy of old? What was formerly the now charming scenery of Switzerland, Belgium, France, and Germany? Nothing but a desert waste. But when man, with his untiring energy and patient industry, set to work, the wilderness was changed into a garden. We may say that God has so disposed nature as to awaken the industry of man, who can, by assiduous labor, remove the vail, which, since the fall, has concealed the beauty of the earth. If man, through indolence and laziness, refuses to obey the sentence of his Creator, he is unworthy of gazing on the beauty of nature, and deserves to live in a desert of thistles and thorns.

*

To the beginner, mental prayer, or *Meditation*, may appear as a desert, without nourishment for the heart. But let him continue with fidelity, and he will, ere long, find the manna of heavenly consolation, which, in that apparently barren region, daily falls from on high. Like the children of Israel, he will then exclaim in astonishment, "Manna?" "What is that?" Can man attain on earth to such a union with God? What can equal the happiness experienced by them that are closely united to their Heavenly Father?

Without buildings or signs of cultivation, the most beautiful scenery of nature is in a great degree destitute of that loveliness and grace which are imparted to it by the efforts of human industry. The same may be observed in the order of grace. The favors lavished upon us by the hand of God may be precious and sublime, even without the concurrence of our will; but it is only when we freely co-operate with them that they adorn a holy life with inexpressible beauty, grandeur, and sublimity.

*

This comparison reminds us of another important truth. Human industry acts by far the least prominent part in forming the beauty and grandeur of scenery, for when man wishes to embellish or originate, he generally draws his ideas from nature. The same holds true of our co-operation with the grace of God in producing works of spiritual beauty and perfection. The principal portion of the work is God's, and even the little that we do, we do by the assistance of His grace.

*

What an addition to the grandeur and beauty of a landscape is a magnificent abbey, with its turrets, and the silvery yet solemn chimes of its bells reverberating through the distant valleys and mountains! Even a little chapel, with its unpretending steeple surmounted by a cross and its tiny bell, gives to the surrounding scenery a charm which no other edifice could impart. It is the marvelous union of nature and grace which produces this effect, reminding us that only Divine Faith can fill the heart of man with consolation.

When human co-operation promotes with untiring energy the work of God, we may behold rising up not only one or two buildings, but a city, well defended against the attack of enemies and adorned with palaces of heroic virtues. Blessed is that city, wherein the Lord resideth, and where all is done according to His most holy will!

*

Would you deem it a real misfortune, if a shower of diamonds should fall upon a field? Certainly not. No doubt the usual crop would be destroyed, but would the farmer regret his loss on gathering in this harvest of precious stones? In like manner we should not lament, though the storm of adversity hail destruction upon our earthly hopes. For by patience and submission to the will of God, we may change the stones of tribulation into jewels of merit, that will forever form our crown in heaven.

*

A careful florist waters his garden twice every day; early in the morning, to supply the plants with moisture during the heat of noon; and toward evening, to refresh them after being parched by the burning rays of the sun. We should be equally attentive to the garden of the heart. In the morning and evening we should, above all, moisten the soil by means of prayer; in the morning, to prepare against the heat of dissipation; and in the evening, to quicken it, after being exposed to the withering influence of our daily occupation. If we are faithful to this practice, earthly cares, far from drying up the heart, will rather promote the growth of merits for heaven.

As, at night, the dew falls to refresh the earth and enable it to bear the heat of the following day, so graces descend during the hours of sleep, to quicken the soul and prepare it for future combats. When a fervent evening prayer and devout reflection have disposed our hearts for the absorption of this dew, we are silently inflamed with the desire of perfection, and, on awaking, we turn almost unconsciously to God. Was it not this dew of grace that revived the spirit of a Xavier, who, during his repose, so frequently breathed the sweet name, "Jesus! Jesus?" Well may we apply to this great Saint the words of Scripture: "I sleep, but my heart watcheth." Oh! how strong the morning found him to bear the heat and burden of the day!

*

A soul which does not live interiorly united with God, by means of prayer, will not be visited during sleep with this dew of grace; and, at dawn of day, it will awaken dry and languid in the service of God.

*

This heavenly dew wonderfully quickens the heart, and prepares us to bear with renewed vigor the troubles and fatigue that we must expect in the service of God.

*

Though a field has been plowed, the seed sown, the grain reaped and stored away, we have yet no savory article of food. The wheat must be ground to flour before it can be made into bread, and the dough must be kneaded and baked before it can be of any service as nourishment. This ought to symbolize the necessity of trials and crosses for becoming true Christians, worthy of the title so much coveted and so well deserved by St. Ignatius, the martyr.

*

In walking through a tangled thicket, it would be foolish to let our arms hang listlessly down and walk along with eyes devoutly raised toward heaven. When the garden of the soul is overrun with wild passions, it would also be of little profit to indulge in contemplative prayer. Where there are so many obstacles to our spiritual progress, meditation, with practical resolutions formed in prayer and strengthened by the grace of God, is far more beneficial. After having at length uprooted our passions, we may indulge in the sweet contemplation of our Lord's love and His adorable perfections.

PLANTS AND TREES.

How many millions of men and animals have trodden the earth for nearly six thousand years past! How many vehicles have, day after day, coursed over its surface! Would it not seem that every sign of vegetable life must have long since disappeared? But no! the earth hides in her bosom a regenerative power, which continually renews the down-trodden vegetation. So men, who lead an interior life, and who are united to their Creator by a strong, active love, suffer no harm from their contact and intercourse with others. The power of grace and their interior union with God compensate for the devotions of a contemplative life, and counteract in a wonderful manner the destructive influence exercised over the heart by creatures, which, in themselves, are liable to interfere with the operations of grace.

*

Nature itself teaches us the importance of living in that place, and according to that vocation, to which God has called us. The tree which develops with a luxuriant growth in a valley would wither and droop at the summit of a mountain. Some plants flourish in sandy ground; others, in heavy bottom-land. So our Lord calls some persons to positions of honor and distinction, while He sanctifies others in the lowly pursuits of common life. Some He tries with aridity in prayer; others he inundates with consolations. A few find Him in the flowery paths of success, but many more must seek him on the thorny road of disappointment. Let us strive to discover that state of life for which God has destined us, and He will mercifully conduct us to the home of eternal blessedness.

*

A tree which is not sometimes pruned, will run into a forest of leaves, and will not yield much fruit. But if the exuberant foliage is lopped off, the tree is likely to bear fruit in abundance. Opposition or obedience may retrench many fair opportunities of action, but, by restraining the wild impulses of self-will, it will promote the growth of virtue.

*

This comparison admits of yet another application. Calumnies, which rob a person of his honor and good name, often do the work of a pruning-hook. If the trunk of the tree is sound, the branches that have been cut away, will soon be replaced by others much more healthy and luxuriant. So if the victim of calumny is a person of true virtue, his reputation will not only be regained, but it will grow in proportion to the injury which it has sustained.

*

The oak rears its giant form aloft, and with gnarly boughs looks defiance at other trees. Yet it is often a victim to the lightning's fatal flash, or the hurricane's fierce onset, while its fruit becomes the food of swine. A striking emblem of earthly greatness, combined with haughty self-deceit and degrading sensuality.

*

How little a wild pear resembles one that is cultivated and raised in an orchard! The good actions of two different individuals are often much more unlike. The one is perhaps in the state of sin, while the other is the friend of God; the one is moved by human respect, the other is actuated by nothing but supernatural motives.

*

Again, impelled by our own excited feelings, we sometimes chide others in so harsh a manner, that our words have an effect very similar to that produced by a sour wild pear. A sharp reproof, however well merited, will only tend to embitter. On the contrary, one that is tempered and sweetened by Christian charity will always be acceptable.

*

Where is the farmer who would not prefer sowing his seed in rich, moist ground to casting it upon a paved street? The hearts of simple country people, and those of the denizens of a great metropolis, often present a contrast no less striking. The former are generally well disposed to receive the seed of divine truth, while the latter are often hardened by the selfish maxims of the world. Too much intercourse with others, the cares of business, and an excessive love of amusements make them so callous that they care very little for the Divine

Word. Why, then, should not the minister of God prefer preaching to these simple souls? Christ Himself has set us the example, and the Holy Ghost has deigned to give it as a mark of His mission, that the Gospel is preached to the poor—" Pauperes evangelizantur."

※

Wild trees, when grafted, yield the most delicious fruit. In the same manner our untrained natural dispositions and inclinations, if grafted with Divine grace and a good intention, bring forth the choice fruits of virtue. If St. Paul had not been, before his conversion, so earnest and energetic in his persecution of the Church, he would not, perhaps, have become one of its most zealous Apostles.

※

The topmost branches of a tree are so very tender and weak, that we are almost led to consider them as of little use; and still, it is they that indicate the condition of the tree. While they are green and fresh, the trunk is sound; but when they wither, the root is decaying, and the tree will soon die. So, little practices of devotion, and small things done with the greatest fervor, are a sure index of the spiritual life of the soul. As long as you are faithful to them, your soul will remain in a healthy state, and will bear in abundance the fruits of eternal life. But when you become careless about them, it is an evident sign that your soul is seriously affected, and in great danger of perishing.

※

The wood of the olive tree is bitter, but the fruit is agreeable to the taste, and the oil obtained from it has so pleasant a flavor, that it is commonly known as *sweet oil*. So penance and mortification are bitter, but their fruit is an unalterable peace of heart, which is sweet, indeed, and gives us, on earth, a foretaste of the joys of heaven.

※

The human race is like a tree which the hand of death is continually shaking. The fruit that is ripe and mellow hourly falls down, but, at the same time, much unripe fruit also drops from the rustling branches. God grant that we may be of the ripe fruit when He sends death to gather us in!

※

When a nut-tree is shaken, those near it take flight to a convenient distance, where they can not be struck by the falling nuts. There are irascible characters, who, when excited, spare no one that comes within their reach. At such times, it is better, as the common saying has it, to "stand from under," lest we suffer from the missiles which they deal around them.

※

To exclude from our houses the burning rays of the sun, we plant shade trees, under whose branches we love to while away the sultry hours of a summer day. For our spiritual comfort, we ought to fly beneath the shelter of the cross. In its refreshing shade we shall not feel the heat of our daily trials and toils.

Pines and firs do not lose their foliage in winter, but retain, in the midst of their leafless comrades, a covering of green. Nay more, unlike other plants they do not suffer much injury from being barked. For they bleed but little, because the sap soon congeals and forms a solid crust over the wounded part. Persons, who, during the time of Divine visitations, change the juice of devotion into the pith of firm resolutions, remain vigorous during the winter of desolation. Even if wounded, they are speedily cured, through the healing power of their strong interior virtue.

*

We may call meditation the root of the virtuous life. Our determination to live solely for God is the trunk of that tree. The different good purposes, which spring thence, are the branches. The generous efforts, to which these give rise, represent the blossoms. Finally, our good actions form the fruit, into which the blossoms soon develop.

*

Fruit does not spring directly from the rough trunk, or from the spreading branches of a tree. No, it develops from the almost invisible little germ concealed within the blossom. See here, how even nature teaches us that the fruit of virtue is produced by the grace of God in the blossoms of holy desires; its germ is humility.

*

In our dealings with others, and especially when exhorting them, we should imitate the conduct of an expe rienced gardener. He does not pour the water in a stream upon the plants, because that would do them more harm than good; but, taking a watering-can, he lightly sprinkles the soil, and allows every drop to penetrate to the very roots. We should use a like discretion when we address ourselves to others, carefully suiting our lessons to their tempers and inclinations, and not allowing our reproaches to descend with a sudden overflow upon their heads.

*

During His triumphant entry into Jerusalem, Christ passed over the branches of olive and palm trees—emblems of meekness and fortitude. It is these virtues that give our sufferings their value and merit.

*

If a person should continuously fix his eyes on the plant growing out from the seed of a tree, he would not see the growth, but nevertheless the tree would grow over his head. So, persons really anxious to advance in perfection, are continually watching themselves; and they grow more and more perfect, though, in their own eyes, they make but little progress in virtue. The tree of sanctity daily becomes taller and more beautiful. Its growth is hidden from the pious souls themselves, but others meanwhile admire their virtues, once weak and flexible shrubs, now tall and stately as the cedars of Lebanon.

*

If a young tree be not properly cared for when it meets with outside impediments, it will grow up crippled and dwarfed. The tree of our good works, in conflict with human respect, if not fostered by a pure intention, will also be stunted, and never attain its full growth.

*

Nowhere is mountain vegetation so luxuriant as in the latitude of the equator. It was the hot climate of zeal, under the equator of an entire conformity of will with Almighty God, that made the hearts of the Saints so fertile, and so beautiful in the majestic trees of heroic virtue.

*

The tree of the cross extends its arms to every loving soul. Extend yours in return, with the desire of a St. Andrew, and press your crucified Saviour to your heart.

FLOWERS AND FRUITS.

THE Gospel, on its first appearance, transformed the moral wilderness of America into a lovely garden; and the first flower which adorned the once desert waste was called "Rose"—St. Rose, of Lima.

※

Some flowers wither, if rudely touched. There are graces of a higher order, which, if handled with too much curiosity, lose all their beauty. Souls that have received extraordinary favors, should imitate the holy indifference of the Saints, and not dive too deeply into the mysterious workings of God.

※

There are some flowers which may be gathered and made into bouquets, and there are others which fade as soon as they are culled. In like manner, there are mysteries of Divine Faith and Love, some of which have been revealed by God for all, and should therefore be communicated to the world at large. Others are intended for the few, and should be known only to God and the favored soul. This will prevent vainglory and show, which would soon deprive the soul of those special communications.

*

What is it that chiefly contributes to the beautiful appearance of a bouquet? A choice selection and a tasty arrangement of the flowers. In like manner, the effect of a sermon depends on a judicious selection, and a proper arrangement of the thoughts and sentiments. If the preacher lacks discretion in the choice, or art in the disposition of his matter, his discourse will resemble an uninteresting medley, rather than a pleasant bouquet of thoughts.

*

The beauty of a bouquet is greatly increased by mingling some green with the flowers. For this purpose, common leaves are, perhaps, the best suited, owing to the contrast which they present. In the same manner, a sermon must not run wholly upon abstruse, though sublime, truths. It must be varied by practical illustrations and familiar examples. While losing none of its dignity, it will thus be listened to with greater interest, and prove infinitely more useful to the mass of hearers.

*

This comparison is also true in an ascetic sense. What rendered the lives of the Saints so charming and attractive? The fact that, while practicing the most heroic acts of virtue, they were studiously careful to perform the ordinary duties of daily life with heavenly sweetness and patience. Though living among men, they seemed to attain to the perfection of the Angels.

*

Still another moral may be drawn from this comparison. Green is the color of hope—flowers are emblems of pure affection. Love of God should be ever mingled with the hope of pleasing Him, and of meriting an eternal reward.

*

In the spiritual life, this mingling of green may also mean the frequent renewal of our good intention, and multiplied acts of hope and humility. As the green is not altogether hidden under the flowers, but shows itself here and there in the bouquet, so those acts of virtue must not be interior only ; they must leave their impress on our whole exterior conduct.

*

As a maiden, filling her flower basket with roses, has no sooner culled one than she extends her hand for another, and still another, so, said our Lord to the blessed Henry Suso, the soul, standing before the rose-bush of tribulations, should pluck one after another, attracted by their fragrance, which, for a soul that loves her crucified Redeemer, is more delicious than the perfume of the roses of paradise.

One of the first flowers that open in spring, is the fragrant *lent-lily*. It is of a yellow color, the symbol of desire, and hence it very appropriately represents the Just, who sprang up and bloomed during the lapse of the forty centuries previous to the advent of Christ. For, were not those forty centuries a real Lent, a season of hunger and longing for the promised Messiah?

After the *lent-lily*, the *forget-me-not* soon rises, a sweet little flower, fit emblem of the martyred Innocents, plucked, alas! by too rude a hand and s rewn on the very cradle of the Infant Saviour. The *pink*, which skirts the borders of our gardens about Whitsuntide, is a type of the Apostles. The *violet*, spread with generous profusion over hill and dale, recalls the endless line of Confessors, who succeed each other through the ages. *White lilies* have always been regarded as figures of those pure Virgins, who cluster around the one spotless Lily of the Scriptures, around Mary, the Virgin without stain. In the *heliotrope*, which, unlike other flowers, hides not its head from the sun, but following his course through the heavens, directly faces his rays, we can easily recognize Christ Himself, who never shrank, like us poor mortals, from the scrutiny of His Father's eye, but always loved to center upon Himself the searching glance of heaven.

*

How sweet the perfume of all these flowers, as it is wafted from earth to heaven. Even here below, we sometimes experience a sense of the Divine perfume of virtue, when we converse with pious persons full of the fragrance of sanctity, but above all, when we read the lives of those servants of God, who have been already transplanted to paradise, to bloom there forever.

Roses bloom in the pathway of God's self-denying children, and they are found in the pathway of the pleasure-seeking votaries of the world. But these roses differ very much from each other. The latter soon lose their fragrance, their leaves fall off, and only the thorns remain. The former always remain sweet and beautiful. The thorns fall off, the flowers remain.

※

Let us all learn a lesson from the violet! This beautiful little flower is always found in some secluded spot, and almost hidden in the brightest green grass. Thus virtue should be unpretentious, and almost hidden by humility.

※

As in nature God has given to different plants their own medicinal properties, so He has also bestowed upon the different Saints, those plants and trees of the heavenly paradise, special power to heal various infirmities and ailments of the soul.

※

When aromatic herbs are put into water and exposed to the influence of heat, the water too becomes aromatic, and acquires medicinal properties. When we meditate upon the life and virtues of Christ, and the truths of Divine Faith are received into the heart, our affections, warmed by the ardor of Divine Love, imbibe this sweet aroma, and exert a wholesome influence upon others.

※

Slight imperfections are very often the little seeds, from which the enormous tree of crime will one day spring up.

*

It is pleasant to inhale the fragrance of a flower. The fragrance of virtue is love; because real virtue is always accompanied by the well-ordered love of God and man.

*

There are flowers which are apparently similar, but, while one fills the air with sweet perfume, the other is without odor. What a difference! Christian virtues are flowers of the former kind; the virtues of unbelievers belong to the latter class. We may, therefore, very properly call them artificial flowers.

*

Let us hear how St. John of the Cross speaks of the flowers of virtue growing in the garden of fervent souls. In the fifteenth stanza of his *Spiritual Canticle*, he says: "God is sometimes so indulgent to the spiritual bride, that through the genial influence of the Holy Spirit, who breathes upon the garden of the soul, He causes the buds of virtue to open and exhale their sweet odor. It is delightful to behold and enjoy the abundance of gifts then displayed before us, and feast our eyes upon the delicious flowers blooming on every side. No language can describe the peculiar fragrance diffused by each. So rich are these odors at times, that the soul seems enveloped in glory and bathed in inexpressible delight. Not only does she herself perceive them, but other persons, versed in spiritual matters, quickly notice their presence. The soul, in this state, resembles a delightful garden, full of the gifts and riches of God." In fact, holy souls nearly always have a certain air of sweetness and dignity, which inspires the beholder with awe and reverence, and is the necessary effect of their close and familiar converse with God.

*

In the blossom the germ of the fruit is formed. The blossom drops off, but the germ remains, develops into fruit, ripens. The same thing happens in the spiritual life. The delicate flower of tenderness and sensible devotion during prayer may fall off, but the germ of a strong resolution is yet left, and grows into the most delicious fruit of virtue.

*

Fruit made of wax sometimes looks more beautiful than real fruit, but how different to the taste and smell! So, the actions of the worldly-minded sometimes wear the semblance of genuine virtue; but they lack the substance, the reality, without which they can have no real value. They are destitute of the fragrance of a good intention, and of the delicious taste of a true, disinterested, Christian charity.

*

Fruits can be better preserved, if dried and pressed. They are all the sweeter for being crushed. Let persecution have a like effect upon you. Be patient under the crushing afflictions which it may please God to send you, and the fruits of your virtue will be far sweeter and sounder.

*

The blossoms of a tree are not an unfailing sign of fruit. They may either fall off, or be plucked by a hand that loves more to gather the fading beauty of a day, than to reap a bounteous harvest. Still, when there are but few blossoms, much fruit is never expected. Blossoms are a fitting emblem of those passing desires for perfection, which diffuse their fragrance over our hearts, and yet often leave us barren in the performance of virtuous actions. At one time, these desires do not become real, earnest resolutions; at another, the resolutions resemble a germ so shrunk and shriveled that it can never come to maturity. However, this longing for perfection is an indispensable condition of sanctity. Without it, we shall never be enriched with the precious fruits of Christian virtues.

*

Some fruits can be easily separated from the stone, and these are generally more sought for than those that cling to the stone. In the moral order, our will is to our works what the stone is to the fruit. If, when obedience speaks, we are ready to obey at once, and to give up our will, our good works are of a superior quality; but if we are self-willed and obstinate, they are of a very inferior kind.

*

By the ease with which the fruit separates from the stone, we may likewise tell whether it is ripe or not. Let us remember that the fruit of good works, which does not possess this quality, must be one day ripened by the terrible heat of purgatory.

*

Christ compares Himself to a vine, of which we are the branches. The grapes produced by a certain species of vine in the Holy Land contain no stone or seeds. If in every action our wills are entirely absorbed in the holy will of God, and no seeds of self-love are found in them, the virtues which we practice are of the rarest and choicest kind.

*

It is often necessary to shake a tree, if we would gather its fruit. Without this, much would remain and decay on the branches. So, vexations and troubles are useful to us. By their means, our virtues, when they are ripe, are gathered by the hands of our Guardian Angels, and garnered up in the storehouse of heaven. Were it not for those blessed trials and crosses, our virtues would wither and decay.

*

Upon the branches of fruit trees there appear in spring certain little lumps, called *eyes*. When these fail, there is no prospect of fruit. In regard to the fruit-tree of life, those eyes are the earnest, good intentions, by means of which we continually look toward God. Where these are wanting, there is no hope of our accomplishing anything meritorious in the sight of God.

❊

Very few persons allow the fruits of their virtuous undertakings for the glory of God to ripen. Too impetuous to wait, they gather, like children, the half-ripened crop. Nay, they often beat it off the tree, and eat it to their own harm, and so find only disappointment, where they had looked for satisfaction and pleasure.

❊

If a man were to mow down his crop while it is still in the bloom, through fear that some accident might befall the growing ear, would he not expose himself to ridicule? Quite as much blame attaches to those timid souls, who, through excessive caution, expose themselves to the very evils which they are over-anxious to avoid.

❊

It would be imprudent to touch roughly the blossoms upon a tree. By so doing, we might blight the fruit in the germ. Again, it would be foolish to make bouquets of them, for how delicate soever their tints, and delicious their odor, we would enjoy them only for a little while, but would never taste the fruit. In the same manner, it is injudicious to touch with too much curiosity the supernatural gifts communicated to the soul by interior union with God. This indiscretion is fatal to our progress, because it engenders vanity and self-conceit, which are very serious obstacles to the grace of God. Better, far better, is it to leave those blossoms of virtue untouched, and wait until, by the grace of God, the tender germ reaches maturity.

*

Rich in the variety of its fruits, and rejoicing in its flowers of every hue, year after year the earth casts off its finery, and yields its treasures into the hands of the Master of the Universe, and yet those treasures never seem to diminish. Fear not to be generous. Give, with a ready hand, of the goods which have fallen to your lot. He that gives to the poor, gives to God, who "loves a cheerful giver."

ANIMALS.

THOU shalt love God above all things, and thy neighbor as thyself." "He that loves me," said the Lord, "keeps my commandments." See what a lesson we can learn from the poor dumb animals! They can not love God, as we can, but they can and do keep His ordinations, and fulfill His holy will, which is the best proof of love. Behold how they all live and act in that sphere, and in strict harmony with that end, for which God destined them! They could not be more faithful than they are. They are all made to serve man in some way; for this they were endowed with their different faculties and instincts. Not even from the motive of love could they do their work better, or correspond more exactly to the designs of Providence. Each lives contentedly in its own place. Not one revolts against the decree which has fixed its end and office. Who ever heard of a fish wishing to live on dry land, or of a quadruped aspiring to the life and movements of a bird?

*

"The second commandment is like unto the first." Love of our neighbor yields only to love of God. In regard to this duty, there is much to learn from the actions and habits of animals. How many proofs and signs of attachment do they not give toward others of the same species? They like to live together. They are animated with the spirit of sociability—that great principle of human life, which can never be realized except through sincere love.

*

Man often has reason to be ashamed, when he considers how submissively and patiently animals suffer, and how they try to satisfy the person on whom they depend for their daily nourishment. They seem to exert every faculty, and to put forth all their strength, to accomplish his will. Look, for instance, at a team that is toiling up hill with a heavy load. How they pull, and tug, and strain, till they have reached the top! If we would employ all our energies to do the will of God, our Supreme Ruler, on whom we depend for time and eternity, what would we not be able to do—what great things could we not accomplish—what difficulties would we not overcome to reach the heights of perfection?

*

Even when suffering from sickness, animals usually lie patiently on the ground, with an expression of passive resignation to their lot. Man, on the contrary, often murmurs against Divine Providence, though he knows the value of sufferings borne for the love of God!

*

How wonderful is the faculty of smelling in animals! Dogs often follow their masters to incredible distances, led only by this power of tracing their footsteps. What fidelity and attachment to their owners! If we would only make use of our faculties to find out the will of God, and then faithfully to follow it with all the affection of our heart, we would never lose Him, nor stray from the path of salvation.

*

The passions and inclinations of the human heart are reflected in the brute creation. In animals, we find the type of nearly every virtue and every vice that distinguish men. Hence the expressions: "Cunning as a fox," "faithful as a dog," "treacherous as a cat," "stubborn as a mule," "lazy as a bear," "hungry as a wolf," "fierce as a tiger," "brave as a lion," "meek as a lamb," "mild as a dove," "busy as a bee."

*

In Paradise, man held the animals in subjection to his will. After the fall, he no longer had this absolute mastery over the animal kingdom. So in regard to his carnal inclinations, and the brute instincts of the body; they were once under his absolute control, but, since the day on which sin entered into the world, they are in rebellion against reason. It is with difficulty that he now restrains these wild beasts by the chains and bars of good resolutions.

*

Holy desires are like the feathers of an eagle's wing. If he has a full plumage, the king of birds sweeps with ease through the air, and breasts even the strongest gale. Clip his pinions, and you cripple him. He can scarcely rise from the ground. So the soul, which is filled with a longing for perfection, flies with ease in the way of perfection, and bravely contends with every obstacle that would retard its progress. But the slothful soul, deprived of these wings of holy desires, plods languidly along, and presents a pitiful appearance in the eyes of God and His Saints.

*

As soon as one little bird begins to warble his sweet notes, all the others take up the strain, till from every thicket and every glen the joyful melody breaks upon the ear, and the woodland seems to be alive with song. Such is the influence of good example, especially in pious conversation.

*

Night birds have large eyes, which enable them to approach our dwellings, under the cover of darkness, and with their dismal hootings to molest us during the hours of rest. But they can see nothing in the day-time, and generally bury themselves in the gloom of thick forests. Here is a faithful picture of the infidels of our day. Very often they are endowed with good natural faculties, and amid the darkness which surrounds them can easily discover occasions to indulge their sinful passions. But they can not abide the daylight of revelation; they can not bear to view things in the glorious light of the Sun of Faith. Like the birds of night, they pursue their way in utter darkness.

Naturalists say that the owl sometimes devours its young in the egg. It is thus that vainglory deals with our good works. It destroys their merit, leaving nothing but the empty shell of pride.

*

Birds pick up every grain with great precaution; yet they show, at the same time, a certain indifference for the future, because they carelessly leave what they do not need at the present moment. Just the reverse is the case with certain animals. They bury in the earth what they can not eat at once, but are far from delicate in the choice of their food. Souls, aiming at perfection, should use earthly goods and pleasures as birds do their food; that is, only when urged by necessity, and then with indifference, leaving to Divine Providence the care of supplying for their future wants.

*

Let us imitate the eagle, which, by the aid of its powerful wings, ascends to a certain height, and then appears to repose upon them in the air. Making use of our intellect and will, let us ascend upon the wings of Divine grace to those heights of contemplation, which the Lord may point out to us; and then let us tranquilly repose in His holy presence.

*

What a difference between the steady and majestic flight of an eagle and the inconstant fluttering of a butterfly! Such is the difference between the firm resolution of a Christian, borne aloft by Faith, and the capricious humors of an unbeliever tossed about by every wind of opinion.

It is said that when the eagle wishes to devour a turtle, he takes it high up into the air, and then lets it fall upon a rock. The devout soul acts in the same manner with temptations against Faith. Imitating the ways of the eagle, she ascends high up into the regions of Divine Love, and casts the obtrusive temptation upon the rock of holy Faith.

*

But we should act thus not only with temptations against Faith, but with all other temptations. When violently assaulted by our evil inclinations, let us raise our hearts to heaven, despising all earthly things and recalling to mind the eternal truths of holy Faith. The violence of the temptation will then diminish at once, according to the promise of the Holy Ghost: "Remember thy last end, and thou shalt not sin forever."

*

No bird ascends with so rapid a flight as the eagle, but when he has reached the highest regions of the atmosphere, he poises himself upon his wings, stretched out in the form of a cross, while his piercing eye is steadily fixed upon the sun. Souls, gifted with the grace of contemplation, resemble the eagle. Having arrived at the blissful state of union with God, they no longer indulge in oral prayer, but remain absorbed in the love of God, and fix their eyes upon the eternal Sun of truth and love.

*

A bird moving through the air with great velocity seems rather to fly by an effort of its will than by the use of its wings. The fish, rapidly darting through the waters, seems to be urged on by the force of the will more than by the motion of its fins. The soul, moving onward to perfection, seems to be impelled by the strength of its own free will, sustained by Divine grace, rather than by its other natural faculties.

*

A bird must move its wings very rapidly and with great force in the lower regions of the air. In the upper part of the atmosphere, the eagle rests upon the mass of air beneath its wings. This points out how we should conduct ourselves in prayer. If God's favors are extraordinary and abundant, it is far better to confine ourselves to a loving union with him, than to labor in vocal prayer, or in the exercise of the faculties in the ordinary way of meditation.

*

As long as a bird keeps its wings folded, it is unable to fly. It can, at best, hop about upon the ground. If it would raise itself on high, it must extend its wings in the form of a cross, and then its ascent toward heaven is easy. In like manner, the soul is unable to ascend to God while its wings, that is, its faculties, are folded in selfishness. It must be filled with a longing desire for heaven, a readiness to forget self, and to suffer whatever God may require as a proof of fidelity. The two wings, the intellect and the will, must be stretched out in the form of a cross; that is, both must be prepared to bear the soul onward in the path of suffering.

*

Worldlings, who seek for sensual pleasures, may be likened to birds of prey feeding upon carrion, and imagining that they taste the delights of real bliss. Souls spiritually united with God, turn with disgust from such food, to partake of a heavenly banquet.

*

The nightingale trills its sweet notes all alone. The lark sings the praises of God in the solitude of the distant sky. They teach us that solitude or retirement best disposes us to lift our hearts in prayer and thanksgiving to God.

*

Listen to the sweet music of the woodland birds. Each one, by its joyous carols, invites all the others to try their best. How pleasant and soothing it is to hear them joining with their many voices in the chorus! So the different affections of the soul should encourage each other to join in the common concert to give praise to God.

*

If we should unexpectedly see a serpent approaching us, a first involuntary impulse moves us either to kill it, or to recoil with horror. The same feelings should actuate us when we behold the hideous form of temptation. Terrified at the thought of committing sin, whose touch is more poisonous than the bite of a serpent, we should either crush the evil suggestion instantly, or seek safety in a speedy flight to God.

*

God has furnished some snakes with rattles, that man may be warned of the presence of those reptiles, and make his escape. In the same manner He usually cautions us, by a variety of circumstances, against the approach of violent temptations.

※

Snakes have two rows of teeth. In some, the teeth are hollow and filled with poison. Behold here a true picture of man's understanding and will, when devoted to the service of the demon. Turned away from God, these powers are hollow and communicate a fatal venom to our entire being. The understanding is hollow, because it lacks reflection; the will, because it is void of the true love of God. When these powers are thus affected, the poison of sin is infused into the soul, and produces death.

✽

The serpent is of a sluggish nature, but no sooner does it perceive its prey, than it springs forward, quick as a flash, to gratify its appetite. Darting out its forked tongue, it seizes its victim, and coiling around it, tortures, before it destroys it. The system of indifferentism, if we may dignify it by the name of system, is of a slothful, chilling nature. Questions of the most vital importance can arouse no interest. But when there is an occasion to gratify the desires of a depraved heart, it becomes at once instinct with life and animation. Remorse of conscience is stifled and crushed at once. It darts upon its victim with its double tongue of falsehood, and loves to torture with calumny, even when it can not destroy its enemy.

Bees are harmless so long as they are not molested, but woe to him who dares trouble them at their busy toil. They have a sting, which they will surely use against the disturber. So there are pious souls, who are apparently all sweetness, without the slightest taint of malice in their nature. Yet cross them in their views, or hurt their feelings ever so little, and presently you will feel their sting.

*

To deprive bees of the fruit of their patient toil, the means often adopted is to raise a smoke about the hive. This blinds the bees, and enables us to take out the honey. The human heart resembles a hive, in which is stored the honey of our good works. Be careful least the devil envelop your heart in the clouds of vainglory, thus blinding you spiritually, and depriving you of the good, which, after much patient toil, you had amassed.

*

The puncture made by the sting of an insect is very small, yet it often has alarming consequences, owing to the virus which has entered the flesh. Thus a single remark, which in itself appears innocent, may, from the malice which has dictated it, prove fatal to the soul.

*

The threads of spiders' webs are curiously constructed and artfully interwoven; but they have no strength, and are fit only to catch flies. Modern philosophical systems bear a close resemblance to these webs; and their authors, as far as regards real merit, are only spiders that surround themselves with the meshes of fine-spun sophisms, to ensnare the thoughtless or worldly-minded. Their subtle theories, often so subtle that the authors themselves have no clear conception of them, are apparently well connected, but they are woven around a false principle. They may glisten for a time in the sunshine of human applause, but, at the first breath of sound argument, they will be torn to pieces, or else, after the lapse of a few years, they will hang neglected upon the walls, covered with the dust of oblivion.

*

Beasts, when attacked, show their teeth, as a sign that they are on the defensive. Whenever the devil begins to tempt you, show him your good resolutions, and your determination to keep them. The infernal enemy fears them, for he knows, that if you offer him a vigorous resistance, he will be conquered, and forced to beat an inglorious retreat.

*

Many of those who aspire to perfection, resemble a bird confined in a cage of wicker work. It is of no avail to the little prisoner to spread his wings and attempt to regain his freedom, unless he has first, with his sharp bill, broken the ozier twigs that inclose him. But when a successful effort has once restored him to the open air, he can soar aloft, and sing a hymn of praise to his Creator. So the soul, that longs to breathe the pure air of sanctity, must not content herself with the mere exercise of prayer. By a generous resolve, she must break the twigs of her many imperfections, and thus attain to the holy liberty of the children of God. She may then, on the wings of contemplation, direct her flight to heaven, and repose on the heights of a blissful union with God.

*

How gorgeous is the plumage of the peacock; how brilliant the many eyes upon its glossy feathers! Conscious of its own beauty, the haughty bird unfolds its splendors to the sunlight, and in its very carriage betrays its self-conceit. But no sooner does it look at its ungainly feet than it droops its head for shame. Thus ought pure intentions beautify our actions in the sight of God; but, lest we grow proud, the view of our own nothingness must furnish us with sentiments of humility.

*

How anxiously the hunted deer listens to the barking of the hounds, to discover from what quarter the danger threatens! How it moves its ears backward and forward, to the right and to the left! Thus should we act at the approach of temptation. Looking back into the past, we should hearken to the whisperings of experience; then, glancing into the unexplored future, we should shudder at the threats of Divine justice. We should consider the right and the left, balance the good and the evil consequences of what we are about to do, and then, with the fleetness of the deer, flee from the seductive temptation.

*

While man continued in the state of original justice, he was raised above the weaknesses of human nature.

But seeking, through pride, to become equal to God, he was cast down from his former dignity, and delivered over to his passions. No longer the sovereign, but the slave of his lower nature, he became in many respects similar to brute animals, so that it might be said of him: "Man was compared with the beasts, and found like one of them."

*

As it is useless to brush off the cobwebs hanging about your room, if you neglect to kill the spider that weaves them, so, though you may resist a temptation, even repeatedly, it will have been all in vain, unless you shun the occasion that gives rise to it.

*

There is no certain preventive against vermin but cleanliness. Without that, you may destroy numbers of them, but you will never succeed in extirpating them. Thus a soul troubled by bad thoughts and desires, will never succeed in expelling them, so long as she remains in the uncleanliness of willful imperfections and inordinate attachments. For one thought or desire driven off gives place to another. How much better and easier would it be to remove those willful imperfections, to break off those inordinate attachments to creatures, and so to destroy at their birth the whole brood of temptations.

*

In summer, we surround our beds with a gauze of thin net-work, as a protection against flies, musquitoes, and other annoying insects. In the same manner, those who wish to enjoy the sweet repose of contemplation, must draw around them the screen of a total forgetfulness of all earthly things. Without this precaution, they will be continually pestered by distractions, and, tossing about in restless anxiety during the whole time of prayer, they will rise more weary, perhaps, and more feeble in virtue, than before they began their devotions.

✱

Many insects have *feelers*, which they extend when they seek nourishment, and draw in when they perceive the approach of danger. We, too, have our *feelers*, which we extend after whatever pampers pride or sensuality, and draw in at the first appearance of a check on our favorite passions.

✱

The truly pious soul also possesses *feelers*, but of a different kind. They are love of God and our neighbor.

✱

The hair of the vilest animals makes very good brushes, with which to clean our clothes. Our imperfections may answer a similar purpose, for they naturally prompt us to sentiments of humility, than which nothing is more efficacious to purify our souls from the defilement of sinful inclinations.

✱

For greater security against the stealthy approach of thieves, we keep a good watch-dog on our premises. The slightest noise alarms him. The dog is an emblem of sincere attachment and fidelity. Sincere attachment to truth, and fidelity to our pious resolutions, are the best guardians at the door of the heart. They will sound the alarm at the least shadow of sin.

*

If a horse is sluggish and will not go, a whip may be of great service. But would it be advisable to apply that instrument of torture continually and immoderately? Certainly not; for, smarting under the pain, the poor animal might run off and plunge headlong down a precipice. So an excess of spiritual chastisement may drive the refractory sinner to despair. Remember the admonition of holy Scripture: "Noli esse justus nimis"—"be not too just."

*

So-called philosophical virtues may be justly compared to the feeble light of the glow-worm, which shines as long as darkness prevails, but disappears with the first bright beam of the rising sun. The virtues of the heathen and the unbeliever vanish, in the same manner, before the sunbeams of holy Faith. Examined in that light, they prove to be nothing but the faint glimmer emitted by the little glow-worm of self-love and egotism, without the heat of that fire which Christ came to enkindle in the hearts of men, to light their pathway up to heaven.

*

Snails carry their houses on their backs, and live surrounded by slime. They are like those philosophers who carry their systems along with them, and dwell, as it were, in the slime of self-conceit, thinking that they have discovered the fountain-head of divine wisdom, and secured the permanent enlightenment of the human race. The hollow shell of their systems may resist the gentle pressure of an infant's foot, but it will be crushed beneath the heavy tread of a strong man. It may seem strong to children, but it gives way before the first blow of a logical argument.

*

There are also snails without shells. These are simply black worms, crawling over the ground. Yet the snail with a house on its back is, in itself, no better than those without one. In like manner, infidelity, with or without the shell of a plausible system, is a vile worm, crawling in the dust of the earth.

*

The shell of the land-turtle is so hard, that a loaded wagon may pass over, without injuring it. That shell is a figure of prejudice. A heavy load of arguments and proofs may pass over it, and yet it will remain as strong and stubborn as ever. But there is a means by which we can remove the shell from the turtle. If we press on it with the foot, the turtle will stretch out its head, which we can cut off, and then remove the shell. The ugly head typifies the hidden sin, covered with the hard shell of prejudiced unbelief; for, as is well known to spiritual directors and confessors, the obstinacy of the unbeliever is not so much the effect of delusion in the intellect, as of a moral disorder in the heart. As soon as the hidden passion is subdued and rooted out, the shell of prejudice, whether against Revelation or the Church, falls away of itself.

*

"Thou shalt walk upon the asp and the basilisk, and thou shalt trample under foot the lion and the dragon," says the Holy Ghost. Every Christian, who subdues the vice of pride, walks victoriously over these four monsters.

*

Pride is typified by the *asp;* for the asp is the emblem of Lucifer, who, the first, has sinned by pride.

Pride is typified by the *basilisk*, of which it is said: "There is death in its very glance." This vice is forever gazing around in search of worldly applause, and thus continually destroys the merit of our good works. Pride is typified by the *lion;* for, as the movements of the lion are imposing, so the vice of pride always seeks to present an appearance, and, with a view to this end, studies its every movement. Moreover, the lion is the most powerful of all animals, just as pride is the strongest of all vices. By its aid, men are even enabled to vanquish the other vices, especially those that would *hurt* their honor and good name. The *dragon*, also, which is noted for its voracity, is an appropriate emblem of pride, which is never satisfied, but continually seeks for new honors. Finally, the asp may be considered a figure of this vice, because this was the form under which the devil—the personification of pride—appeared to tempt man to sin.

When we see flies hovering around the most exquisite delicacies, we might be led to suppose that they are very dainty in their taste; yet we know well that it is not so. They are just as willing to partake of the most loathsome and disgusting food. Here is a good picture of worldlings, whom St. Francis used to compare to flies.

*

The raven which Noah let fly from the ark, did not go back, while the dove, which he sent forth some time after, soon returned, because it could find no resting place. Why this difference? The raven, finding the bodies of men and animals left by the waters of the flood, glutted itself upon them; but the dove could not live amid such infection. In like manner, sinners delight to feed upon the filth of moral corruption and sensual gratifications. But the pure and holy soul finds no attraction for these disgusting and loathsome pleasures.

*

A single grasshopper is a harmless creature. But let a swarm of them come down upon our fields and gardens, and they are a terrible plague, devastating entire countries, and exposing them to the danger of famine. The grasshopper is an emblem of levity. To indulge in occasional trifling is not dangerous for our spiritual advancement; but woe to us, if our frivolity should become habitual and taint all our actions. It will soon be as pernicious to the harvest of virtue, as armies of grasshoppers to the teeming fields.

*

The principal object of penance is to extirpate from the soul all the inordinate affections and desires of self-love. It would, therefore, be of little spiritual profit to us, were we to perform many acts of exterior penance, yet secretly indulge our own caprice, vainglory, and self-satisfaction, by following the dictates of our own unstable fancy, rather than the wise counsels of our spiritual advisers. This would be as foolish as to attempt to kill a fish by throwing water on it. Draw the fish upon the dry land, and it will soon die.

*

Noxious weeds and dangerous beasts of prey are comparatively rare. Moreover, man may destroy and exterminate those that do exist, and, in their stead, cultivate wholesome herbs, and rear useful animals. If he neglects to do so, he alone is to blame. The same holds true in a spiritual sense. If we allow the poisonous weeds of our sinful inclinations to grow up, if we nourish dangerous passions and vicious habits, we alone are at fault. It is in our power to extirpate them, and replace them by practices and habits of virtue.

*

We have an instinctive aversion to reptiles or creeping things. They may be taken as the type of those men who, through human respect, or in a spirit of abject flattery, degrade themselves before others. Or, again, they may represent those who forget their high destiny for heaven, and crawl in the dust of the earth, seeking only what is below, not what is above.

It is said that no quadruped ever looks higher than a few feet from the ground, unless when frightened by some accident. How many men, solicitous only for that which is below, and living, as Scripture says, "like the horse and the mule," never elevate the eye of the mind more than a few feet! They have, perhaps, a few principles of morality, but scarcely rise to the height of the ten Commandments. They feel satisfied, if they live like good Pagans or good Jews. They hardly ever think of heaven, unless frightened by some sad or untoward incident.

*

In animals, we remark one or all of these passions prevailing, viz: greediness, anger, sensuality. So, among sinners, these are the three predominant passions: gluttony, anger, sensuality.

*

To deter wild beasts from attacking us, when they threaten an assault, we are advised to look them resolutely and steadily in the eye. In the determined gaze of man, they, as it were, behold his superiority, and are subdued. In like manner, a firm look at the hideousness of vice and crime subdues temptation. It gives the devil to understand, that the shamefulness of sin is fully understood.

We may say, therefore, that as a look directed continually toward God, a ceaseless walking in his presence, makes us advance with zeal on the path of perfection; so, an intrepid, unquailing glance at the "abomination of iniquity,' frees us from the danger of the allurement of temptation, and keeps us removed from the way of perdition.

Wild beasts are especially terrible on account of the strength which resides in their claws and teeth. Hence it is, that when menacing man, they open their mouths and raise their paws. The open mouth symbolizes the temptations of the tongue and taste; and the elevated paws, those in which the hand is the instrument of sin. If we could pull out the teeth, and cut off the paws of these beasts, they would become harmless. Happy the soul that, by mortification, controls the tongue and subdues gluttony, thus gaining a mastery over the mouth; and that knows how to suppress every temptation to sins in which the hands lend themselves to evil deeds.

*

Is it not a strange and humiliating fact, that, as anatomists inform us, the internal organization of swine is the one, among all quadrupeds, that most nearly resembles the internal structure of man. Unfortunately, many of the children of men appear outwardly refined and honest, but, interiorly, **in the moral order, they are like them, unclean animals.**

*

Swine are not fastidious in their taste, either as to the kind of food, or the place where it is to be found, provided it satisfies their appetite. There are men so eager to satisfy their cravings for money, or for sensual pleasure, that they will seek it, no matter where it is to be found, or by what means, how foul soever, it is to be obtained.

*

Animals that seem to live on the best terms with one another, suddenly become enemies when food is thrown before them. They are ready to fight, and to tear each other to pieces. How often do we see something of the same kind among men! A question of money, business, property, or inheritance, has often severed the bonds of a life-long friendship, and made even brothers and sisters enemies for years. The ties of money are sometimes stronger than those of blood, and cause men to sacrifice not only their friends, but their own lives, and even their souls.

*

As in the vegetable, so in the animal kingdom, the most useful species are not those that are remarkable for beauty and variety of color. Panthers, tigers, and snakes are beautifully striped or mottled; domestic cattle are rather plain in appearance. The same holds good in regard to birds. Those of the most gorgeous plumage, especially the gaudy birds of South America, are generally poor singers. The analogy may be found also among men.

*

The embraces of this sinful world are like those of a boa-constrictor. As this huge serpent is able to crush in its folds even the bones of a lion, so the caresses of the world, its applause and favors, can break the strong resolutions, even of one whose virtues proclaimed him a king among men.

*

The snake does not masticate its food, but swallows it slowly and with much exertion. So prejudice, whether of heresy or unbelief, gorges itself with the most incredible calumnies, and swallows down, without examination, the most improbable stories.

*

As soon as the leech has glutted itself with blood, it falls off. So the sinner may for a time succeed in satisfying his appetite for pleasure, but after a short while he feels sated and disappointed, and drops the object of his sinful passion. The pleasures of sin are as short-lived and as unsatisfactory in the end, as the feast at which the leech gorges itself with blood, only to lose it a moment after.

*

Bears are said to be plunged in a profound sleep during winter. Whilst in this state of torpor, they live on the fat which they gained during the previous summer. Like them, are those persons, who were once faithful, practical Christians, but who, falling into the sleep of religious indifference, retain for a long time some sense of religious feeling and esteem of Christian virtue. By and by they lose even these, and retain naught but the skeleton of a pagan honesty.

*

Bull-frogs, in the slime, by the edge of a pool, gazing with their big eyes in one direction, and continually uttering their croak, are dignified representatives of those business men, stationed in the mud of traffic, whose eyes are fixed constantly on their goods, and whose lips incessantly repeat the croak of " money," " money."

*

Owls possess large eyes, but can not see during daylight. Yet they open them, and move them now up and then down, and from side to side. They are a type of those worldly men, who are endowed with talents, and who see well in the darkness of earthly affairs, but who appear blind in the daylight of revealed truth.

*

We may, in a special manner, compare *heretics* to owls. Those opposed to our doctrines, seem to be big-eyed when searching the Scriptures for texts that may appear to favor their tenets. Devoutly they turn their eyes to heaven and to earth; they seem to be absorbed in piety, and yet how pitifully blind are they when it comes to recognizing and acknowledging the only true rule of Faith—the infallible authority of the Church!

*

All animals, even the wildest, fly before fire. In like manner, the wild beasts of temptation shun the consideration of everlasting flames. Never forget the admonition of the Holy Ghost: "Remember thy last end, and thou wilt never sin."

*

Naturalists tell us that the worms which crawl on the ground are blind. Yet, when prevented from going straight-forward, they elevate their heads toward heaven. It is the same with those men who call themselves Christians, and yet grovel in the dust of earthly desires, and never look to heaven, except when they meet with some unexpected calamity.

*

A lion-tamer once said, that when entering a den, he felt more fear of the lioness than of the lion. It was remarked in turn, that this was not strange, since a woman in ill temper is always more to be feared than a man. And the same analogy holds among animals.

THE INTERIOR OF THE EARTH.

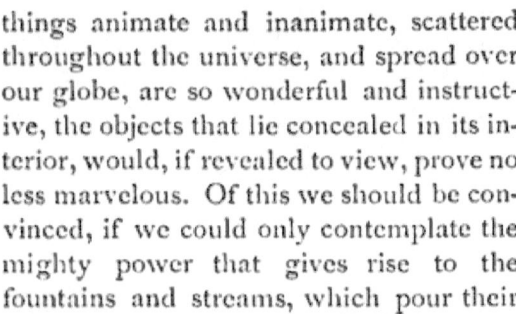

IF things animate and inanimate, scattered throughout the universe, and spread over our globe, are so wonderful and instructive, the objects that lie concealed in its interior, would, if revealed to view, prove no less marvelous. Of this we should be convinced, if we could only contemplate the mighty power that gives rise to the fountains and streams, which pour their waters into the ocean, whence, returning, they are again discharged into the deep. Or, if we beheld how the internal heat of the earth diffuses itself, continually renewing the productive power of the globe. Considering those subterranean depths with the eyes of Faith, what have we to say? May we not look down into them as containing Purgatory, the Limbo of unbaptized children, and Hell? O, those mysteries of the globe beneath our feet! What a world of wonders!

*

Under the surface of the globe, it seems that there is nothing but the natural inertia of inanimate dust; and yet what a grand, majestic, uninterrupted activity reigns there! So the existence of contemplative souls, living a hidden life in the midst of the world, may seem to the children of earth to be rather of a quiet, idle nature; nevertheless, what an active life they lead before God, and how intimately this hidden life is connected with the active life of the Church Militant!

*

How indispensable is the use of metals in civilized life! They are no less important than those substances that may be found on the surface of the globe; yet, these metals lie hidden under the surface, God's providence having so disposed things that man should be obliged to study the works of the Almighty, and to use his reason, if he would live in comfort on earth.

*

Those hidden treasures of the mineral kingdom, on whose use depend the wealth and splendor of social life, oblige men, who search for them, to humble themselves so far as to kneel down in the mining pits, where they are engaged in digging. How many are there who find it hard to kneel in a church, during a quarter of an hour, that prostrate themselves the whole day before the mammon of gold!

*

The finer are distinguished from the baser metals by greater ductility and permanence of lustre. Similar properties belong to the higher and nobler kinds of virtue. When ordinary virtue comes in contact with the world, it knows not how to accommodate itself to circumstances, and easily contracts the rust of impatience, inconstancy, vanity, and self-esteem; but solid virtue is proof against vain applause, as well as against contempt, and readily yields to others without yielding to their vices.

*

Seldom are metals found pure; they are usually mixed up or amalgamated with other substances, and only after being subjected to different chemical or mechanical processes, the pure metal is obtained. In like manner, we seldom find natural virtues pure in practice. They are, more or less, accompanied by other motives, and we need not expect to separate them from the alloy, except by the careful process of Christian asceticism.

*

Gold is often found associated with quartz. Men undergo hardship in digging, pulverizing, and washing the mixture, until the gold is separated and obtained in a pure state. So, too, in regard to the gold of perfection. We shall never acquire it, except by passing through much hardship and labor in pulverizing our imperfections, and separating them from the pure ore of virtue.

*

Certain articles glitter like gold, though they are only alloys of the inferior metals. There may likewise be works which shine like the pure gold of virtue, but which are, nevertheless, only a mixture of custom, natural inclination, caprice, and human respect. The fire of which St. Paul speaks, will one day test such compositions, and melt them like wax.

Stalactitic caverns present a magnificent appearance. The pillars and walls are formed by the crystallization of water constantly dripping down. A heart, in which the tears of penance and devotion crystallize into firm resolutions, and determined purpose of amendment, presents a still more glorious sight.

*

There is yet a part of creation on the globe almost unknown to man—the depths of the sea. Could we only behold the bed of the seas and oceans, some of which are covered with corals and unknown marine vegetation, and could we but view the myriads of animate beings that glide with the rapidity of lightning through those watery realms, great would be our pleasure. We shall one day, when united with God, have that satisfaction. Then we shall see all in Him, all the fullness of created perfection, as reflected in the universe; as well as the fullness of His own infinite perfection.

*

The different forms of life among fishes and other aquatic beings are, for the most part, unknown to us; yet there is one peculiarity observable, very similar to what obtains in human life and conduct: fishes devour one another, and so do men. The interests and gains of one person are sooner or later swallowed up by others. Men really live upon one another.

*

Christ Himself compares the Apostolic vocation to that of the fisherman; but with this difference, that fishes are caught by earthly fishermen to be killed. On the contrary, the fishes caught by Apostolic labors are destined to live in everlasting bliss.

*

We can form but a very imperfect idea of the immense activity that prevails among the countless forms of living things found in the depths of the sea; yet all this is hidden from the eyes of men. But if it is unseen, it is not therefore useless. So with the activity and energy of the soul—living, "though hidden with Christ in God," a contemplative, but at the same time a most useful life in the communion of Saints.

Part II.

NOTHING in the universe attracts our attention so powerfully as man—because he is the noblest being in the visible world—because he is a rational being, and therefore an image of God—and because we ourselves belong to this category of beings, created by God and for God. Man is composed of a body and a rational soul. He is placed in society, has the power of communicating with his fellow-creatures, and is endowed with talents to make the exterior world subservient to his will and wants.

THE BODY—ITS SENSES AND MEMBERS.

WOULD you know the true value of the body as compared with the soul? St. Paul tells us, that "the body burdens the soul." How often do we not experience this truth, that the body is a clog, and an impediment in the practice of virtues and good works?

*

There is a defect of the eye, called squinting, which mars the appearance of the whole countenance, and prevents it from being beautiful, in spite of the regularity of every other feature. In the moral order, this defect is envy, which disfigures a character otherwise beautiful.

*

Always fearful of running against something, a man that is blindfolded, gropes his way timidly along, even on level ground. Every little unevenness is enlarged by his imagination into a hill; if he steps into a gutter he receives a severe shock. Here is a true type of a scrupulous soul.

The devil puts on our eyes, according to circumstances, two different kinds of spectacles. In the hour of temptation, he furnishes us with convex glasses, to diminish our aversion for the sin into which he seeks to draw us; at the time of confession, on the contrary, he furnishes us with concave glasses, that, frightened by the greatness of our offenses, we may be prevented, by a false shame, from declaring them to our spiritual director.

*

Persons absorbed in reflection, now raise their eyes to heaven, now cast them down to earth, or even close them entirely. When we are to determine about some weighty matter, we should first look toward heaven and consider what is the good pleasure of God; then cast our eyes upon the earth and reflect upon the vanity and nothingness of everything transitory; and, finally, closing them upon all purely human considerations, decide by the light of eternity.

*

Humility and pride resemble two perspectives. In the former our merit appears distant and insignificant, our imperfections near and enlarged. In the latter, on the contrary, our merit stands forth in undue proportions, while our imperfections dwindle away in the dim distance.

*

How sad it is that we generally do not see the things of this world in their true light, until the shadows of the tomb thicken around us and the finger of death closes our eyes forever.

Some persons can distinguish an object only when it is near them; others can see it better at a great distance than when it is directly before their eyes. A like diversity may be noticed in the capacities of men. Some are very far-sighted, divining, with astonishing precision, possible future contingencies, but, at the same time, they seem to have no eyes for the present, and often neglect the means now within their reach. Others may be called short-sighted, because, though fully alive to the wants of the present, they are so improvident of the future, that they incur the risk of losing, owing to some untoward circumstance, what it has cost them great sacrifices to acquire. Both classes would do well to use the right kind of spectacles.

*

When the minutest particle enters the eye, tears begin to flow, and generally soon remove the annoyance. The heart may, in some respects, be called the eye of the soul. If it is so very sensitive as to wince at the slightest faults, the tears of repentance will soon wash them away.

*

We may say that tears speak, because they are as expressive as words. Perhaps we should say that the language of tears is often far more eloquent than that of the tongue. What the most earnest words fail to effect may be accomplished by the tear silently stealing down the cheek.

*

How powerful is the voice of tears! How eloquently does it plead for pardon! St. Mary Magdalen experienced its virtue when silently weeping at the Savior's feet. How sweetly came the assurance from His Divine lips: "Thy sins are forgiven thee."

*

St. Aloysius used to walk with his eyes modestly cast down. This gave his whole exterior an expression of innocence. How many are there who seem to fear meeting the gaze of others, and who walk along with downcast eyes! Is it through modesty? Ah! no, the voice of conscience unceasingly reminds them that they have lost the precious charm of purity.

*

St. Aloysius carefully kept his bodily eyes bent toward the earth, but not so the eyes of his soul. These were directed toward the object of his longings. Indeed, no one gazes more upon heaven than he who closes his eyes upon the passing vanities of this world.

*

When persons pray, they frequently close their eyes in order to be more recollected. They do well. But they should not forget to give a piercing glance into the depths of their weakness and nothingness. Many fail in this respect, because, when praying, they close not only their corporal, but also their spiritual eyes, drawing no practical benefit from their prayers.

*

Others, when praying, raise their eyes to heaven. That, too, is well. But would it not be a sad thing, if, on account of their progress in perfection, they would only look to heaven, and neglect the occasions of gaining merit on earth, watching the opportunities to work for God?

*

Others, finally, always look toward the earth, without ever closing their eyes; that is, in their devotions, they have only their earthly wants and desires in view. Their prayer is not so much an elevation of the heart and a conversation with God, as a depression of mind and intercourse with their worldly cares.

*

The tear shed through penance and devotion, is Holy Water blessed by Christ himself. Salt is mingled with Holy Water as an emblem of wisdom and perseverance. Salt is also contained in tears, which, shed in the spirit of true contrition, are a certain index of heavenly wisdom and perseverance.

*

Such tears are good for the soul. St. Francis of Assisi and St. Ignatius esteemed them more than the light of their eyes. They are the Holy Water which terrifies the devil and protects us in the hour of temptation. They are the "Asperges," which prepares our souls for the devout celebration of the Divine Mysteries. Ah! never let the shrine of your heart be without this Blessed Water.

*

The thread of a needle is inserted through a hole, which in English is called the *eye*, and in German the *ear*. The devil makes use of the eye and the ear, to fasten the soul with the thread of temptation.

*

A mother removes with the utmost care a plaster, which adheres to the person of her child. By gentle applications she soothes the pain, which would probably have been extreme, had the operation been performed by hands less tender than hers. Thus should we employ great care and circumspection when called upon to free others from their inordinate affections and evil habits. By conciliating their favor and occasionally dropping a word of consolation and encouragement, we may greatly lessen the pain connected with the spiritual cure.

*

There is a German proverb, which, literally translated, means: "He is a thorn in my eye." It expresses how great is the annoyance caused by the presence of one whom we dislike. Unfortunately, we ourselves are often the cause of the thorn that deeply wounds our eye, by sins against brotherly love, by envy, by anger, and by lascivious looks.

*

According to experience, blind men are generally rather of a gay and joyful temper; on the contrary, deaf persons are usually sad. What is the reason of this? I would answer: Because real joy of heart is communicated to man through Faith, and Faith comes through hearing. All that we see will change and pass away, and the blind are free* from so many impressions of objects which are nothing more than vanity. It is better not to see them. The blind may be gay; the deaf have reason to be sad.

*

St. John of Constantinople acquired his honorable surname of *Chrysostom*, which means *golden-mouthed*, by an eloquence, wonderfully persuasive in instilling into the hearts of his hearers a contempt for gold, and a desire to amass the treasures of heaven. The children of this world also merit the title of *golden-mouthed*, but in a far different sense. They speak and think of nothing but *gold, gold! money, money!*

*

There was another John, so celebrated for keeping his tongue, that he was called *The Silent*. God placed before the eyes of the children of His church, so extraordinary an example, that they might be ashamed of their unrestrained and almost wild talkativeness.

*

God has placed the tongue under the eyes and brains. Let this be an admonition to us, that we should see and understand before we speak.

*

The tongues of two Saints have remained in a state of wonderful preservation; that of St. Anthony of Padua.

and that of St. John Nepomucene. The tongue of the former was judged worthy of this honor, because it spoke so frequently for the glory of God; that of the latter, because it maintained a perfect silence for the glory of God.

*

When a person is buried in serious thought upon the course advisable to pursue in an important affair, he often involuntarily places his finger upon his lips. This instinctive motion should admonish us not to be too communicative when we are about to perform an important work for the greater glory of God, for our own sanctification, and the salvation of other souls; because, by talking, we give the devil a chance to know what we are about to do, and to put obstacles in our way.

*

The sense of taste is much affected by the state of the health, and by the humors of the body. This should teach us that, in our intercourse with others, we should accommodate ourselves to circumstances, choosing our time before we venture to impart instruction, and modifying our remarks according to the occasion. A reproach, which would be in season now, might argue a great want of discretion under other circumstances; and language calculated to correct some characters, would only tend to irritate others.

*

To ascertain whether a person is in good health, the physician asks him to show his tongue. So, to learn the state of a man's soul, we need but listen to his conversation. In many instances a few words from his lips will reveal how he stands in regard to charity, piety, and Christian perfection.

*

Many can not remember sermons. But they must not thence infer that the words of the preacher are void of practical effect for them. After we have ceased to eat, we no longer taste the victuals that we have taken; nevertheless the food still nourishes us.

*

Sick persons often feel no appetite whatever; they nauseate even the most exquisite viands. What wonder, then, that sinners who are sick of a spiritual malady, have no taste for practices of devotion, the food of the soul; that they loath even that most delicious banquet—the Body and Blood of Jesus?

*

Keen hunger gives a savor to a dish that would otherwise be insipid or disagreeable. This fact may serve to explain how worldly or sinful souls may gorge themselves with carnal pleasures. Deprived of the spiritual food of devotion and union with God, yet goaded by an insatiate craving for some absent good, they devour whatever Satan or a seductive world presents, and glut themselves with the offal of sin.

*

There are gourmands, whose stomach is the sole object of their thoughts, who "live to eat," instead of "eating to live." With their food and drink, all their ideas apparently bury themselves in the stomach, which, usurping the right of the brain, seems to have become the seat of the intellect. The Apostle uses still stronger language, and affirms that "their God is the belly."

*

Strange to say, the more we hunger after holiness, the more abundantly we are supplied with whatever will satisfy our craving; but when we feel no hunger, the greatest scarcity and even famine ensues.

*

There are gourmands, who will not eat venison unless it is already in process of corruption. They declare that its taste is then most delicious. In the moral world, there is an immense number of gourmands, who like to perform good actions, but only when infected with vanity, vainglory, and love of praise. God preserve us from such a taste!

*

One who expects to grow in grace before God, without actuating his pious desires by practical resolutions, is like a man, who thinks that he can give the necessary sustenance to his body, without using his teeth to masticate his food. He swallows his food without relishing it, and, instead of invigorating the system, he rather ruins it.

*

We speak of " the tooth of time." Time, well employed for the glory of God, is a healthy tooth, strong enough to break the hardest nut of Christian duty and self-denial. On the contrary, time spent in idleness and sin is a decayed tooth. The remorse of conscience, caused by the remembrance of time lost or ill-spent, may be compared to the agonizing pain of toothache.

*

As nourishment, sleep, and exercise are the three great requisites for physical life and health, so vocal prayer, meditation, and active labors are the three requisites for our spiritual life and well-being. Now, as we allow less time to taking food than to repose, and less to repose than to our daily labors, so we should devote ourselves less to vocal prayer than to meditation, and less to meditation than to active duties.

*

The patient parched with fever is always restless; he tosses about from side to side, to find a more comfortable place; but all in vain. The fault is not in his couch, but in himself. So the sinner, in his feverish paroxysms of passion, is ever seeking to quiet a guilty conscience by new objects of pleasure. But peace has forever fled from his bosom. The fault lies not in the created pleasures, but in him who abuses them; and hence, instead of delight, he finds only bitterness in his indulgence.

*

Exterior wants and vexations can give us no idea of the interior trials that sometimes prey upon the soul. If you feel cold in your body, you can, at pleasure, kindle a fire and warm yourself. If you are hungry, you can purchase, or, at least, beg some morsels to satisfy the cravings of your appetite. If you find yourself in the dark, you can light a candle; besides, you are certain that the sun will soon rise again. But if your soul is benumbed with cold, it is not so easy to find the means to send renewed vigor through its torpid faculties. If you experience the pangs of spiritual hunger, it is not so easy to satisfy its cravings. If you grope in mental darkness, you may remain, perhaps for years, uncheered by a ray of consolation. But there is one solace, which soothes every pain; there is one remedy for every ill, whether of body or of soul, and that is death. There is another death, which spares the body, whilst it relieves the soul in her acutest interior pains. This is the death of *self*, which lies in an entire, unreserved submission to the holy will of God. But how few, alas! how few, are willing to undergo this death!

*

To detach the heart from creatures, nothing is more efficacious than to consider them apart from their outward covering. How loathsome is the appearance of the human body from which the skin has been removed by the surgeon's scalpel! Every one turns from the sight in disgust. Apply this to creatures. Disregard the fascination of their exterior—remove the covering. Doomed to perish, and of no real value in themselves, they ought not to exercise a deceitful charm over a being destined for immortality.

*

There are two kinds of love for our neighbor—the one real, the other feigned. The two are as different as the ruddy glow, which health pours over the countenance, and the artificial bloom with which vanity colors the cheek. The one adds an untold charm to the character, and bears the test of sacrifice; it is the ardent love that the precious Blood of our Savior communicates to the heart. The other betrays an ungenerous soul, and disappears in the hour of trial; it is the hollow love of a selfish spirit, which borrows the exterior appearance of genuine virtue.

*

The heart is continually palpitating and imparting life to the whole body; yet it remains ever in the same place. Our zeal should be guided by the same rule. Though ever active, and calling forth all our powers, it should never allow itself to be disturbed, but rest immovably in God.

*

A sigh is a breath drawn from the depths of the lungs, accompanied by a heaving of the chest, which enlarges to give room to the expanding heart. This physical act should serve to remind us of heaven, which is the only thing that can fill the capacity of our hearts—of heaven, which shall forever unite us to Him, who must be our portion, if we would enjoy true beatitude, according to the words of St. Augustine: "Lord! Thou didst create our hearts for Thyself, and they will never be at rest until they repose in Thee."

*

Tender feet, or corns on the feet, are to be found among all classes. Few persons are entirely free from that inconvenience. In the moral order, those may be said to have tender feet, who find much difficulty and pain in walking on the hard way of self-abnegation. The different forms of self-love, so easily hurt by humiliations, may be likened to corns on the feet.

*

Scripture tells us that, after the fall of our first parents, God clothed them in the skins of wild beasts. This was to serve as a sign, that after losing the garments of sanctifying grace, they had become similar to the beasts, and subject to the assaults of shameful carnal passions.

*

Even our first parents, Adam and Eve, did not observe the precept of abstinence. No wonder that their children are not fond of abstinence or of fasting! While some, under various pretenses, try to obtain a dispensation from the obligation, many more, like Adam and Eve, dispense themselves.

*

Tall men often walk rather inclined a little forward, whilst, on the contrary, very small persons generally carry themselves as erect as they can, and try to appear taller than they are. So, real moral greatness is always more or less accompanied by a certain sense of dependence, free from all appearance of haughtiness, while weak and mean characters "put on airs," and try to appear better than they are.

The ills to which the human body is heir, and the sicknesses it is liable to catch, are almost innumerable. We have no doubt they are all so many types of those from which the soul is liable to suffer.

✻

As long as a disease tends outward toward the skin, it is not so dangerous as when the poison remains within and attacks the vital parts. So in regard to the soul; the most dangerous diseases are those which remain concealed, and even for a time assume the appearance of health.

✻

He that enjoys good bodily health sleeps calmly and soundly. His rest is the image of a happy death. For the soul that is in good health, in the evening of life, sweetly falls into that last sleep which knows no waking. Sometimes even the lifeless remains wear a smile, that speaks of the eternal repose of the happy spirit, just escaped from earth.

✻

It is hurtful to health to be always either sitting or walking. Similarly, it would not be advisable to give oneself to meditation, to the exclusion of vocal prayer, neither would it prove beneficial to engage only in vocal prayer and never to make any meditation. Either method should be used as a help and a relief to the other.

✻

This comparison may also serve to show, that we must not give ourselves entirely to contemplative repose, but combine prayer with an active life, employed in the service of God, according to our opportunities.

*

A single exposure to cold may bring on a fatal illness. In like manner, the neglect of a single grace admonishing us not to expose ourselves to temptation in a single case, may prove fatal to our salvation.

*

For the good of our bodily health, it is advisable to keep the feet warm and the head cool. In like manner, for the health of the soul, it is highly important to keep the feet warm by the practice of an ardent charity, and the head cool by a perfect indifference to worldly applause.

*

The mere sensation of heat or cold does not betoken a coming illness; but the repeated alternation of the two is an almost infallible sign of a serious, perhaps fatal attack. Thus, too, continual changes from zeal to sloth, from imperfect repentance to sinful indulgence, is a dangerous symptom in a Christian soul.

*

When we stand, sit, or lie, the body may remain motionless; but in the interior, the vital organs are ever busy. So, an expression of quiet and calm should always appear in our exterior, while, within, a never-ceasing activity should give evidence of our zeal for God's glory.

*

No matter how well-proportioned may be the human frame, it produces a frightful monstrosity if united to the limbs of a beast. The same thing holds true of our actions. A good work, vitiated by a sinful motive, must necessarily appear, to the pure eyes of God, like a hideous deformity.

*

Nature itself seems to indicate, by the very structure of our bodies, that we should not be selfish, but should labor for others with the same zeal as for ourselves, seeking in all only the fulfillment of God's holy will. For man has two eyes, two ears, two hands, two feet. Even the heart, the lungs, the breast, and the shoulders, consist of two parts united together. Reflect upon this suggestion, and see how it may be applied in the virtue of charity toward your neighbors.

*

The various members of man's body move at the bidding of his will. Thus should we be always subject to the holy will of God. Happy shall we be if such is our disposition, for it is an evident sign that our soul is in good health, and ready to perform every action for the love of God.

*

Persons awaking in a strange place, to which they were carried during sleep, gaze around to discover where they are. How great, then, will be our surprise, when we awaken on the last day from the sleep of death.

*

The first death, that occurred among men, was not a natural, but a violent death. The hand of a murderer, and that murderer a brother, shortened the life of Abel. A sad confirmation of the truth, that " sin brought death into the world."

*

Death does not deprive us of self-knowledge. On the contrary, it only closes the eyes of the body to open those of the soul. At the very moment, when it would seem that all our consciousness is lost, we, for the first time, see ourselves truly, and awaken to a full consciousness of what we are.

*

THE SOUL—ITS FACULTIES—SOURCES OF KNOWLEDGE.

WE do not see the air, but, by its wonderful effects, we are just as sure of its existence as if we could see it. In the same way, we know the existence of the soul without seeing it. It proves itself by its operations, and by the results of its activity.

*

Experience, Reason, and Authority are the three fountains from which all acquired knowledge flows. Hence they beautifully typify, by their inseparable union, the triune nature of God, who is the eternal source of all truth and knowledge.

*

Experience is, no doubt, a great source of knowledge. It introduces knowledge and makes it practical. Experience is nothing but the perception of facts falling under a man's personal observation, and it derives the power of imparting knowledge from the principle: " Factum infectum fieri nequit," what is done can not be undone. If once you question the force of this principle, you make all experience useless, and leave a man, after years of observation, as ignorant as if he had never come in contact with the outer world. But as long as you admit this principle, so long also must you regard experience as an undeniable means of certainty. In truth, experience is the very starting principle of all acquired knowledge. Hence it may very appropriately symbolize the principle of uncreated truth and knowledge in the Blessed Trinity. This principle is the self-existing personality of the First Person, God the Father.

*

The second fountain-head of human knowledge is Reason, whose researches into abstract truths constitute the science of Philosophy. Reason typifies the second source of eternal truth, that is, the Second Person of the Most Holy Trinity.

*

The very name "Logos," by which God the Son is called in the Sacred Books, confirms the truth of our position. For of the Logos it is written, that it " enlighteneth every man that cometh into this world." Now, man is man, in virtue of his reason—the enlightening faculty of his soul; consequently, it is his reason that points to the *Logos*, or Second Person. As reason accepts the truth communicated, and assumes it as its basis, so the existence of the Son presupposes the existence of the Father, by whom He is begotten. Were you to eliminate all experience, you would make philosophical inquiry impossible; for "reason," as a philosopher rightly observes, "would then be like a fool in fairy-land."

Were you to deny the existence of God the Father, you would, of course, be forced to deny the existence of the Son.

*

The third source of human knowledge is Authority, or the testimony of persons vouching for the truth. It springs from the two preceding as from an undivided principle. Like the first, it can witness an historical fact; like the second, it can warrant an abstract truth. Hence it typifies the third eternal source of knowledge, namely, the Holy Ghost, who proceeds from the Father and the Son, as from His undivided principle.

*

Hence we may justly say, in regard to eternal truth, which is the Divine essence itself: "There are three that give testimony in heaven, the Father, the Word, and the Holy Ghost, and these three are one."—(St. John, v. 9.) There are also three that give testimony on earth—Experience, Reason, and Authority; and these three are one in regard to human knowledge, which is but the reflex of Eternal Wisdom.

*

We are not wanting in respect for that science which has always claimed for its votaries the name of *wise men*, or *lovers of wisdom*. True, genuine philosophy we venerate as much as we do the human mind, whose exponent it ought to be. But, because we respect man, it by no means follows that we owe the same consideration to the monkey. Many of those who arrogate to themselves the title of *philosophers*, show even less resemblance to them than monkeys to man!

*

In the development of a science, especially of Philosophy, we seek for what is called a first principle, namely, an axiom or postulate, to which all else can be referred. But this principle must be to the point, and it must be generally received; otherwise, the appeal to it is a "vicious circle," as logicians term it. Men often try to excuse their evil deeds by referring them to false principles, which the devil instils into their hearts. But let them not think themselves justified before God, for such principles themselves are condemned by His holy Law.

*

Such persons are much given to talking of "progress, enlightenment," etc., but they do not, in fact, advance a single step in the path of real progress, in the path of true human happiness. Like a blind horse turning a mill-wheel, they move in the circle of wickedness, and their so-called progress is a mere illusion by which they endeavor to satisfy their animal passions. They make the round of their customary pleasures, and, without perceiving it, tread, at the bidding of the devil, the mill-wheel of their sinful habits.

*

"Nosce teipsum"—"know thyself"—the celebrated axiom of the old heathen philosophers, contains a more important advice, a much deeper meaning than they themselves ever suspected. It is grounded in the Divine Nature itself. *God knows Himself:* this expresses the constitution of His essence, this is the source of His beatitude. No wonder that this axiom should be of so great importance to man, who was created according to the image and likeness of God.

*

"How sweet and pleasant it is for brethren to dwell together" in peace and harmony! This is the idea expressed by the Royal Psalmist. The same may be said of the different powers of the soul. How beautiful it is when the memory, understanding, will, and imagination are harmoniously united; when the will seeks for nothing except what is suggested by the memory or understanding as good for the soul; when the imagination does not confuse, but rather assists it to perform with zeal and joy whatever it undertakes for the honor and glory of God! And how can this perfect union be brought about? By an ardent love of Christ, a desire to live only for Him in this world, and so to be spiritually united with Him, even before entering heaven.

*

Consider, on the other hand, how sad it is to see a continual warfare between the powers of the soul, the understanding suggesting what is right and the will refusing to act in accordance with its dictates, while the imagination draws many a picture of sensual pleasures to stifle the remorse of conscience, awakened by a relentless and faithful memory.

St. Teresa compares the interior life of a soul to a castle. The image is very truthful. The spiritual, as well as the material castle, is built upon the top of a high hill, and surrounded by a deep moat; that is, it is elevated, by contemplation, toward God and separated by a total detachment of heart from the rest of the world. But these are by no means its only defense. It is further protected against the assaults of its enemies by the ramparts of good resolutions, and the wall of a well-regulated life. This wall encircles the whole building, and is strengthened by the powerful turrets of heroic acts, performed from time to time by those aiming at perfection.

*

The walls of a castle are provided with loop-holes or embrasures, at a fixed distance from each other. Through these the inmates may observe the movements of the enemy's forces, and victoriously repulse them when they attempt an assault. True devotion is not blind; on the contrary, it expands the intellect, according to the proverb, "Pietas dat intellectum." In the citadel of the contemplative soul, as in castles of ancient times, subterraneous passages are dug, with prudence and skill, as avenues of escape from the violence of temptation. Profound self abasement never fails to obtain extraordinary help from God.

*

The doors of this castle are the five senses. They should be locked, but not barred, for they must be opened from time to time, as circumstances may dictate. Before every one of these doors, a draw-bridge is suspended, which may be raised or lowered on the ropes of holy discretion. On account of all these means of defense, the castle presents a frowning aspect from the outside, but the interior is fitted up with exquisite taste. Its splendor and heavenly delights are described in Holy Writ. The Apostle enumerates the arms kept in its arsenal, when he thus addresses the faithful: " Stand, therefore, having your loins girt about with truth, and having on the breastplate of justice, and your feet shod with the preparation of the Gospel of peace; in all things taking the shield of faith, wherewith you may be able to extinguish the fiery darts of the wicked one. Seize the helmet of salvation, and the sword of the spirit, which is the word of God."

*

The four beings mentioned in the vision of the Prophet Ezechiel may be regarded as typical of will, memory, understanding, and imagination in man. The Angel signifies the will, which enables us to do the wil of God, by our own co-operation, as the holy Angels do it in heaven. The calf, which is a ruminating animal, is emblematic of the memory. The eagle typifies the understanding, which, aided by Faith, gazes upon the Sun of Truth. Finally, the lion symbolizes the imagination, which inspires the heart with true courage and enthusiasm. The four beings in the vision moved each by its own effort, and yet together.

*

So, likewise, those four faculties of the mind, though distinct from each other, are closely united, and belong but to one soul or spirit. The creatures of the Prophet's vision were also furnished with wings, and covered all over with flaming eyes. Through faith and love, wings are given to those four faculties to follow the inspirations of grace, and eyes to perceive every occasion of doing the will of God. Under the wings were hands, showing that the true service of God does not consist in idle promises, but in action, in the diligent and faithful performance of duty. The movement of the four beings was accompanied by a noise as of rushing waters. Our faculties, in the service of God, must move with the strength and steadiness of a mighty stream, overcoming and sweeping away all obstacles.

*

There are two kinds of obscurity in regard to religious truths: that of Faith, and that of infidelity—the one leading to God, the other away from Him. If the mysteries of Faith are incomprehensible to man, infidelity is a still greater mystery; because it is certainly more incomprehensible that man should close his eyes to the light of revelation, than that the object of Faith should transcend his natural powers. We readily perceive that human reason, which is finite in its very essence, can not, of itself, fully comprehend Divine truths. A God, completely within the reach of a human faculty, would be a finite being, and no God at all. In a Divine religion, reason itself looks for incomprehensible truths. The choice lies between incomprehensibility and contradiction, and, of the two, Faith accepts the former in preference. Infidelity, on the contrary, selects the latter, and like a well-known philosophic system, goes so far as to proclaim contradiction the principle of certainty, and the characteristic mark of truth.

God, in His creative power, said: "Let there be light," and there was light. He repeats the same words in the world of grace, and light illumines the faithful soul. So, by the light of Faith, we understand much, where unaided reason gropes in the dark. On the contrary, when, in the obscurity of unbelief, infidelity proclaims, "Let there be light," it is overwhelmed with darkness. Infidelity dims the light of natural reason itself, or, rather, it often seems to extinguish it altogether, making man, in point of religious truth, similar to the animals. "Man," says Holy Writ, "was compared with the beasts, and found like one of them."

*

Quicksilver is a poison found under several different forms. Its principal qualities are mobility, coldness, and a silvery lustre. What a truthful emblem of Indifferentism, now so widely spread! This fatal plague of modern society is exceedingly changeable, because it is destitute of a solid foundation, and wholly dependent on the caprices of passion and public opinion. It is cold; for in its code the love of God and the real love of our neighbor hold no place; there is nothing but self-love. It knows how to assume the appearance of truth, yet nothing is more false and treacherous. When Indifferentism mingles with the actions of daily life, a most dangerous poison is instilled into the souls of men.

*

St. John the Baptist, the precursor of Christ, exclaimed: "Prepare ye the way of the Lord, make straight His paths; every valley shall be filled, every mountain and hill shall be brought low, and the crooked shall be made straight, and the rough ways plain." The precursors of Antichrist, in our day, continually cry out: " Prepare ye the way of our leader. All that is wrong and iniquitous shall be called right and just, and every obstacle presented by religion and morality shall be removed, leveled, and smoothed by the motto: 'Liberty, Equality, Fraternity.'"

*

Luther often contemptuously called reason "a saucy, deaf, dumb, and blind prattler," an old "weather witch." "a treacherous invention," and yet he elevated reason to the throne, and allowed it to decide as a queen in matters of Faith. Luther's reason was such a one, without yielding to any other authority. No wonder, then, that his faith, the religion of his reasoning, is deaf and dumb, blind, boastful, variable, and utterly illogical.

*

Is it possible to imagine that a rational soul, which lives only for God and his glory, should be doomed to annihilation? Even if such a rational creature had not been originally destined to live forever, its life for God's glory alone would merit for it immortality.

*

The civilized nations of the world ridicule the Turkish idea of heaven, and they are right. Yet, is it not foolish in them to imagine, that, after living for years upon earth in a sort of Turkish paradise, they shall share after death the glories of the Christian heaven?

There are persons gifted with praiseworthy moral qualities, but not enlightened by the lamp of Faith. These sometimes go so far as to sneer at religion, and make their natural virtues a pretext for considering themselves better than others that believe. The devil is only too much pleased with their self-conceit; and, reluctant to disturb the spiritual sleep in which they indulge, in the vain assurance that they may be saved without Faith, he bids temptation pass cautiously and lightly by them, lest, perchance, they should awaken to a sense of their danger.

*

Every sin finds its excuse and apology in some false principle, or in a true principle wrongly applied.

*

"He that digs a pit for another, frequently falls into it himself," says a German proverb. This is invariably the case with those skeptics, who indulge in theories, and, as we may say, dig ditches of objection to the truths of Faith. Their object is to prove that Faith is contrary to reason, but they only succeed in proving that they themselves are opposed to sound reason.

*

A rod, even though it be made of diamonds, appears to be bent when immersed in water. In the deep waters of religious indifference, the most convincing arguments and reasons look no less warped and crooked. The fault lies not in the arguments, but in the bad disposition of the listener, who is willfully deceived by his prejudices.

The unbeliever of modern times may be compared to the young man, who, when seized in the garden of Gethsemane, left his cloak in the hands of his assailants and fled. Unbelievers, feeling the grasp of our arguments, frequently leave nothing but the victory in our hands; and, without being converted, depart hastily, ashamed of their incapacity for logical reasoning.

*

How strong is the net of Peter! It has captured, for centuries, fishes of the greatest weight, and drawn them from the ocean of this world. Yet it does not break, while the web of worldly philosophy gives way under the smallest weight. Never could its frail threads drag, from the sea of sin, those monsters of human depravity. To attempt it would be the sheerest folly

*

Christ said: "Do you think that the Son of Man will find Faith when He comes again?" Christ, then, foretold that infidelity would be rife at the end of time. Its existence, therefore, so far from raising in our minds a doubt concerning the truths of our holy religion, furnishes us with an additional proof. For thus is accomplished the prophecy of its Divine Founder.

*

MAN CONSIDERED IN SOCIETY—LANGUAGE.

LANGUAGE is the great motive power in our intercourse with men, and it is now universally admitted that a mysterious relation exists between language and the history of mankind.

*

The principal word in every language is the *substantive*, which signifies *self-subsisting*. It may be taken as an emblem of man himself, who is too often impatient of restraint, ready to declare himself his own master, amenable to no superior, and owing fealty to no fellow-mortal. Even the slave tries to gain, in his limited sphere, a sort of irresponsible position. The various orders of society are like so many paradigms of regular and irregular declensions, exhibiting the different modifications of this inborn propensity of perverse nature.

*

In the Latin language, the substantive is regularly *declined* through six *cases*—that is, it is made to pass through six *falls*. There is something analogous to this in the history of the world.

The first period, or epoch of time, dating from the creation of the world until Noah, may be called the *nominative case.* It is marked by the first *fall*, that of our first parents.

*

The second period, comprising the years that elapsed from Noah to Moses, forms the *genitive* of the world's existence. It recalls the almost total fall of the human family, possessed and governed by sin and vicious passions.

*

The third period, extending from Moses till the coming of Christ, being the epoch during which God gave to man the positive Law of the Old Covenant, may be appropriately styled the *dative.* Like the two preceding, it also has its *fall*. The chosen people often rebelled against God and stoned the prophets sent to them.

*

The fourth period, embracing the time from the coming of Christ till the vocation of the Gentiles, deserves more than any other to be called the *accusative.* It stands forth the witness and the accuser of ungrateful man. After the copious rain of graces which Christ has showered on the sons of Adam, by His advent among them, they have no longer any excuse to offer, if they yield not in abundance the fruits of salvation. He himself will be their judge and verify the solemn declaration made by the mouth of the Prophet: "Now I will show you what I will do to my vineyard. I will take away the hedge thereof and it shall be wasted. . . . . . And I will make it desolate. . . . . . And I will command the clouds to rain no rain upon it."

*

This epoch also reminds us of a *fall* that invokes on the guilty the wrath of heaven. Sinful man imbued his hands in the blood of his Savior. Not only the cast-off race of Israel, that uttered the fiendish cry of " *Crucify Him! crucify Him!*" but every one who has ever fallen into mortal sin, " has crucified Christ in his own heart."

*

The fifth period is that in which we live, and is appropriately designated as the *vocative*, because, during it, the Gentiles have received the call to the Faith.* It is the golden era, when all are invited to a participation in the blessings of truth. Alas! that this epoch should also have its *fall*. Innumerable souls still grope in the darkness of infidelity, or, through their willfulness, cut themselves off from the Communion of the Saints.

*

This fifth period shall last until the end of the world, which is very aptly termed the *ablative*. For then time shall be no more, and those who will be found fallen from grace shall be carried off by Satan into the yawning abyss of hell.

*

In most languages, the *pronoun* ranks next in importance to the substantive. In a figurative sense, that is, transferred to the moral order, the relations which it expresses are second only to those expressed by the substantive. What more important, in its application to the spiritual life, than the force of the personal pronouns, *I, thou,* etc., of the possessives, *my, thy,* etc., or, finally, of the interrogatives, *who, which, what?* Every one must be sensible how powerfully the meaning of these words bears upon the tenor of our lives, and how much they contribute to give even the substantive its practical significance and importance.

*

It is a remark sometimes made by masters of spiritual life, that God looks more to the *adjective* than to the substantive; that is, more to the quality than to the thing; more to the manner than to the action. There are, in the adjective, three degrees of comparison—the positive, comparative, and superlative. We may, hence, draw this very consoling and instructive conclusion, that we should not so much desire to do great and extraordinary things, as to perform, in the most perfect manner, the ordinary duties of our state of life.

*

Curiosity and inquisitiveness being leading features in the character of man, how can the *interrogations* fail to hide a spiritual meaning far beyond what the words seem, at first view, to imply? Alas! man is only too prone to ask questions, and, by so doing, lays himself open to an infinity of temptations. Was it not an interrogative, of

which the devil availed himself to draw Eve into sin?—
"Why hath God commanded you that you should not
eat of every tree of paradise?" Was it not an interrogative which transformed Judas from an Apostle into
a traitor?—" What will you give me, and I will deliver
Him unto you?'

*

Man, generally speaking, asks too much about creatures, and too little about the Creator. According to the
testimony of the Holy Ghost, he is too much devoted to
his material interests, and to useless profane learning.
" He hath busied himself with many questions;" but, at
the same time, he is too careless about the one thing necessary, the only important affair of his eternal salvation.
He seldom exclaims, with the repentant Saul: "Lord!
what wouldst Thou have me to do!"

*

Terror, grief, and joy find vent in *exclamations*, of
which the children of this world are generally fond, because they know not how to restrain their feelings, and
often allow themselves to be hurried beyond the bounds
of moderation. Many, also, pride themselves in the use
of expressions of admiration, flattery, and immoderate
affection.

*

The paradigm of the Latin *verb*, as generally given by
grammarians, begins with the words, *amo, amas, amat—
I love, thou lovest, he loves.* This may serve as a model
for our lives. For, according to the very pertinent remark of St. Augustine, " there is but one sun that illu-

mines the heavens, and there is but one virtue that enlightens all our actions. This virtue is a well-ordered love of God and man. Every other virtue that shines in the soul is but a ray, emanating from this sun of love."

*

I love—these were the words that God uttered, when He called the universe into being. They expressed the nature and motive of the creative act, an act due to no force or compulsion, but the result of pure love for those rational beings, on whom, by an eternal decree of His will, He freely chose to bestow existence.

*

I love—this is, more evidently still, the motive of the Redemption. The Word of God, made flesh, immolated Himself, as a holocaust, on the altar of love, in order to restore us to the love of His Heavenly Father, forfeited by our repeated infidelities. The Sacred Humanity of Christ is the very embodiment of love: "Charitate æterna dilexi te, et miserans attraxi te."

*

I love—listen to the words of Jesus crucified. He loved us in the past, He loves us in the present, and He will not forget us in the future. He longs to draw us still closer and closer to Himself, until that blessed moment when we shall be wholly consumed by the flames of Divine love, in the kingdom of heaven.

*

The most infallible means of reaching that kingdom of love is love itself. The Holy Ghost affirms: "Love is strong as death," and "many waters can not quench charity."

*

In the conjugation of the verbs, the *present* tense plays the most important part. It must be considered first, before we can form a correct idea of the past or future. Applying this to the spiritual life, we may infer that we should endeavor to make a good use of the *present*, assured that it will soon exercise a salutary influence on the past and the future.

*

The *future* tense expresses what is yet to come. Man constantly hankers after some distant good, and lives, so to speak, in the future rather than in the present. This solicitude about what is yet in store for him, is a necessary consequence of his present imperfect condition. Unfortunately, however, his anxiety is too often bounded by the narrow limits of time, and, in very rare instances, extends beyond the grave, which, after all, is the real beginning of our future. What a sad and painful delusion!

*

The names of the *imperative* mood and the *participle* suggest this reflection: Every one exercises, at times, some authority, and every one participates, to a greater or less extent, in the good or bad actions of others. Who can calculate how much harm is daily done by abusing this moral influence to the ruin of others, and becoming accessory to their guilt.

*

Not unfrequently the etymology of a word contains a practical admonition. Thus, to *convince* the mind of a certain truth, it is necessary to defeat the opposite error. The Latin word *vincere*, to vanquish, from which the word *convinced* is derived, bears us out in our assertion. Until the stronghold of error has yielded, conviction is impossible.

*

The fanatical agitators of women's rights would do well to consider this fact: That, in almost all languages, the words *man* and *mankind* are, by extension, applied to the whole human family, while the words *woman* and *womankind* never admit of such an application.

*

The word *reflection* indicates, with accuracy, what is necessary to make the act of the intellect, which it expresses, useful to ourselves. It is not sufficient to dwell, in thought, upon any particular subject. It is necessary to turn it over and over again, to revolve it in mind, until we have viewed it from every side, and examined its every phase.

*

Is it not remarkable, that, in almost every language, the word *passion* has the twofold meaning of violent *affection* and *suffering?* This fact would seem to argue a sort of relationship between the two feelings. This connection does in fact exist, our ill-regulated affections being the cause of all our sufferings. How happy should we be, if, in the midst of exterior trials, we were entirely free from passion! We should then experience the unalterable peace, which always reigned in the hearts of the Saints.

*

The words *explain* and *develop* contain an important lesson for the teacher. It is not enough for those charged with the instruction of others, to touch lightly upon a point of doctrine, as if their disciples were already familiar with all its details. They must propose it in so plain a manner, as to enable them to perceive its full bearing. They must proceed slowly with their demonstrations, and always have regard to the capacity of their audience.

*

The English word *instruction*, traced back to the Latin root, from which it is derived, means a building. The teacher must, therefore, build in the minds of those under his care a structure of knowledge. Now, in erecting a building, the materials are not thrown pell-mell on each other, but placed according to a plan, or a design, with art and skill.

*

Contrition, from the Latin word *contero*, means, in its literal acceptation, a bruising or crushing. In order to make so fervent an act of contrition, that the heart may be really bruised with sorrow, nothing is more efficacious than the thought expressed by the Holy Ghost: " Remember, man, that thou art dust, and into dust thou shalt return." The first part of this sentence brings before us the original nothingness from which the hand of Omnipotence drew us. Ought not this to humble us to the dust? Ought it not to excite us to sorrow, for having raised our hands against our greatest Benefactor? The other part, " and into dust thou shalt return," serves to remind us of the approach of death and judgment.

*

Many persons, who *possess* earthly goods, are *possessed* by them, and through their inordinate affection for wealth at last become possessed by the devil, who abuses them and leads them according to his fancy. This kind of possession, so far from being feared, is rather desired; and yet, it is worse than real possession. In the latter case, an exorcism of the Church may be successfully applied; but, in the former, it is of no effect. In case of real possession, the evil spirit dwells in the body of his victim and makes it his home. But, when man is wrapt up in an inordinate love of wealth, he himself dwells in the house of the devil, who is called " the prince of this world."

*

The gift of language raises man far above all other beings in this world. He should, therefore, employ it before all to praise God, his Creator, who has placed him so high in the scale of existence. If language is used to announce to our fellow-men the truths of Faith, to instruct, to advise, to encourage them in the service of God, in the love of Him and of our neighbor, and to deter men from sin and everlasting perdition; the sounds of human language are sweeter than all the melodies of birds, and more powerful than the thunders of heaven.

*

Yes, language is a Divine gift. Without the special assistance of God, a child could never learn to express itself in language. Perhaps, besides the ordinary interpretation, we may understand in this sense, also, that passage in the beginning of St. John's Gospel: "Erat lux vera," etc. It is the Personal Word of God, which helps man to speak, and which, by the intervention of language, illuminates every rational being that comes into the world.

*

Next to the word spoken, the written word is the means of communicating to others our thoughts and knowledge. To write, we use paper. Egypt, the mother of learning, was also the first to supply the world with paper.

*

How extensively, and in what varied forms, paper is used! What a vast amount is daily called for in institutions of learning! Letter paper is daily sent in every direction, North, South, East, and West, conveying the most important business-news, communicating orders from one person to another, and cementing the ties of friendship. In all court-houses and state offices paper may be found in abundance, containing acts, decrees, orders, accounts of promotions and appointments, deeds of trust, etc. Think, also, of the numberless books which are daily issued from our thousands of printing presses; think of the newspapers and journals which are sent to the four corners of the globe. See how beautifully paper adorns the walls of our houses, how effectually it protects us from the heat of the sun, when it hangs in the form of blinds before our windows. Reflect how it amuses us in the shape of cards, and how it often decides the question of loss or gain. Above all, do not forget that in modern times paper, in the form of bank notes, checks, drafts, etc., is the representative of money, that idol of the world. Paper relates our actions after we are dead, and by means of our last "wills and testaments" transfers our wealth to others.

*

The communication of our thoughts to others has been wonderfully facilitated by the invention of printing. What Adam and the patriarchs could not do through the many years of their protracted life, we now accomplish in a few days by the help of press and telegraph and steam. Would to God these inventions of human genius were always employed in a good cause!

*

Some writers use their pens well nigh as scavengers do their brooms. There is nothing of which they are so fond as of collecting from the street of daily life the filth with which they bespatter and sully the truth.

*

What a fearful account will be demanded of those writers who make use of the press to blacken the reputation of others, to scatter the poison of immorality, or to spread principles of disorder and impiety! "Blind leaders of the blind," they are accepted as teachers and guides; but they lead their confiding victims to destruction.

*

The press is a powerful means of spreading falsehood. Nevertheless, we have to thank God for this means of communicating to others truth also, and of spreading the kingdom of God so rapidly, and with so much fruit, over the globe. The abuse made of so efficient an instrument should increase in our hearts a lively zeal for its right use. It were a shame that the enemies of God should show more zeal and activity for Satan and hell than we for God and heaven.

SOCIAL INTERCOURSE.

FAITH, Hope, and Charity, are strongly linked together. He who really believes, hopes, and loves as a child of the Church, and whose Faith, Hope and Charity exert a practical influence upon his conduct, merits, even in a purely human view, our faith, confidence, and love.

*

Faith, Hope, and Charity are a mystic bond, that unites the children of God in the same religious family, and exerts a practical influence upon their progress in perfection. Even in the purely natural order, these amiable virtues would form a golden chain, linking the sons of men in a fellowship of interests. Without their influence, there can be no public or private prosperity, no comfort in the domestic circle, no happiness in social life

*

Without natural Faith, what would become of science and civilization? What disorder would pervade all ranks of society, if the pupil would dispute the assertion or information of his teacher, or the apprentice question the skill of his master! Evidently, all education would be impossible. Furthermore, if one man would not rely upon the word of another, all commercial transactions would at once cease, all confidence in the just administration of the laws would be destroyed, and even the sanctity of an oath would be without effect.

*

The same remarks are applicable to Hope. Hope is the great stimulus to action and enterprise. Were there no hope of success, no reasonable being would engage in any business. A person deprived of all hope, wanders about without any definite object or aim, in the gloom of despair.

*

Charity is no less necessary. Is love a stranger at the family hearth? Then, too, is happiness. Banish this sweet virtue from the domestic circle, and it will become a hell on earth. Banish it from public life, and society will present the most dreadful scenes of discord, hatred, and bloodshed. All the bonds of union will be broken, enmity and strife will ravage the world.

*

The Apostle says that he became "all to all" to save souls. Alas! there are many apostles of Satan, who know how to accommodate themselves to others, and become all to all in order to ruin souls.

*

Our conversation should always, as the Apostle desires, be fragrant with the good odor of Jesus Christ; that is to say, it should promote the spiritual interests of those whom we address. All, whether sinners or saints, should become better by being in our company.

*

A certain reserve, and sometimes even a certain independence of manner, is advisable, when conversing with very worldly and over-refined people. Such a manner is for the soul what a set of furs is for the body in winter time. We do not mean that, in our social relations, we should be rough and repulsive; for, as furs may be quite ornamental, if prepared with taste, so a certain abrupt manner, tempered with prudence, may adorn our social habits, and make us more powerful for good.

*

In many respects, our position in life must modify our deportment. It would be as ridiculous for a princess to demean herself like a peasant maid, as for a peasant maid to ape the manners of a princess. Great tact is requisite, not to overstep the bounds of strict propriety in our dealings with others.

*

In our intercourse with the world, our memory should resemble a sieve. All vain, trifling, and idle words it should instantly forget, and retain only those that are edifying and instructive. Alas! the reverse is often the case; the good grain passes quietly through the sieve, and only the chaff of worldly and frivolous tattle remains.

*

When a person carries a precious liquor through a crowded thoroughfare, he is very careful not to spill it. This precious liquor in our hearts is sanctifying grace, which has to fill it to the very brim. How carefully should we not guard it, not to spill a drop of it when men press upon us in our daily intercourse with them in business and conversation! Alas! how often, in conversation, a mortal sin is committed and sanctifying grace poured out to the last drop! The loss of the whole universe can not be compared with the loss of God's grace.

*

How many streams flow into the broad channel of the Mississippi! And yet, despite the volume of water, a single snag under the surface can destroy a beautiful and majestic steamer. Learn from this, that a soul may enjoy an affluence of graces, and yet, by unrestrainedly indulging one single passion, may incur eternal destruction. Again, vessels may come into collision and be wrecked upon the rivers, and even on the high sea. What an admonition for us to be guarded in our intercourse with men, for fear of meeting with some disastrous accident!

*

A single unsightly object mars the beauty of a lovely landscape. The conversation of persons possessed of many excellent qualities sometimes grows insupportable, owing to one single vice or fault which continually shows itself, and infects even their happiest strokes of pleasantry.

*

When we wish to catch birds, we do not run after them in order to attract their attention. On the contrary, after throwing grain on the ground, we generally retire, and, by imitating their song, endeavor to decoy them into our nets. We should act in a similar manner, if we wish to gain souls to Christ. St. Francis Xavier, St. Francis de Sales, St. Philip Neri, and other "hunters of souls," were skilled in the art of adapting themselves to the characters of men.

*

The very posture of the body has much to do with the charm and grace of conversation. Too great an inclination, either backward or forward, is unbecoming; an erect posture is the most proper. The same ho'ds good in the moral order. All appearance of pride, or of affected humility, is to be avoided. The proud man throws his head back with arrogance; the sycophant, on the other hand, inclines his head with affected meekness. Both only succeed in making themselves ridiculous. A noble uprightness of character can alone win the approbation of mankind.

*

It is good to season our conversation with wit, for this renders our intercourse with others more agreeable. But we should regard it as salt, which, when moderately used, improves the flavor of a dish; but when mixed too abundantly, renders our food entirely unfit to be eaten. The same effect is produced by salting our conversation with overmuch wit. In the beginning it may please, but after a while it can not fail to disgust.

*

Objections and reproaches should be considered as stones cast at us. We should look at them, in order to avoid being struck by them. But if they miss their aim, and we find that they have fallen harmless to the ground, we should let them remain there, and not run after them.

*

A person who is able to substantiate his arguments, is by no means disconcerted or displeased at objections brought against them. He is like a tennis-player, who lets the ball fall to the ground, not in order to leave it there, but to strike it anew when it rebounds, thus giving it fresh impetus and sending it farther than ever.

*

The staves of a barrel must be well joined, that the liquid may not flow out on every side and be lost. Still, some opening must be made, if we wish to draw out the contents of the vessel. In like manner, we must so far check our inclination for idle gossiping, as never to exceed the bounds of a moderate reserve. On the other hand, however, we must guard against an excessive taciturnity, if we would not lose many an opportunity of benefiting our neighbor.

*

Glass is very hard, and yet very brittle also. In the same manner, there are characters, whose haughty bearing gives them an air of inflexibility and firmness, and whose virtue is withal very fragile. Their firmness is the fruit of obstinacy, which can not co-exist with solid virtue. The worst of it is, that, as glass once broken can not be made to adhere again, so the virtue of such stubborn, yet weak-minded persons, when once shaken, scarcely ever becomes as firm as before.

*

The same cork does not fit every bottle, and the same advice does not suit every person. Though it be ever so good in itself, of what use can it possibly be, if it be unintelligible to the listener? But as, by a slight alteration, the cork may be made to fit another bottle, so, by a slight change, you may adapt to different characters an advice that is substantially the same.

*

Prejudice resembles a cork. For, as it is impossible to pour any liquid into a bottle before drawing the cork, so is it impossible to instill true principles into a mind closed to them by prejudice. Now, as to draw the cork, we should not use a knife but a corkscrew, so, to eradicate prejudice, we should not employ sharp but gentle means.

It is more prudent, as well as effective, to begin in a mild and insinuating manner, gradually employing all our forces, until we are enabled to direct a last and vigorous attack against our obstinate adversary.

*

He that is guilty of excessive harshness in correcting others, resembles a person, who, in breaking a nut, strikes the shell with such violence, that both the shell and the kernel are bruised and made equally useless.

*

When a person has trodden upon our feet, we generally feel very much vexed, and do not reflect whether he has done it purposely or through want of attention. We have been unexpectedly hurt, and we feel annoyed, because we ascribe it to the awkwardness or impoliteness of the offender. A similar impression is made on our moral sensibility, whenever we are wounded by a remark or offensive personality. We may have merited reproof; yet we seldom fail to resent it, on account of the unexpected and impolite manner in which it is administered.

*

When a man readily perceives the point of a remark, or the difference between right and wrong, we call him *acute*. In conversation, this quality is usually connected with another, usually called wit; but it is a sad truth that very often this wit is so pointed and *acute*, that others are severely wounded by it.

A hasty correction is calculated to do more harm than good. Suppose a child were holding a knife by the blade; would you, to prevent it from cutting itself, snatch the dangerous weapon quickly away? Certainly not; for you would thus occasion the very misfortune which you seek to avoid. It were far better to coax the child to give you the knife. So, in leading a wanderer back to the path of righteousness, be not harsh, but try with gentle, loving admonitions to move his heart.

*

The most convincing arguments are lost on him who is incapable of understanding their bearing. If they are so profound that his mind can not fathom them, they only serve as a precipice of doubt, into which the truth is hurled down and bruised.

*

Think you it is only the rough and uneven path, which presents dangers and obstacles? If so, you are mistaken. May not an even road expose you to an unforeseen misfortune? May not even the polished floor of a palace conceal a fatal trap-door? You see, then, that some degree of care in walking is always necessary. This is also true with respect to our journey along the highway of perfection.

*

It is an act of politeness, and even a real kindness, to offer a drink of cool water to one to whom we think it would be acceptable; but to force it upon a person who does not wish it, would be very impolite and offensive.

We may learn from this, how much depends upon the manner in which we give good advice to others. If we use tact and discretion in administering it, they will thank us for it; but if, on the contrary, we are imprudent, they will only be incensed, and will derive no profit from our words.

*

Every question is like the center of a circle, equally distant from every point in the circumference. Every good answer may be compared to a point in the circumference; it must not be too far removed by affirming too much, nor too close by affirming too little. The same thing holds true of our actions. The real center lies in avoiding every excess, and doing neither too much nor too little.

*

We nowhere find more real littleness than among the great ones of this world, who, by the observance of petty formalities, politely termed *etiquette*, subject themselves to an endless variety of annoyances.

*

By indulging in self-praise, we patch, with the rags of vanity and folly, the precious garment of grace, in which we are arrayed, and thus, of our own accord, adopt the guise of beggars.

*

It often happens that the reconciliation of a sinner to God draws upon him the ill-will and persecution of man.

Thus the friendship of the Creator is followed by the enmity of the creature. Truly, "the judgments of God are not as those of men."

*

There have been fools, who died of starvation, because, from a constant dread of being poisoned, they would not take the necessary sustenance. In Lisbon, some years ago, two persons, fearing that the world would come to an end next day, cut their throats, through fear to die the next day. In a spiritual sense, the world is full of maniacs, who, through cowardice, throw themselves in the midst of great and real evils, in order to avoid small and imaginary dangers.

*

How wonderful is the effect of order! A single fo'd out of place sometimes destroys the appearance of the whole garment; while, in its proper place, it would have added dignity and grace to the dress.

*

It is the custom of blacksmiths to accompany their work with a resonant play of the hammer, and so to enliven their toilsome hours. Thus a certain cheerfulness should always distinguish our efforts to be virtuous. Such a disposition, besides lightening our labor, will increase our merits; because, according to the words of Holy Writ, "God loves a cheerful giver."

*

The renewal of old and long-forgotten offenses often has an effect similar to that produced by discharging a gun which has been a long time loaded. He that fires it off is sure to receive an unpleasant shock, even though he hits his mark. Just so, the renewal of an old attack upon another serves only to stir up angry feelings again. You may wound the other, but you yourself will not escape unhurt.

*

When a match is applied to powder in the open air, the explosion generally does not cause much serious injury. In like manner, indignant feelings may often pass away in a burst of passionate words; while, if shut up in the heart, they become stronger, and if some day the slightest spark touches them, they may explode with the most disastrous consequences.

*

"Strike the iron while it is hot," says an old proverb; that is, lose no time in advancing the spiritual interests of others, while they are in a condition to profit by your advice. Another practical lesson may be drawn from this saying, namely, that when we give counsel, we should first make the culprit warm with the consciousness of the fault committed, for then the reproof will have a wholesome effect. Never, so long as he is cold or indifferent, can his heart be touched with sorrow.

*

According to the Apostle, the wisdom of the Gospel is foolishness in the eyes of the world. The wisdom of the world, on the other hand, is folly when compared with the maxims of the Gospel. The world laughs at the teachings of the Gospel, because it *does not* understand them; the Gospel laughs at those of the world, because it *does* understand them.

*

Are you surprised that the world looks upon the maxims of the Gospel as folly? Did you ever see a fool who thought himself a fool? Did he not rather consider every one else out of his senses? In ages past, the world declared the Author of the Gospel a fool. Witness the white garment, with which it clothed him in derision, when he was sent from Herod to Pilate. That garment explains the mistake of the world. The doctrine which the world inculcates is stained and soiled, and its votaries are pleased with it. Hence they look upon the pure white of innocence as folly.

*

Among the many toys with which children amuse themselves, there is one which consists of little figures of cork with pieces of lead attached to their feet; and the sport of the little ones lies in this, that, in whatever position the toy is placed, it will instantly get on its feet again. We may compare to these little figures, the characters of those who, though not favored with too sound a judgment, hold themselves in the highest esteem, and will never relinquish their opinions, no matter in what position you may place them by your arguments. Demonstrate to them their self-contradiction, and they will nevertheless return to defend their views. Refute them a hundred times over, and they will still persist in holding them as before.

*

Persons, who perform their good actions that they may be seen, are like those who have no house to live in, but encamp under the open sky, and are always in danger of losing their goods. Those, on the other hand, who conceal their good deeds, wishing them to be known to God alone, are like people who dwell in strongly built houses, protected by guards; or, we may also say, that the former expose their treasures on the highway, while the latter lock theirs up in a safe

*

A tree, bending under the weight of its fruit, is a very beautiful object. We may gaze upon it, and partake of its gifts. But it would be foolish in the proprietor to dig around the roots in order to show how the earth's moisture is absorbed, and the fruit brought to maturity. For this would ruin the tree. Just so, our virtue may delight and benefit numbers of men, but its root, that is, our interior life in God, must not be exposed to the gaze of the crowd. The tree of life, planted in the soil of the heart, would be seriously injured by the blighting influence of vain ostentation.

*

If we have an aversion for a person, we very often dislike even those actions of his which are good, and which, in another, would be most pleasing to us. See how we are blinded by our passions!

*

Persons who are somewhat deaf, usually speak very loud. So those who are deaf to admonitions, are generally very violent when they reprehend others, and exceedingly loud in their own defense.

*

You complain that you suffer from great interior dryness. What can be the reason? Is not your heart, perhaps, too often exposed to the oppressively hot atmosphere of worldly conversation and dissipation? If so, you may take it for granted that there lies the source of your complaint. It is your duty to remove it by prayer, solitude, recollection, and meditation. These will soon draw down upon you the refreshing dew of devotion, and quicken you with heavenly consolations.

*

To induce men to be charitable to the poor and afflicted, it is found necessary to dress benevolence in the garb of pleasure, to invite them to picnics, suppers, and balls. What an idea! To amuse oneself in order to aid the suffering poor! Is it not a sad sign of languishing charity?

*

You are laughed at for your piety and zeal! Well, then, laugh with your revilers. They laugh at you, because they despise religion and consider it worthless; you may laugh at them, because you understand its priceless value. They laugh at you, because they think you are a fool; you may laugh at them, because you know that they are fools in reality. If, when laughed at, you betray your vexation, they will ridicule you all the more; but if you appear unmoved, they will soon leave you in peace.

*

With what eagerness do men listen to generous promises, whose fulfillment is calculated to promote their earthly happiness—promises of elevation to dignity, promises of rich estate, promises of a large donation. They are equally anxious about threatening misfortunes; the fear of losing their property, or of falling ill continually haunts their minds. How is it, then, that even Christians remain so cold and indifferent about the great promises and threats of holy Faith? Is it not well nigh incredible?

*

"The sensual man perceiveth not the things which are of God. They are foolishness in his eyes and he understandeth them not." So affirms St. Paul. Hence, to ask advice from the children of the world, for our spiritual guidance, would be the greatest of follies. It would be as if a professor of philology were to take advice of one who has scarcely mastered his A, B, C. It would be as if a Parisian belle were to take lessons in the art of dressing from an uncultivated savage, or a professional cook request instruction from cannibals, or a member of the *beau mond* learn the rules of etiquette from a Hottentot.

*

"Qui nimis probat, nihil probat"—he that proves too much, proves nothing—is a very ancient philosophical maxim, of great importance to all who impart knowledge. For he that disregards it seems to the hearer to be fond of exaggeration; and thus, instead of convincing, he only succeeds in rendering himself and his proof alike suspected.

*

When you have offended another through *rudeness*, with what readiness do you not apologize? Yet you experience no remorse of conscience when you have given scandal to your fellow-creatures by excessive *affability*.

*

Who are our most dangerous enemies? Very often they are those whom we call our "best friends." And why? Because, by engaging us in idle conversation, they at least rob us of time; and how terrible for *eternity* is the loss of *time!* Considering this loss with the eyes of Faith, we may easily understand why Jesus, our Lord and Judge, will require so rigorous an account of every idle word. Were it to lead to no other evil than a loss of time, this alone would be sufficient to make us deplore it for all eternity.

*

When two walk out together, each must accommodate himself to his companion's step; otherwise, they will annoy one another, and find no pleasure in the walk. A like readiness to yield and defer to the opinions of others, should always be noticed in us when we exchange thoughts, that so our conversation may continue to be pleasant and entertaining, as well as instructive.

*

When passing along the most frequented streets in large cities, we find it necessary to look carefully ahead of us, in order to avoid running against others. We should use the same precaution whenever we are thrown into a large company engaged in a lively conversation. In the rapid interchange of thoughts, much tact is requisite to avoid coming into collision with others, in their principles or feelings

*

Speak little, be brief in your answers, and you will greatly diminish your responsibility to God and man. This advice can not be too often repeated to all. The Scripture inculcates the same lesson in these words: "Be in many things like one who hears and is silent." Alas! the great majority of mankind act quite otherwise; they speak, but do not hear.

*

Blessed is he who never contradicts himself, for he is a man of truth, and therefore a man of God.

*

Rejoice, if, while you try to do your good actions from the pure love of God, the world repays you with censure and abuse. These are certificates sent you from heaven, to testify that your efforts are recorded above, and that your good works are garnered up in the storehouse of paradise. Unmerited persecution is a pledge of salvation.

*

A pithy proverb says: "Hasten slowly." By this means you will not only move onward more surely, but even more speedily, avoiding the many delays and impediments occasioned by injudicious haste.

*

Medical men lay it down as an axiom, that "whatever is appetizing, nourishes"—"quod sapit nutrit." If this is true of the body, it is doubly so of the soul. It should, therefore, be our study to excite, in those whom we have to address, an appetite for hearing us. If they have no relish for the dish which we present to them, they will either refuse it, or, if through complaisance they partake, they will not be benefited by it.

*

St. John Chrysostom deserved his glorious title, partly, and perhaps especially, for the boldness and impartiality with which he denounced crimes and criminals. It mattered not to him if golden crowns decked the brows of the offenders, or jeweled scepters sparkled in their hands.

He valued not such earthly grandeur. How different is the conduct of those whose idol is gold! They are ever fearful of offending the wealthy, especially those by whose assistance, favor, or friendship they hope to acquire place or riches. They will allow everything, no matter how sinful, to pass unnoticed, if they fear that a candid expression of their disapprobation would draw upon them the displeasure of their pretended patrons. The Apostle says that, for Christ's sake, he looks upon everything here below as dross and filth.

*

"Everything has its time," says the Wise Man. He that forgets this truth will surely make himself odious, and will never achieve anything great in the service of God. His ill-timed works of zeal will wither like premature blossoms, before they grow into the ripe fruit.

*

This discretion is especially desirable in those who are preparing themselves for the active duties of the ministry. Such persons must not seek to quit their sacred retreat before the time. They must first be well grounded in virtue, and be so far proof against the allurements of the senses, that they will not suffer from contact with the world. A young cleric, who does not bide his time, but prematurely leaves the asylum of his yet feeble virtue, resembles one who handles newly painted objects. He will certainly bear away with him traces of his folly and inexperience.

*

"Honor flies from him who seeks it, and pursues him who flies from it," very truthfully remarks St. Jerome.

*

Some hurt their heads, because, from an excessive fear of stumbling, they fix their eyes so intently on the ground at their feet, that they see nothing else. Very often persons, too solicitous to avoid some slight evil, rush recklessly against a great one, which prudence would have taught them to avoid.

*

How often do we discover, to our great regret and mortification, that those who promised to take us under their patronage are the first to turn against us, and that we would have been much better off had we not relied on their pretended favor! They are like people who invite us to walk under their umbrellas during a shower, but who, to our great discomfort, allow the drippings to fall full upon us.

*

The displeasure of the bridegroom at the faithlessness of his bride would be all the greater, if she were to use, for the purpose of attracting others, the very presents, dresses, and ornaments, received from him. So it is with Christ, if we employ the gifts of nature and grace to please men, instead of referring them all back to Him who is the "Giver of all good gifts."

*

During the prevalence of an epidemic, it is advisable to keep an aromatic spice in the mouth, while visiting infected quarters. Our morning meditation, rightly made, recalls to our minds those salutary truths, whose frequent remembrance during the course of the day is a powerful preservative against the tainted air of moral corruption.

*

In hot weather, we seek relief by putting the air in motion with a fan. How is it, then, that, oppressed by the heat and burden of our daily occupations, we do not have recourse to frequent short, but fervent aspirations, calculated to refresh our souls fully as much as a fan does our bodies?

*

He, who wishes to strike another violently, first draws back his arm. It would appear that this motion should indicate no intention of hurting any one; yet, in reality, it is made to give greater force to the blow. This is very like the conduct of those who, in order to inflict a heavy blow on the honor of another, first affect to praise him; because, then, the censure and the cutting remarks which follow, will be all the more keenly felt.

*

The same comparison holds good of the manner in which you should admonish others. When you have an occasion to administer a reproof, let the culprit first feel that you are aware of the good qualities which he possesses, and that you censure only what is blamable. He will then feel the reproof much more than if you are harsh, and completely ignore the good which lies hidden under his imperfections.

*

A few drops of a chemical substance can instantly clarify a troubled liquid, by precipitating the solid held in solution. In like manner, some words, uttered by a true servant of God, can, in a moment, settle a troubled heart.

*

If we place a pitcher directly under the spout of a pump, and at the same time pump violently, the water will be thrown far beyond the vessel, and, instead of filling it, will only wet it slightly. It is thus with respect to the communication of heavenly truths. If we try to convey religious instruction, without considering the mental caliber and acquirements of our hearers, our labor will be altogether useless, or, at least, it will be attended with very little profit.

*

Again, we may place the vessel too far away, or pump with so little effort that the water can not reach it. Here, too, it is not hard to draw a very useful moral. If we have no regard to the disadvantages under which the hearer is placed from want of previous religious instruction, we may fail to produce any beneficial result. For great exertion is requisite to reach the understanding of one who is a total stranger to the teachings of our holy Faith.

By using the snuffers carelessly, it often happens that, instead of cleansing the candle and improving the light, we extinguish the flame altogether. A similar effect is often produced by inconsiderately reproving a person for his failings. If the offender deems us harsh or unnecessarily severe, he will be vexed at the injustice of the reprimand, and, losing sight of his fault, will think only of excusing himself, while he might have acknowledged himself guilty, and repented, had the reproach been administered in the spirit of charity. Generally speaking, it is advisable to lead the sinner back by kind and gentle treatment.

*

Even a small quantity of dust falling into a large flask filled with the clearest liquor, is liable to render the whole turbid. It is thus that the slightest imperfection sullies a virtuous life and makes it repulsive to others.

*

When a liquor is allowed to stand, the sediment falls to the bottom of the vessel, and leaves a pure, limpid fluid on the surface. But if the contents of the vessel are ever so slightly shaken, they presently grow muddy. Thus, some persons have a smooth, even temper, so long as nothing occurs to ruffle it; but let the hand of fortune touch them somewhat rudely, and instantly they are stirred up, and all their apparent composure is at an end.

*

The Holy Ghost admonishes us to restrain our love of talk and bridle our tongues. How few, alas! follow this advice! The greater number of Christians, living as if they had no knowledge or fear of God, allow their tongues to run off at pleasure; and if conscience seeks to curb them, they champ the bit of self-control, and, under the most specious pretexts, still permit their tongues to move.

*

Our conversation should always be suited to work a conversion; that is to say, it should always promote the spiritual interest of those whom we address. All, whether sinners or saints, should become better by being in our company. This is evidently the tenor of the Apostle's words, directing us to carry about with us, at all times, the good odor of Christ. Did we but comply with this instruction, the children of this world would soon be converted, and the children of God be still more sanctified.

*

You complain that others have too little regard for you, and stand in your way. But may not the truth be that you have too little regard for others, and stand out of your place?

*

When we take a visitor through a city, we are careful to lead him to that point from which he can have the best view. How sad it is that, when we are exhibiting the character of our neighbor, we are not always so ready to call attention to his good qualities, but often find a sinful satisfaction in showing him in an unfavorable light!

*

The fisherman baits his hook with something of which the fish are fond. If we wish to catch men, and save them for Christ, we must likewise adopt, as far as in us lies, those means that are most in accordance with their natural dispositions and inclinations.

*

To see and to be seen is the aim of the children of this world. Their lives are wholly given up to frivolous pursuits, and turn out a mere comedy. "I have played my part; friends, give me your applause." Such were the last words of one of earth's departing heroes, as the curtain fell upon the closing scene of his life.

*

"I will lead thee into solitude, and speak to thy heart," says the Holy Ghost. There is a solitude in which the Christian hears the inspiration of the Divine Spirit. But the spirit of Darkness would fain introduce him into another solitude, that of egotism, in which he speaks loudly and constantly to the soul, till it withdraws far into the fatal seclusion of selfishness.

*

One who seeks to make a display of learning and erudition, by high-sounding words far beyond the comprehension of those with whom he speaks, resembles a man that would present himself with a long, trailing robe at a friendly, social party. Before long, such a pretentious appendage would draw the greatest mortification upon the wearer. Either some one would step on it, or he himself would entangle his feet in it, thus making himself ridiculous, in place of attracting the admiration of the company.

*

The fondness with which the votaries of fashion frequent balls, and especially masquerades, is only a reflection of the ordinary daily manner of men's living. Men seldom appear in their true colors; in dealing with others, they usually wear masks, and skillfully disguise their real sentiments. Moreover, they seek only for amusements, and throw themselves headlong into the wildest pleasures of the world, whose principles, maxims, and customs are the music to which they dance. So, social life in general is stamped with the character of a masquerade.

*

In a certain part of Hungary, there was once a splendid castle, and near it a poor Capuchin monastery, whose inmates lived on the charity of the faithful. One of their greatest benefactors was the lord of the castle. Whenever the purveyor of the monastery came, he received a generous alms. But this good and pious Count went at last to enjoy the reward of his liberality; and his son, a worldly youth, succeeded to the inheritance. He was fond of dress, and took particular care of a very long and carefully trimmed beard. According to custom the purveyor of the monastery came to solicit his wonted *dole*. The young Count very politely replied in Latin— the language used at the time in conversation between the clergy and nobility—" videbimus," we shall see; and then lifted his jeweled hand to his face and complacently stroked his whiskers. The good old times had passed away, and the Count, like a true child of this enlightened age, had quite other opinions than his father's upon the subject of alms-giving. The old prior, tired of the unsuccessful application, and the unfailing " videbimus," at last answered: " Illustrious sir, in your departed father's time, I used to hear another word. He, too, would smooth his beard when I accosted him, but instead of your unmeaning 'videbimus,' he would answer with a hearty 'dabimus.'" So saying, the good father stroked his own long beard, and departed, leaving the worldly young Count overwhelmed with confusion.

*

Those who rail and scoff at religion, pour out their venom in particular upon Religious Orders; and yet they organize societies of their own, which they call *Orders*. Thus they have an Order of Free Masons, an Order of Odd Fellows, an Order of Knights of Malta, all under officers whom they distinguish as high-priests, priests, etc. They are fond of imitating religious vestments, emblems, banners, and ensigns; they have constitutions and rules, and, instead of vows, they take oaths, by which they bind themselves to a blind obedience such as was never exacted by any Order of the Church. They have a Novitiate, or kind of probation, and their own peculiar kind of Profession. The devil is still what the Fathers used to call him—"the ape of God"—trying to use for man's perdition, what Divine Providence employs for his salvation.

*

According to the testimony of Holy Writ, Cain was the first to build a city. Unhappily, the morals of our cities give only too plain a proof of their origin. Nowhere are sins against charity and brotherly love so common as in large cities. Nowhere is there more selfishness; nowhere less regard for the rights and feelings of others.

*

If every pastor were to watch over those whom he has brought back to God, with the same care that Satan does over those whom he has led astray, how few of his spiritual children would be lost, and for how little would he have to answer before God!

*

It is not often that we see a missionary who has traveled over the whole globe, even once in a lifetime. The devil, in his apostolic zeal for hell, does it daily, not once only, but many, many times. What a sad reflection! Should it not make even the most fervent among us blush?

CIVILIZATION—THE FINE ARTS.

THE development of the arts and sciences, their application to the requirements of daily life, and the corresponding improvement in taste and social habits, constitute the principal elements in what we call Civilization. In all the branches of science, the light of Faith discovers moral truths hidden beneath the surface. These it singles out, takes their picture, and holds it up to the eye of the soul. We have already had occasion to touch upon some of these views presented in Philosophy, Astronomy, Chemistry, Natural History, etc. We shall now, in a special manner, devote some space to the moral and practical reflections suggested by the Fine Arts.

PAINTING.

OUR virtuous and meritorious life may be compared to a painting. In a painting we distinguish the picture or scene, the work of the artist, from the canvas. The picture could not have been painted, if the canvas had not taken and retained the colors. So it is with the soul. The graces which adorn her are so many lines or touches of God's hand. They are truly the work of God, as the Church teaches, when she affirms that, "crowning the virtues of His Saints, He crowns His own gifts." Yet they belong to the soul too, and are hers. She has taken them in, as the canvas does the colors. But more than this, she has made them her own by active and free co-operation.

*

A person who, by true charity, becomes all to all, may be compared with those pictures, which leave upon every spectator the impression that the eyes of the figure are constantly directed toward him.

*

Though a painting should, in the main, be executed with great skill and correctness, yet one single stroke, passing the proper limits, would mar the beauty of the whole, and convert it into a caricature. Hence, in the use of the brush, the artist is especially careful to give well-defined outlines to the different parts of his work. Thus ought we to avoid, in the salient points of our character, even the slightest excess, which might give those uncharitably disposed some cause to blame our lives, though, in other respects, our conduct challenges their well-deserved admiration.

*

The use of very bright and glaring colors argues a bad taste, or a very slight acquaintance with the great masterpieces, which are all distinguished for their truthful simplicity. In the spiritual life, an extravagant or eccentric demeanor, calculated to strike the eyes of men, shows a want of judgment, and a departure from the practice of the Saints, who always made it their study to hide their good works from the gaze of the world.

*

Both light and shade are necessary to impart correctness, beauty, and expression to a painting. A cheerful confidence in God, mingled with holy fear, must also appear in every action of our lives, if we would make them correct, beautiful, and expressive copies of the great original.

*

Did you ever see a painter engaged in copying a great masterpiece? He does not draw a single line without looking at the original. Such should be our conduct. The model from which we have to copy is the life of our

Lord Jesus Christ. What a masterpiece is thus placed before our eyes, and how much care is requisite to succeed in our undertaking! Let us, then, frequently ask ourselves: How did Jesus act while upon earth, and how would I act if I now saw Him here present? Alas! how few are thus anxious to imitate their Lord! How many, on the contrary, resemble a man, who copies a painting with his eyes closed, or who never glances at the original, but follows the dictates of his own wayward fancy!

*

Some painters possess the art of portraying persons of repulsive looks in such a manner that the deformity almost disappears, while the likeness is sufficiently truthful to be easily recognized. It should be our constant care to conceal as much as possible the defects and faults of our neighbor, not by defending what is wrong in him, but by throwing over it the mantle of Charity. Happy is he that has this skill of masterly charity.

*

Many objects, considered from one point of view, are commonplace, perhaps even unsightly; while, from another, they appear attractive or magnificent. At one extremity of New York, for instance, nothing meets the eye but groups of small, sooty tenements; while, at another, long rows of the noblest edifices rear on high their marble fronts and lofty stories. An artist may paint, at choice, either of these two parts, and, with equal justice, call his picture, *a view of New York*. They are views, but they are partial or incomplete, and therefore liable to misrepresent. So we may misrepresent facts and characters by giving only a partial view, painting only the dark or the bright side.

*

Oil paintings are generally intended to be seen from afar. If you stand close to tthem, he colors blend confusedly together. Virtues, too, wear an additional charm when viewed through the distance of time or place. One who makes profession of piety, is rarely appreciated according to his merits by those among whom he lives. Not until seen from afar does his life appear what it really is, a masterpiece of grace. God wisely allows this, to preserve humility from the dangers of worldly applause.

*

An artist painting in *fresco* loses no time, but tries to finish his work before the plaster becomes too dry. This ought to be a lesson to us, that, if we wish our lives to resemble a beautiful painting, we must set to work promptly and resolutely, according to the words of St. Ambrose, "Nescit tarda molimina Spiritus Sancti gratia"—"The grace of the Holy Spirit knows not tardy efforts."

*

The likeness of an Angel, drawn upon a transparent ground, may be so disfigured by a piece of black stuff put behind it, as to be almost changed into the effigy of a devil. Our actions are liable to meet with a similar fate. For often the evil tongue of the calumniator, ascribing them to sinister motives, gives to the charming picture of virtue the hideous appearance of crime.

※

If we do not perform our apparently virtuous deeds purely for the love, honor, and glory of God, but rather from a vain desire of gaining the applause of others, we ourselves are the fools who place the black ground under our actions, so that, in the sight of God, they become deformed, and are not numbered with the works of light, but with those of darkness.

※

A valuable painting placed at the mercy of every one, will soon be damaged and torn. It is far better to keep off the hands of visitors, by having it framed and hung up against the wall. This will enhance its beauty and preserve it from injury. In like manner, by shunning the applause of men and remaining attached to the walls of humility, we shall be secure against the fatal touch of vanity, while at the same time we shall render ourselves more agreeable to those with whom our lot is cast.

※

It is usual to varnish a painting to preserve the freshness and beauty of its colors. The substance used for this purpose is cheap and common, and the manner of applying it is very simple, requiring but little attention compared with that which has been already bestowed on the painting itself. Varnish may serve as a fit emblem of that unpretending modesty, which best preserves the lustre of a virtuous life.

*

A single picture, no matter how finished, can never make upon us so solemn an impression as a whole gallery, in which each piece is a *chef d'œuvre*. The same holds true of sanctity. Any one act, however heroic, can not give so much edification as an entire life illustrated by the practice of every virtue.

*

When the celebrated Greek painter, Apelles, drew the portrait of Philip of Macedon, whose face was disfigured on one side, by the loss of an eye, he ingeniously took a profile of the other side. Thus he produced a faithful likeness, while concealing the deformity of the original, and art was true to nature without copying its defects. So should we draw the likeness of our neighbor, calling attention to his good qualities rather than to his imperfections. In this manner we do not sanction his faults, but merely hide them from view, so long as there is no necessity of disclosing them to others. Alas! how few possess this art! When there is question of our neighbor's good qualities, most men prefer to represent him *in profile*, but when there is question of his defects, they take him *in full face*, criticising, with an air of zeal and justice, whatever is defective.

*

A painter, who has but imperfectly mastered his art, may employ the richest colors and yet produce only a caricature. So, too, a speaker may gather from the writings of others the choicest specimens of eloquence, and yet produce a work that deserves ridicule, because he can not use well what has been well thought or said by others.

*

The delivery of a sermon is, as it were, a canvas on which the speaker paints that feeling or sentiment which is at the time uppermost in his mind: the order and arrangement of the thoughts supply the light and shade. The mere painting or coloring is not enough; the proper admixture of light and shade is absolutely necessary to a good discourse.

*

Speakers, whose highest aim is to excite enthusiasm by strong appeals to the imagination only, have the taste of a savage, who judges of the merit of a picture by the prevalence of glaring colors, especially of red, the emblem of enthusiasm. Those, again, who do not address themselves to our feelings, produce a mere drawing, not a colored, life-like painting. Finally, those who pay no attention to the order and disposition of their matter, lose all the effect of light and shade, and expend their strength upon points of minor importance.

*

In order to appear to advantage, the painting requires the light of the sun to fall upon it. In the same manner, to appreciate fully the beauty and importance of a sermon, the heavenly light of faith is required.

*

A good sermon is like a picture of scenes or places that require to be explained. The preacher, who undertakes this task, should guard against standing before the picture and obscuring the view. He will be only too likely to fall into this fault, if he is more anxious to appear eloquent than to be understood.

*

They that listen to sermons without any desire to gather spiritual fruit from them, resemble children that hastily turn the leaves of a picture-book, and then lay it aside forgetting entirely what they have seen.

*

Sermons which speak to the heart, are never wholly forgotten, but, like cherished pictures, remain treasured up in the memory, which we may call the soul's album.

*

In a good painting the shade predominates over the light. So should it be in your life. Humility, which is well represented by the shade of a painting, will relieve the bright coloring of your other virtues and bring them out to better advantage.

Painting. 217

If, in a sermon, an idea which deserves only a passing notice is dwelt upon with too much emphasis, it will have the same effect as a painting too much colored in one particular spot. It needs not an artist's skill to know that such a painting is not only defective, but a caricature.

*

By using colors, which are too bright and glaring, or by using any particular color too much, a painting, which, in other respects, has claims to considerable merit, is sometimes completely ruined. A similar result may be feared for the words of a preacher, who deals in exaggerations, or shows a want of taste in the management of his figures and illustrations.

*

If we wish to prepare colors for oil painting, we must carefully grind them and mix them with oil on a stone plate. So, before we can make a profitable use of our natural faculties, in adorning our lives with the bright colors of virtue, we must first crush out their imperfections by penance and self-denial, and then unite them with the oil of Divine Grace. The Lord Himself, in His providence, often brings about this union by the pressure of adversities.

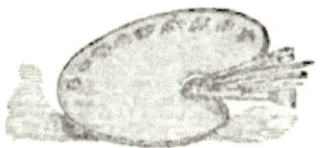

MUSIC.

ACCORDING to the myth of the heathen poets, the music of Orpheus tamed the most savage beasts, and so charmed the very trees and plants, that they bent their heads in silent wonder to listen to his lays. The music of the voice of Christ, the heavenly Orpheus, the soft whispering of the Holy Spirit, can subdue the fiercest passions, and bend all our faculties and feelings to the practice of virtue.

✱

Harmony does not require that all the instruments in an orchestra should be of the same kind, or have the same tone. On the contrary, it supposes a variety of instruments and tones. Only one thing is indispensable, viz: that each instrument should play correctly its own part, after they have all been tuned to the leading note. The same holds in society. It is by no means necessary that all the members composing it should have the same temperament or the same calling. It is sufficient that each perform well the part that has fallen to his lot, and that all should be in accord with the leading note, that is, with truth; with truth as expressed by the words and example of Christ. In that case, the diversity of tempers and characters only contributes to the harmony of life.

*

None but a very skillful artist can perform, with any degree of correctness, on an instrument whose strings are not in perfect order. This remark has its application in the moral world. He that is zealous and exact in the performance of his duties, no matter what may be the state of his mind, is no common artist, but a perfect master in the science of the Saints.

*

There are within the compass of the human voice four kinds of tone, namely, *bass, tenor, alto,* and *soprano.* Rendered with the requisite clearness, flexibility, artistic skill, and force, each in its way is agreeable to the ear. There are, likewise, in the human soul four principal varieties of temper: the phlegmatic, the melancholic, the nervous, and the sanguine. Each one of them may make our mutual intercourse agreeable and promote our advancement, if, like masters, we can attune it to the others, and regulate its proper time. A perfect unison of tempers among those whom a similarity of tastes and interests, or the same religious vocation, has drawn together, would be like the skillful blending of voices in a band of practiced singers.

*

A musician displays his artistic taste by his manner of attending to the *time* and to the different *expressions*, marked or unmarked, required by the nature of the musical thought. What taste is to music, that discretion is to our actions. It prompts us to avoid with equal care the two extremes of rash precipitancy and listless indolence. It teaches us to accommodate ourselves to circumstances, and thus to lead a life edifying to our fellow-men, and unspeakably pleasing to our heavenly Father.

*

Like the obstacles which prevent us from attaining perfection in music, are those that stand in the way of our progress in virtue. One possesses great ease in fingering, but has no ear for music; another is gifted with a correct ear, but can not learn to execute; a third unites both of these qualities, but, not having a love for the art, can throw no feeling into his performance. This one is too timid to play a *solo;* that one can not keep time with others; one plays too loudly or too softly, wholly inattentive to the musical signs; another practices difficult and stylish pieces, but can not play at first sight everything that is put before him. Here is an illustration of the different hindrances on the score of temperament and talent to be met with in the spiritual life. One has considerable ability, but, unwilling to take advice, conducts himself as if he had no ear; another is docile to instructions, but is awkward in executing them. A third seems to have no feeling; his heart is cold, his manner austere, his look forbidding. This one is too timid to undertake anything difficult in the service of God; that one can not agree with others, and, far from making himself "all to all," he acts as if he alone were to be consulted.

Another does not know how to accommodate himself to circumstances; regardless of all propriety, and seemingly doomed to overdo everything, he sometimes astonishes and pleases, but more frequently tires and disappoints us. Another aspires to extraordinary sanctity, but he pursues the even course of virtue only so long as nothing unusual occurs.

*

Nothing can be more monotonous or disagreeable to the ear than the continued repetition of two successive notes of the scale. Yet, performed *prestissimo*, it produces a *trill*, which is one of the graces of music. So it is with acts of love to God and to man. Performed slothfully, with indifference and languor, they tire and displease; but done with fervor and intensity, they produce an effect quite charming to the spiritual ear.

*

Yet it must be remembered that the trill is not in itself music, but only a grace or an accomplishment of a skilful performance. In like manner, the mere acts of love of God and our neighbor can not be called the music of a holy life. The performance of our various duties constitutes the real music of this virtue.

*

Musical *transitions*, separated from the rest of the composition, are mere discord; but taken in connection with the succeeding chords, their merit and beauty become apparent. With these transitions may be compared unexpected temptations and interior or exterior trials.

which we often look upon as great misfortunes, but which, viewed in relation to the good resulting from them, can not fail to strengthen our virtue, and increase its beauty and value.

※

Praying without preparation is like performing on a stringed instrument, without having previously tried whether the strings are in tune. Anoying spiritual discord must be the result.

※

The majesty of the organ is due principally to the power and strength of the pedals, which are pressed by the feet. What the pedals are to the organ, humiliations are to the soul, which is, as it were, trampled under the feet of others.

※

If even one string in an instrument is out of tune, harmony becomes impossible, and the whole effect of the music is lost. In the same manner, a single defect in our virtue greatly mars its beauty, and prevents the beneficial influence of an example otherwise very edifying.

※

Every touch of the *virtuoso* argues his skill, while the dissonant thrumming of the beginner as plainly betrays his first imperfect efforts. Indeed, we derive far more pleasure from hearing some simple air played by a master, than from listening to a splendid piece of music performed by an inferior artist. What causes this striking difference? Practice—assiduous, untiring practice. This not only teaches the musician to remove every imperfection, but also enables him to throw his heart and soul into the performance. As much may be said of the study of virtue. For in the science of the Saints, as well as in everything else, " practice makes perfect." It is not surprising, then, that we find more delight in seeing truly pious souls go through their ordinary duties, than in beholding careless Christians perform extraordinary and apparently sublime acts of virtue.

*

This remark holds equally true of prayer. They who, like St. Aloysius, notice every fault committed during their spiritual exercises, and who try to avoid it, will shortly become real masters in their art. Their ordinary devotions will be far more beneficial to them, and tend more to the edification of others than the extraordinary efforts of such as are less studious to correct the slightest failings.

*

Self-esteem, united to an inordinate love of praise, may be called the drum of conceit, which vain people always beat as an accompaniment to the fife of flattery, blown by their supposed admirers.

*

Virtues, practiced without any regard to our sanctification, are like bells swung without a clapper, and incapable of producing any sound which can charm the mind and elevate it toward heaven.

The perfect regularity of the cast gives sweetness to the tone of a bell. Our pure intention of laboring exclusively for the glory of God, likewise imparts to our actions all their merit. Even the least flaw in the largest bell gives it a harsh and grating sound. The slightest admixture of self-love in the most virtuous actions destroys, to a great extent, their value in the eyes of God.

*

What is more disagreeable than the repeated striking of the same note upon an instrument, especially if it is out of tune? In the moral order, the same effect is produced when self-love is the leading note of our actions, and self-praise continually sounds it.

*

To a person who does not understand music, the care taken by a violinist in tuning his instrument may seem excessive and unnecessary. Having no ear for music, he may consider the tone good enough. But the musician, accustomed to perfect harmony, can detect the slightest discord. So, to the lukewarm it may seem that fervent Christians carry their piety too far. Often they style them enthusiasts and fanatics, and say that they evince neither reason nor judgment. The cause of all this is, that worldlings know nothing of the harmony of virtue, and therefore faults and imperfections do not grate on their moral sensibilities.

*

The director of a choir must make the members observe the *time* and the *signs*. If all follow the leader, the musical composition will be rendered with better effect than if every one is led by his own caprice. If every one would attempt to direct, and induce the rest to follow him instead of the leader, there would be nothing but discord; and the effect would be worse in proportion to the loudness and rapidity with which each musician plays. In the same manner, society is better conducted when all follow the direction of the lawful superior, than when every individual, deeming himself more capable than his neighbor, takes upon himself the management of things. Nowadays, the world frequently resounds with such caterwaulings.

*

What are all the precepts and admonitions of Ethics without the grace of the Holy Ghost, whose influence Christ compares to a breath of wind? Philosophical systems of morality, deprived of that breath of the spirit of grace, are like an organ with empty pipes.

*

One of the charms peculiar to a stringed instrument is the quivering vibrations of a tone in the middle of a performance. It is then that the purity of the sound is most perceptible, and the musical taste and feeling of the performer displayed to the best advantage. Behold here an emblem of that holy fear and self-distrust which usually accompanies the heroic deeds of the most virtuous souls. It is grounded on true humility, joined to a tender but firm confidence in God's providence, which causes them, notwithstanding the deep conviction of their own nothingness and insufficiency, to advance with zeal in the pursuit of virtue.

✻

An *adagio* played quickly, or an *allegro* played slowly, destroys the effect of a composition. The delivery of a sermon has its own *tempo*. In order to produce the effect intended, some parts must be spoken with vivacity, others with deliberation. The heart of the speaker, and his skill in reading human nature, must dictate his style of delivery.

✻

The heart of the priest may well be compared to a sounding-board. His power of elevating the hearts of his hearers depends upon his own union with God. By the practice of meditation and zeal, his heart should beat in perfect accord with the will of God; then his words will reverberate in the hearts of his hearers with full force and success. Two preachers may deliver the same sermon with a very different result. The words of the man of God will be heard with eagerness and delight, while those of a person not deeply impressed with the importance of his mission will be received with indifference, or even distrust. What the one says will reverberate in the soul for years, while the remarks of the other will be quickly forgotten.

✻

The heart and the interior life of the hearer may likewise be compared to a sounding-board. If, by a holy life and intimate union with God, he is well prepared to listen to the Divine word, it will resound in his heart; and the preacher, perceiving his good disposition, will be greatly encouraged, and almost instinctively speak words all aglow with the fervor of Divine love. But if he should not receive the preacher's advice as the word of God, but only as that of an ordinary man, he would not be much benefited, even if a St. Paul were preaching; but, as the Athenians, he would probably remain indifferent and irreverent. Let both the speaker and the hearer beg God to animate their hearts with perfect dispositions, and the effect can not fail to be most consoling.

*

Who has not noticed the effect produced by observing the signs of music? The best song is spoiled by a monotonous singer. His voice may be true and well sustained, his time may be perfect; and yet, for want of the delicate shading, and the variety of expression, given by the musical signs, the piece will not produce half the effect of which it is capable. Learn from this, that, to impart a charm to social intercourse, our conversation should not be marked by monotonous sameness; it should not always be very low in tone, nor always very high; not always fast, nor always slow. It should be varied in tone and in time, in loudness or softness, according to circumstances. Nothing but a good education, and intercourse with those who are themselves familiar with the art, can teach us to observe the *signs* of conversation.

The remembrance of the presence of God is for prayer what the key note is for music. The strings of all the affections of the heart should vibrate in harmony with it, that so our prayers may be as sweetest music ascending on high, to mingle with angelic strains before the throne of God.

*

Whispering galleries are so constructed, that even the faintest sound made within their walls is distinctly audible at a certain point called the *focus*. The universe was framed on the same principle, by the hands of the Almighty Architect. All the prayers, all the sighs, that come from the heart, floating, like so many waves of music, along the vault of the firmament, meet at last before the throne of the Lamb, where innumerable Angelic voices swell the sweet chorus, and the Immaculate Mother of Jesus joins her voice in supplication to Her Son.

SCULPTURE—ARCHITECTURE.

THE perfection of works of art depends on carefully excluding whatever does not enter into the design of the artist. This is especially manifest in sculpture. For wherein lies the magic virtue that transforms the raw unshapen material into a statue! The secret consists in the skillful removal of those parts of stone or wood that prevent it from being a perfect copy of the ideal. The more finished the statue is intended to be, the longer and the more carefully must this labor be continued.

*

A tall, stately tree, felled to the ground, seems to have lost all its usefulness and beauty. But the artist thinks differently. He knows that, at some future time, it will be wrought into lifelike forms by the sculptor's hand, and that, as a statue, it will adorn some palace hall, or pay silent homage in the house of God. Was it a loss for that cedar of Lebanon, used for the tabernacle of the Old Testament, to fall beneath the stroke of the woodman's axe? Need I mention the tree, whose wood serves as a tabernacle in the church of the New Covenant, inclosing the God of heaven and earth Himself? Need I allude to the tree upon which the Saviour consummated the work of Redemption? Had it remained standing, lovelier than even the trees of paradise, would it ever have become the object of so much reverence and devotion? No; in the course of time, it would have moldered into decay and mingled with the dust of the earth So God sometimes demands of us humiliating sacrifices, from which our frail nature recoils with horror. Yet He destines them for our greater exaltation, and He will certainly accomplish His ends, however unpromising, according to our views, the means which He employs. Let us, then, rest assured that we shall derive great advantage from ever patiently submitting to the afflictions sent by Eternal Wisdom.

*

As the followers of Christ, we must, according to our different callings, strive to reproduce Him within our souls. He Himself has pronounced these emphatic words: "If any one will come after me, let him deny himself, take up his cross daily, and follow me."

*

The first and most essential step, toward the imitation of Christ, is the practice of self-denial, which may be very appropriately compared to the work of the chisel. If we are unwilling to make any sacrifices of our natural feelings, and courageously to use the chisel in removing our imperfections, we shall remain, despite our apparent polish, like mere shapeless blocks of marble, without bearing a trace of resemblance to our Divine model.

*

If the block of native marble were capable of feeling, how it would writhe beneath the chisel that molds it into form! Its pains would be in proportion to the perfection which the piece is designed to reach. The first rough and heavy strokes of the chisel, which give the general outlines to the figure, would perhaps cause less agony than the last delicate touches which impart the finishing grace. Yet, how much the marble has gained! But lately a shapeless block of raw material, it now stands before us a perfect statue, that almost seems to live and breathe. Soon it will grace a princely court, or, from a sacred altar, recall and fix the wandering thoughts of adoring multitudes. A similar change is wrought in the Christian, who labors with persevering efforts to acquire perfection. The struggles undergone by nature in vanquishing its evil passions, are like heavy blows inflicted upon his heart, while the ever-recurring acts of self-denial are as final touches, all the more painful, because they curb even the lawful feelings of his bosom. But then, how happy is his lot, when he has succeeded in producing within himself a perfect copy of his model, so that, with the Apostle, he may exclaim: "I live, now not I, but Christ lives in me!" I was a child of earth, but I may now be justly called a child of God.

*

Scripture compares the acquisition of virtue to the building of a house. The strength of the whole edifice depends on the solidity of the foundation and the perfection of the arches beneath. Both typify the practice of humility, which must be the basis of the building of Christian perfection. The emptiness of the arch, particularly, is a beautiful symbol of that interior renunciation of self, which must underlie the whole structure of sanctity.

The strength of the arch depends much on the two side walls, which are, in the spiritual building, great *diffidence* in our own strength, and great *confidence* in God. For we can do nothing of ourselves; but "we can do all things in Him who strengthens us." If these two walls do not give way, through presumption or despondency, the arch will stand any pressure from above.

*

The labors, preliminary to the erection of a palace, are neither very pleasant nor of a character to attract notice. The foundation must be dug, the rubbish removed, and the wall commenced with rough unhewn stones. So, in rearing the fabric of Christian perfection, we must first dig, by meditation on that important truth: "Remember, man, that thou art dust, and into dust thou shalt return;" we must clear away the rubbish of vicious habits; we must practice acts of humiliation and self-denial.

*

A building without windows would be as unhealthy as a damp cellar. A light could scarcely burn there, and everything would wear an aspect so dismal that few would be willing to take up their abode in the place. Behold here the picture of a soul given to that gloomy sort of piety, which makes war on all innocent mirth, and shuts out from the heart every ray of cheerfulness and joy. In the murky atmosphere that soon gathers in such a soul, the lamp of devotion may perhaps, for a time, cast around a feeble light, but it will never burn with a brilliant flame.

Sculpture—Architecture.

It is advisable, therefore, to allow ourselves some innocent recreation, after which we shall return, with renewed vigor, to the duties of our religion, and more cheerfully tread the paths of virtue.

*

To make a building strong to withstand the elements, it is not sufficient to lay the stones on one another; they must, moreover, be closely cemented together with mortar. In erecting the edifice of Christian perfection, our good works must, no doubt, serve us as stones, but to have strength and consistency they must be cemented with the mortar of humiliation and self-denial.

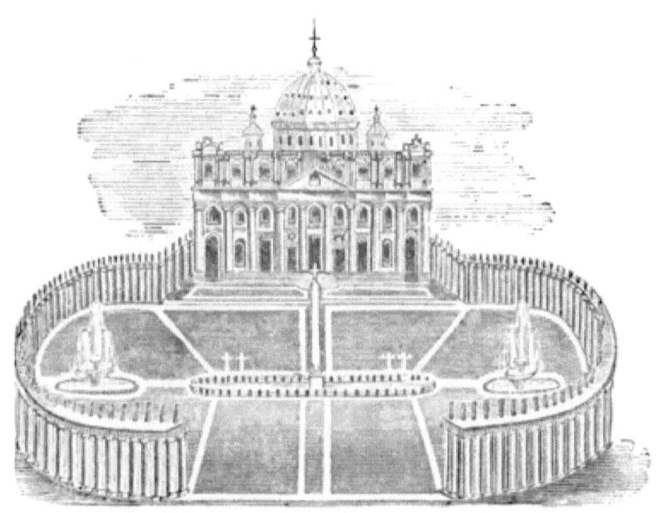

Part III.

The word *Jehovah*, by which God called Himself in the Old Covenant, is well suited to express His essence. According to its etymological composition, *Jehovah* means "He who shall be, who is, and who was," the syllable *Je* being taken from the future, *ho* from the present participle, and *vah* from the preterite. How well does this name express that the Almighty is not subject to time!

*

In various parts of Holy Writ, God invites us to seek Him. Let us not fail to answer His call with alacrity, relying upon the infallibility of the promise, "Seek, and you shall find."

※

God, the Triune, is essentially light. There is also a threefold light, by which He is known—the light of reason, the light of faith, and the light of glory.

※

God lives wholly within Himself, and His own essence is for Him the source of infinite felicity. Happy you, if you retire into the innermost recesses of your heart, and find there God alone! Once possessed of him, you will have in yourself a foretaste of heaven, and will no longer ask for the mite of earthly comforts to complete your bliss.

※

The eyes of God are continually upon us. Ours should be continually on Him.

※

Yet, alas! how few are thus united with God, and, therefore, how few rest in God! The vast majority is wholly devoted to vain pursuits, and absorbed in them, and carried off by them with never-ceasing agitation.

※

God watches over us, not only by His Omnipotence, but also by his Providence. How happy shall we be, if, with the reliance of a babe reposing in the arms of its mother, we commit ourselves entirely to the guidance and care of His Providence!

*

St. Augustine appropriately says: "Lord, Thou hast care of every individual, as if he were the only one over whom Thou watchest; and Thou hast care of all, as if all were only a single individual."

*

So we should take care in all our actions to do all for God alone, as if on every single action depended the whole glory we have to give to God; and we should take care to do all for God, as if His glory depended on all together.

*

How diligently that servant works who is aware that his master is near, particularly if that master, though a man of high standing, is kind enough to lighten the burden of his servant! What influence should not the presence of God, and His assistance given to us in every action, exercise on us!

*

God lives in an eternal present. The future as well as the past are intimately connected in Him with the passing moment. We should likewise make use of the present in such a manner as to associate it with the past and the future. We should consider the future as already come, and look upon the past as still in our possession for we can profit by its experience.

*

"I will lead thee into solitude, and speak to thy heart," says the Holy Ghost. Listen, devout soul, and allow yourself to be conducted by the hand of God. Though you may not be able to quit home and bury yourself in the deep recesses of a forest, you can erect a little sanctuary within your own heart, and thus be alone with God. But remember that this, too, is impossible, so long as you seek only your own comfort. Self must die before you can feel so truly alone as to desire no witness of your actions but God. Let not the apparent difficulty of the sacrifice deter you. A generous effort on your part will be liberally rewarded, even in this world, by the peace of heart which you will experience. For God will speak to your heart, you will listen to Him in secret, and no one will ever hear the loving words which He will address to you.

*

To the soul that has chosen retirement in God as her portion, these words of the spouse in the Canticles may be well applied: "My heart dissolved within me." The blissful union and happy converse which she enjoys in that interior solitude with God, is melting all her affections into one, and that is—*Love*.

*

The devil also sometimes leads men into solitude, to whisper, with greater freedom, his wicked suggestions. Hence that dismal loneliness experienced by the soul, when she has turned away from God, to listen to the unholy proposals of the tempter. She is alone with the evil one. O, frightful solitude! Alone with no companion but the devil!

*

Is God merciful? Ask the heavens. They remain silent. When Lucifer raised the standard of revolt, the hand of God's justice fell heavily upon the mighty hosts of Angels, though not one of them was ever guilty of more than a single sin. No mercy was displayed in the punishment of the rebel host. Is God merciful? Ask the immense universe. Ask the starry firmament, with all its numberless worlds. Ask the globe, with its towering mountains and deep seas, its plants and animals and jewels. No answer. Profound, breathless silence. They are incapable of sin, and never offend God.

*

Is God merciful? Ask man the question. Hark! exultant cries are heard throughout the universe, mingling in harmonious chorus, and verifying the words of the Psalmist: "Miserecordias Domini in æternum cantabo"— "I will sing the mercies of the Lord forever." That Divine attribute did what could scarcely have been believed possible. It made Him man for the sake of men, in order to celebrate the triumph of infinite mercy in regard to him.

*

Yes, the Angels give us a glimpse of the infinite beatitude and majesty of God. The exterior world proclaims His wisdom and beneficence. Hell testifies to His justice. But man, frail, sinful man, manifests the triumph of His mercy. What a motive for us to glorify God by acts of mercy, especially by the spiritual works of mercy, imitating this gracious attribute of God, by zealous endeavors to gain souls for heaven!

*

The whole life of Christ is stamped with evidences of this Divine attribute. It drew Him from heaven, to clothe Himself in the form of a little child. It checkered His earthly career with sorrow and sufferings. It subjected Him to the painful consequences of sin, and finally fastened Him to an ignominious gibbet; that so, as St. Paul says: " He might show Himself to us a merciful High-Priest, who has compassion on our infirmities." To the Church, also, which continues to live His mystical life, as the impersonation of His maxims and doctrines, He has left a legacy of sufferings and persecutions, that her children might be more thoroughly imbued with the spirit of mercy, which thrives best where suffering abounds.

*

" Charitate æterna dilexi te "—I have loved thee with an everlasting love—says the Lord by the mouth of His prophet. These words are applicable to the Angels as well as to men, for they, too, can taste their sweetness and rejoice. But the succeeding words: " et miserans attraxi te "—in mercy have I drawn thee to myself—have special reference to man. Man alone is permitted to exclaim, with the exultant Church: "O felix culpa, quæ talem ac tantum meruit habere Redemptorem"—" O happy fault which has won for us such a Redeemer!"

*

"O mercy! O Divine mercy! O God of mercy!" were the exclamations that burst from the lips of St. John of God, moved to penance by a sermon to which he had been listening. Day and night he would repeat these words, and throw himself into the arms of the Divine mercy. Thus he came to be the founder of an Order, whose members bind themselves by a special vow to the performance of works of mercy. And because mercy is synonymous with God, the Saint himself is now called John of God.

*

Considering the infinite justice and holiness of God, we have reason to fear His judgments; but considering the malice of men and their injustice, we have cause to rejoice and feel confident; for it is not man, but God, who will be our Judge.

*

The Apostle says: "In God we live and move and have our being." God is truly the life of every creature, and all things are dead to him who does not see and seek God in all. When we use created things for God's sake, they are productive of health and vigor; but when we use them for their own sake, they become dangerous and even fatal to the soul.

*

There is scarcely any motive, which acts so powerfully on the mind, as the thought: "God is my Creator." The whole universe should therefore serve to kindle our zeal for His glory; because all things speak of God the Creator, living for His glory. We are therefore inexcusable, if, knowing our Creator, "we have not glorified Him as God, or given thanks."

*

What a shock to our feelings, when we find ourselves deceived in one to whom we have given our entire confidence! On the other hand whenever persons come to us for assistance and place complete reliance upon us, we can scarcely refuse to lend our aid. Can we, then, wonder that when we approach God in this manner, He should receive us with open arms, and that Ho'y Writ should speak in the strongest terms of the power of hope and confidence? If we trust in God, we almost oblige Him to hear our prayers. In His infinite goodness and mercy, He will not allow any one to trust in Him in vain. He will not permit our confidence to surpass His generosity. We have His own words for it: "Because he has hoped in me, I will help and deliver him." And again: "Look around, ye children of men, if there is any one on earth who has ever trusted in me and been confounded?" Indeed there is no better or more efficacious prayer than an act of heartfelt confidence.

*

Diffidence dishonors God. It may be considered a practical denial of the attributes, which He most loves to manifest, namely, mercy, goodness, and truth.

"Perfect love casteth out fear." Fear is advantageous, if rightly directed. It is the point of the needle, with which we work at our heavenly attire. It should not stick in the cloth, but penetrate through the tissue and draw after it the thread with which the garment is sewed. In like manner, fear is efficacious in piercing and penetrating the obstacles and difficulties, with which we meet, in the practice of virtue. But it should be transitory and lead the way to the love of God. Then shall our heavenly attire be soon finished and richly adorned.

*

A mother may carry in her arms a child still too feeble to walk, and at the same time lead by the hand another, which, though perhaps more beloved, is strong enough to follow at her side. Thus Almighty God sometimes bears up with spiritual favors and consolations a soul still weak in virtue, while He conducts the child of His love along the common road of temptations and sufferings. Let us, then, recognize in every trial a special mark of love.

*

Nothing is more painful than to live away from those on whom all our affections center. How happy, then, are we in always having near us the two objects of our most ardent love—God, who by His immensity fills all space, and Jesus, who is everywhere present to us in the most Holy Eucharist!

*

If the consideration of your many imperfections weakens the sentiment of confidence within your heart, remember the words of the royal Psalmist: "As the father hath compassion on his son, so hath the Lord mercy on those who fear Him." He knows full well that we are but dust and ashes. Fear is indeed commendable; but it must not expel hope. Fear should guard us from the precipice of foolish presumption, hope should bear us aloft to the heights of confidence.

*

God made the world. Be not troubled in the midst of strange changes and threatening calamities. Leave to the Creator the care of His own work.

*

God Himself is simplicity personified, and He manifests that characteristic quality in the creation. Gold, silver, and other metals are simple bodies, and nothing but what is simple in nature is called an *element*. What is the diamond, but the simple essence of coal? We should be distinguished for the same quality, and adorned with the brilliant diamond of a pure intention, doing all for God.

*

Every Christian need not be clad in a complete suit of theological armor, and protected with the shield of controversial knowledge, in order to combat the enemies of the Kingdom of God, which is the Church. But every one should prepare the sling of David, with its five stones, and be ready, by steadiness and a sure aim, to defeat his adversary. The five stones are the five marks of the Church; namely, her Unity, her Sanctity, her Catholicity, her Apostolicity, and her Unchangeableness. By a judicious management of these stones, the doctrines of our holy Faith may be defended and its enemies defeated.

*

In time, nothing is more dreaded than death; in the eternity of the damned, nothing is more to be dreaded than life. On earth we lament that life is so short; in hell the devils lament that it is so long. "O death, where is thy sting," is the thought full of consolation for the good, on this side of the grave, but full of despair for the damned in the other world.

*

The devil never had a chance to hope, after he once fell; man has always had the strongest motives for hope. How much greater, then, must be the pain of despair for the reprobate soul than for the rebel Angel!

*

An Italian proverb says:

"Non si lascia senza dolore,
Quello che si possede con amore."

You can not sunder without pain,
The links of fond affection's chain.

We should, therefore, love nothing for itself, except God, from whom nothing, not even death, is able to separate us.

The will of God is the standard to which we must conform every desire of our heart. Those who are ever seeking, even in the service of God, to do their own will, may be compared to those waxen Angels, which we fasten with wires to the Infant Savior's manger. In their exterior conduct, they often resemble Angels; but their virtues are as wax, and their all-pervading self-love attaches them as by wire, to their own convenience. They seem to fly, yet they always remain in the same place, always at the cradle; that is to say, at the beginning of their spiritual life, without ever advancing a step in the imitation of their Lord.

*

The Lord said to His prophet: "Constitui te hodie ut destruas et disperdas et ædifices et plantes"—"I have appointed thee to-day, that thou mayst destroy and scatter and build and plant." Our first care should be to destroy the dominion of sin and scatter the temptations of Satan; then to establish the reign of justice within our hearts, and, by daily progress in the way of perfection, to adorn the garden of our souls with all kinds of sweet shrubbery and flowers.

*

St. John of the Cross says: "Since I have wished for nothing, nothing has been wanting to me." God and Nothing! All that is not God, or for God, should be as nothing to us.

*

St. Paul styles avarice idolatry; and the term is not too strong. The worldly-minded too often ascribe to money Divine attributes, and pay it an homage due to none but God.

Faith tells us, God is Almighty. Avarice declares, money is almighty. Faith exclaims: In God is my trust. Avarice affirms: I place my trust in money. Faith cries out: God is my hope. Avarice returns: Money is my hope. Faith counsels us, to seek first the kingdom of God. Avarice urges us to strive first for wealth. Faith asks: "What doth it profit a man to gain the whole world, and lose his own soul?" Avarice inquires: What does it avail a man to pray and go to church, if, by so doing, he lose an occasion of making money? In fine, Faith embraces all its teachings in this one precept: "Thou shalt love the Lord thy God with thy whole heart, and with thy whole soul, with all thy mind, and with all thy strength." But Avarice only cries out in reply: Money, I love thee with my whole heart and soul. Thou art my thought from early morn till close of day. Even in my dreams, I own thy sway. For thee I labor, for thee I live. Thee I love, thee I desire above all things. Thee I worship. Money, thou art my God!

*

The proof that we really love God, is the keeping of His commandments. The Law of God was written in the hearts of men, before it was written on the tablets of stone. But now, as well as in the first ages of the world, the sinful children of men interpret those Divine precepts according to their own liking, or rather according to the views of the devil, the father of lies.

*

Have you done much for God? Perhaps you will ask in surprise: How can one so weak as I, do much for

God? St. Francis Xavier answers: "If you have done all in your power, little though it be, you have done much." God considers not the greatness of the work, but the intensity of the *love*. If you seemed to do much more than others for God, because He gave you more facilities and occasions than others, in His eyes you did less, if the others, with fewer means and fewer occasions worked harder, and with more zeal, and with a purer intention than you.

*

The life of St. Francis affords us still another criterion, by which we may judge of the value of our labors. If, forgetful of what we have hitherto done, we earnestly press *forward*, we are doing *much* for God.

*

The Christian, who wishes to render God none but great and brilliant services, and neglects the daily and ordinary duties of his calling, gives the clearest proof that he has neither the right idea of God, nor a good will to please Him. In the service of God, no actions of ours can, of themselves, be called either great or small. The object or end for which they are performed imparts to them their real dignity and merit. All that lies in our power is to keep that *end* constantly in view and leave nothing undone to further it.

*

St. Ignatius used to say: "One act of heroic virtue is of more value in the sight of God than a great many ordinary ones," and Holy Writ frequently extols its heroes, for having performed one noble deed. Witness Abraham, Joseph, Moses, David, Judith, Esther. The same is to be observed of the Saints in the New Testament. Their holiness often took its rise in one heroic action. You may see this truth illustrated in St. Augustine, St. Benedict, St. Bernard, St. Ignatius, St. John of God, St. Francis Xavier, St. Teresa, St. Alphonsus Liguori, and in a greater or less degree in all the rest.

*

The man, whose life gives no promise of such heroic actions, has not yet firmly planted in his heart the tree of a holy life.

*

"Because thou hast done this thing," said the Lord to Abraham, "I will bless thee; and in thy seed shall all nations of the earth be blessed." The same consoling words are addressed to the Christian, eager to sacrifice everything for God's sake. "Because thou hast done this, I will multiply my graces, and thy merits shall shine as stars, adorning thy heavenly crown, and all the blessed shall be made partakers in that glory, with which I will crown thee in Heaven."

*

Who can understand the wondrous generosity, liberality, and munificence of God? For every work, even the most trifling, done for Him, He gives a reward which can not be compared with any price in this world, even if it would be the whole world for a cup of cold water. And for every moment of work done for Him, He gives a reward which shall last through all e'ernity. And this reward is nothing less than Himself, who is infinite beauty and bliss.

*

"Are you afraid of God?" asks St. Augustine. No doubt, we have reason to fear when we consider His holiness and His justice, when we see the scales of judgment in His hand, and reflect that our eternity is at stake. But there is another thought that will inspire us with confidence. "Fuge a Deo ad Deum," says that holy Father. Fly from the infinite justice of God to His infinite mercy.

CHRIST.

E that does not love the God who created him for heaven, merits hell. But he that does not love the God who descended from heaven to redeem him from hell, deserves a dobled hell.

*

"I know that my Redeemer liveth." This was the motive of holy Job's confidence in the midst of his manifold afflictions. This, too, should be the ground of our hope. Christ is our Redeemer, and "Christ, being risen, dieth now no more."

*

If God had bestowed on you all created goods that you could desire, how favored would you deem yourself, and obliged to thank Him! He has done infinitely more. For through Jesus, who is possessed of the same Divine nature with the Father, He has given himself to you. How comes it that you do not overflow with gratitude?

*

Have you ever seriously reflected on the great dignity to which human nature was raised by the Incarnation? Of none of the Angels, not even of St. Michael, can we say: That Angel is God. But of Christ we rightly say: That Man is God. The Angel can only exclaim, O my God and my Lord! Man can exclaim, O my God and my Brother!

*

Adam's transgression spoiled the likeness of God in our soul. Christ's atonement not only renewed, but perfected that likeness. Through Christ and the unction of grace, it has received the finish of a beautiful oil painting, bringing out the resemblance, and giving to the whole picture the vivacity of life.

*

Divinity dwelt personally in Jesus Christ. Hence the remarkable words of St. John the Evangelist, who speaks as if his bodily senses had come in direct contact with the Godhead: "The Word was made flesh and dwelt among us, and we *saw* His glory."

*

According to philosophical principles, the means must be proportionate to the end. Now, the mystery of the Incarnation was the means by which the salvation of man was effected. Of what priceless value, then, in the eyes of God, must not our salvation be, since He chose such a means to secure it?

*

"Where sin abounded, grace hath more abounded." We have, indeed, gained more in Christ than we lost in Adam. The first man was invested with royal dignity, as an image and child of God. Every created object, so far from injuring him, did him homage. The ransomed soul is raised to the brotherhood of the Incarnate Son of God, and as St Paul affirms: "All things co-operate unto good for those who love God." The very resistance of nature displays the superiority of man, who, strengthened by faith, forces her to aid him in carrying out his designs. Passion may struggle for the mastery in his heart, but by manfully resisting its attacks, he can secure to himself a more glorious crown.

*

Earth changed its aspect after the transgression of the Divine command. Instead of sweet flowers, thorns sprang up, and guilty man was doomed to earn his bread in the sweat of his brow. Still, by patient toil, he can beautify the earth, and cause the wilderness to blossom like the rose. By offering up his fatigue in the spirit of penance, he can increase the joys of the celestial garden of paradise, to which he may aspire after passing through the wilderness of life.

*

The garden of Eden was lost; but it is replaced by the paradise of the Church on earth. The four streams which water that paradise are the four Gospels, flowing from the fountain of the revealed Word of God. The tree of the knowledge of good and evil is no longer a forbidden tree, because, by the grace of Redemption, we can act according to the knowledge of good and evil. The fruit of the tree of life is Christ Himself. No cherub stands before the gates to prevent us from entering. No, we are sweetly invited by the words of our Lord: "Come to me all ye that labor and are burdened, and I will refresh you."

*

No wonder that David, who styles the creation of the firmament the work of God's *finger*, should attribute the Redemption to the *arm* of the Almighty, as if to intimate that a word sufficed to call the universe into being, but that all the power of Omnipotence was required to restore fallen man to grace.

*

What was the first prayer uttered by Jesus on the Cross? One of forgiveness for His enemies. To partake of the infinite merits of our Lord and Savior, we should first ask of God forgiveness for our enemies. Our worst *enemies* are our *sins*.

*

Few reflect how consoling death has become for man, through the power of Faith. That primitive curse, pronounced against sinful man, has been changed by the Redemption into a great blessing. Death is but the gate through which we enter into everlasting life.

*

Christ descended from heaven to cure men, who were mortally wounded by sin. He styled Himself the Physician come to heal the sick. For this end, He allowed

Himself to be wounded and put to death. How hopeless must have been the condition of man since so extraordinary a remedy was needed to cure him!

*

What a difference between us and Christ! He freely chose to suffer; He sighed with earnest longings for the Cross. We fly from it, and shun it as much as we can. He wrought miracles to increase His sufferings; we would willingly work them to be free from all sufferings. He left heaven for earth, in order to suffer; we decline to suffer, even for an eternal reward in heaven.

*

Why did our Lord choose a carpenter for His foster-father? Why did He select that trade in preference to any other, and often labor at it Himself? Perhaps, because, in working in wood, He had before His eyes a continual remembrance of the mystery of the Holy Cross, by which He had resolved to save the world. How often, even in His tender years, would not the form of two pieces of wood stretched over each other present a vision of that Cross, on which he was one day to consummate His bitter passion!

*

He that knows and loves Christ, can never want words to speak of heavenly things, because his mind and heart are the abode of God's living Word. Such a person may say, in the language of David: "I believed; therefore I spoke."

*

On entering into the world, Christ, as the Apostle tells us, already said to His heavenly Father: "Thy will be done." After completing His mission here below, and commencing His bitter passion, with an exhausting sweat of blood, He still repeated, with an agonizing voice: "Thy will be done on earth, as it is in heaven" Would you know whether you are imbued with the spirit of Christ? Examine if, in all your prayers, in all your labors, in all your sufferings, your only aim is to do the holy will of God. Here is the touchstone by which you may judge of your proficiency in the school of Christ.

*

Under the Old Law, nothing was more consoling to men than to look forward to the day on which the promised Messiah should make His appearance among them. At present, nothing is more consoling than to look back upon the days forever vanished, when the Savior confirmed His lessons of wisdom by His own example. Powerful was the testimony of prophetic faith, in the mission of Christ; more powerful still ought to be the testimony of retrospective faith in His teachings and examples, and in His own prophecies of the coming events at His second advent.

*

Again, under the Old Law, nothing was more consoling to man, than to look forward to the day on which the promised Messiah should come. Now, for the true child of God, nothing is more consoling than to look forward to the day on which He shall come again to take us with Him.

*

Often, perchance, you lament, in the bitterness of your heart, that your zealous labors produce little or no effect, that your sermons work but few conversions among your hearers. Look at Jesus! Notwithstanding the numbers to whom He preached, how few, alas! profited by His loving words! How few felt the full force of His miracles! Can you reflect on this, and not derive thence motives of consolation?

*

If your courage begins to fail when you behold the fruit of your labor suddenly blighted, look at Jesus! In the hour of His triumph, He was greeted by the people with jubilant *Hosannas;* and but a few short days after, His ears were stunned with the deafening cry of *Crucify Him, crucify Him,* bursting from the same ungrateful multitude. Nevertheless, Pentecost came, the Church was founded and souls were saved. The fruit of your labor will not all wither and die; much of it will grow up, and, reaching maturity, will be gathered by faithful souls in the harvest-season of grace.

*

Christ was pleased, that His apostles, too, should taste the bitter chalice of disappointment. St. James made but few conversions among the people, to whom he bore the tidings of salvation. Fortunately he had learned to center all his hopes and desires in his Divine Master alone. Let us imitate his example. The greatest disappointment will then be unable to cast us down, because we are united to Him, who knows no change, and is, as the Apostle affirms, " to-day, to-morrow, and yesterday, always the same."

*

Christ, whose every action is replete with instruction for us, did not perform all His works alone; for many of them He used the Apostles as instruments. He foretold that, in His name, His followers should work greater prodigies than He Himself had wrought during His mortal life. Moreover, in the establishment of the Church, He admitted human co-operation. Yet this very circumstance shows in bold relief the Divine character of His work. Though propagated by feeble instruments, the Church has now existed for eighteen centuries, and it will exist until time shall be no more. Where can you find a more convincing proof of its Divine origin?

*

Several important moral truths receive additional light from this example of Christ. The first of these is the obvious fact, that the Saints appear to the greatest advantage precisely by the side of other holy men. They were not solitary mountains rising from a level plain; they were rather lofty peaks towering high above an elevated chain of mountains.

*

How mean and contemptible, then, are the whisperings of envy, which would persuade us to guard from the knowledge of men our undertakings for the glory of God, through a vain fear that others may divide with us the honor of the work, or, perhaps, eclipse the lustre of our renown. All this apprehension is illusory. The chief merit of a work always belongs to the master-mind which originated, planned, and directed it. It is not usual for the commanding general to engage in person; frequently he does not even fire a shot. But the whole body moves by his orders, and, therefore, the glory of the victory is his. The architect of a great church or palace does not labor alone. But, as he draws the plan and watches over its execution, the building is pronounced his work. Had Michael Angelo, through selfishness, refused to employ the labor of skillful workmen, would h have ever been able to rear the mighty basilica of St. Peter's, whose colossal proportions stand as an eternal memorial of his genius?

*

Learn, then, to live in a spirit of friendly intercourse with others who labor to promote the glory of God, and of His kingdom, the Church, and you will be able to do much more than you would by your own unassisted efforts.

*

Christ "humbled himself, becoming obedient unto death, even the death of the Cross. Wherefore, God also hath exalted Him, and hath given Him a name which is above every name: that in the name of Jesus every knee should bow of those that are in heaven, on earth, and in hell." If we are moved by the spirit of Christ, we must perform our actions with humility, obedience, and a desire of the cross. All things, in heaven and on earth, will then aid us to serve God and to increase in merit.

*

Christ entered not the palace of the ruler, whose son He had been asked to heal, but He often repaired to the cottages of the poor, to dispense His heavenly favors. You, on the contrary, find it hard to live among the poor, while you delight to visit the rich and even deem yourself highly honored, if they tender you an invitation. Do you resemble your Savior?

*

Do you know that Christ denounced the rich, exclaiming, "woe to the rich"? And yet you look upon wealth as a blessing, and cringe to those who are favored with the gifts of fortune. Evidently, you did not learn such sentiments in the school of Christ. You are aware that Christ said: "Blessed are the poor;" and yet you regard poverty as a curse, and look down, in contempt, upon those who do not possess the riches of earth. Oh! the sad, the unaccountable contradiction between the faith and the conduct of many Christians!

*

When Christ had refused to change stones into bread, Angels came and ministered unto Him a food which was, no doubt, infinitely more delicious than the one which He had rejected. We may experience something similar ourselves, when, through a spirit of self-sacrifice, we spurn the offers of the tempter, who holds out to us the allurements of earthly pleasures. As a reward for such fidelity, God is accustomed to overwhelm us with His grace and unite us more intimately with Himself.

Falsehood or lying contradicts truth. No wonder, then, that Jesus Christ, the Incarnate Truth, was styled by the prophet Simeon, "a sign which shall be contradicted." The world, which is nothing but a tissue of falsehood and lying, would fail in its fiendish mission, were it disposed to enter into an alliance with Christ. Hence the war of contradiction, which it incessantly wages against Christ and His followers.

*

In the words: "Thou shalt love thy neighbor as thyself," our Divine Savior lays down the standard, by which we should model our conduct toward our felllow-man. The position that he fills and the relation that he holds toward us, may vary, to a considerable extent, the exterior marks of respect due to him; but nothing can ever dispense us from interiorily entertaining for him that same love, which we cherish toward ourselves.

*

In connection with this subject, St. John asks: "How can he who loves not his brother whom he sees, love God whom he does not see?" Even if you see in his character traits that are repulsive to you, Faith will furnish you with innumerable motives for loving him. Is he not the image of God? Is he not ransomed at the price of Christ's suffering and death? Is he not, like yourself, an heir to heaven? Viewed in this light his failings may move you to compassion, but they can never exhaust the supply of love flowing from the Sacred Heart of Jesus.

*

Who has not read that celebrated little book on the *Imitation of Christ*, by the venerable Thomas à Kempis? Next to the inspired pages of the Bible, it is the most precious book that has ever been written. Would you know which is the most valuable edition of the *Imitation?* It is that which is printed in the heart, and stereotyped by the constant practice of its maxims and holy teaching.

*

Christ assures you that at the hour of death He will come, "like a thief in the night," to bear away your soul, whether you wish it or not. But during life He will not enter your heart by stealth. He will not take it by force. He asks for it through love. He wishes it to be a free gift.

*

"I will give to thee the keys of the kingdom of heaven," said Christ to Peter. He says it in another sense to every soul that desires to be united with Him in the heavenly kingdom of His love. But that these keys may open the door of the Sacred Heart, Christ demands, as a condition, that you, in turn, give Him the keys of your heart, so that He may enter it whenever He wishes, at any moment of the day or night.

*

The new world has now been brought into very direct communication with the old. The electric spark flashing along the cable has removed the barrier of distance, and made man almost ubiquitous. Ever since its discovery, America has been connected with Europe, and every other part of the earth, through the Communion of Saints, which forms a system of electric wires, all meeting in Rome, their common center.

*

Not only are the different parts of the globe thus connected, but, through Christ's infinite merits, there is a telegraphic communication between heaven and earth. Dispatches are transmitted every moment, and are often answered by enlightening grace.

*

We may compare the five wounds of our Savior with the first five books of Holy Scripture, because, in His infinite merits, we may find analogies to the characteristic qualities of those books. Thus we may consider that the wound of the right hand answers to the first book, called Genesis, or the book of creation. The merits of Jesus Christ called into existence the creation of grace, in which the Church is the new paradise, Christ Himself being the heavenly Adam. The wound in the left hand may point to the second book of the Pentateuch, called Exodus. Through the merits of Christ, we leave the Egypt of a carnal life, and journey toward heaven, our destined home. Christ is the manna, with which we are nourished and sustained during our pilgrimage through the desert of this life. The wound of the right foot may be referred to the third book, called Leviticus, which contains the rites of divine worship in the Old Covenant. The infinite merits of Christ impart to the ceremonial of the New Covenant, especially to the Holy Sacrifice of the Mass, and the Sacraments of the Church a really Divine character and dignity, typified by the rites and sacrifices of the Old Law. The wound of the left foot may correspond to the book of Numbers, so called because it contains the list of those men who were able to bear arms. Through the merits of Christ, we become soldiers—members of the Church militant. The wound of the Sacred Heart may answer to the book of Deuteronomy, which lays down the laws of God's chosen people. The law of the children of the Church is the law of love written with blood in the Sacred Heart of Jesus. The open wound in the side of Jesus is the most evident and consoling pledge of Divine love.

*

In the natural order of things, a bitter substance mixed with one still more bitter does not become sweet, and a heavy burden added to one still heavier does not grow light. But in the supernatural order, another law holds: Our bitterest sufferings, united to the still more bitter sufferings of Jesus, become sweet; and our heaviest burdens, united to the heavier burden of His Cross, become ineffably light.

*

Who does not wish, with St. Bernard, to breathe out his last sigh in the open wound of the Sacred Heart of Jesus? Who does not join in the loving and beautiful aspiration, expressed by the Saint in the following lines:

> "Hora mortis, meus flatus
> Intret, Jesu, tuum latus:
> In hac fossa me reconde,
> Et cor meum ibi absconde."

> "Jesus, God, when death is nigh,
>   Listen to my latest sigh:
>   In Thy ever-open side,
>   Let this heart of mine abide."

*

From a desire of plucking the forbidden fruit, Eve extended her hand toward the tree of knowledge. Christ extended His arms on the tree of the Cross to expatiate Eve's transgression. But oh! how infinitely stronger was his yearning desire to gather for us the precious fruit of life!

*

Concerning the inscription upon the Cross, "Jesus of Nazareth, King of the Jews," this beautiful and ingenious remark has been written: "Behold the title respectfully conferred on Christ, at His birth, by the Magi, mockingly applied to Him, at His death, by Pilate, jealously assailed by the Jews, but, in opposition to them, confirmed by the Holy Ghost, when Pontius Pilate replied: 'What I have written, I have written.'"

*

Listen to the admonition of Blessed Margaret Mary, concerning the devotion to the Sacred Heart of Jesus: The Heart of Jesus is an abyss, where you will find all that you need for your comfort, relief, and support, in all the troubles, temptations, and miseries of this life. If you are in an abyss of privation and desolation, bury yourself in the Heart of Jesus; this Divine Heart is an abyss of every consolation. If you are in an abyss of dryness and powerlessness, go and bury yourself in the Heart of Jesus; it is an abyss of power and strength.

If you are in an abyss of poverty, and stripped of everything, bury yourself in the Heart of Jesus; it is an abyss filled with treasures.

If you are in an abyss of weakness, relapses, and misery, bury yourself in the Heart of Jesus; it is an abyss of mercy.

If you find in yourself an abyss of pride and vain self-esteem, bury yourself in the Heart of Jesus; it is an abyss of humility, and deepest self-annihilation.

If you are in an abyss of ignorance and darkness, bury yourself in the Heart of Jesus; it is an abyss of light and knowledge.

If you are in an abyss of inconstancy, bury yourself in the heart of Jesus; it is an abyss of fidelity.

If you find in yourself an abyss of ingratitude, bury yourself in the Sacred Heart of Jesus; it is an abyss of gratitude and thanksgiving.

If you are in an abyss of agitation, impatience, and anger, bury yourself in the Sacred Heart of Jesus; it is an abyss of gentleness and meekness.

If you are in an abyss of dissipation and distractions, bury yourself in the Sacred Heart of Jesus; it is an abyss of recollection and fervor.

If you find yourself plunged in an abyss of sadness, bury yourself in the Sacred Heart of Jesus; it is an abyss of joy.

If you are in an abyss of trouble and disquietude, bury yourself in the Sacred Heart of Jesus; it is an abyss of peace.

If you are in abyss of fear, bury yourself in the Sacred Heart of Jesus; it is an abyss of sweetness.

If you are in an abyss of despondency, bury yourself in the Sacred Heart of Jesus; it is an abyss of hope and confidence.

If you are, as it were, buried in death, bury yourself in the Sacred Heart of Jesus; is is an abyss of life.

If you are, as it were, buried in hell, bury yourself in the Sacred Heart of Jesus; there is the foretaste of heaven.

In fine, in everything, and on all occasions, plunge yourself in the ocean of love and charity, and, if possible, do not quit it, until, as a sponge in the sea, soaked with its waters, you are penetrated with the sentiments of this Heart; or, like iron in the furnace, you glow with the fire of love, with which that Heart is burning for God and men.

Behold, here, the shortest way to reach the heights of Christian perfection!

*

He who follows Christ in an imperfect manner, often seeks rest and happiness in worldly pleasures and vain amusements; but, far from finding in them the desired repose, he only augments his interior anxiety, and sharpens the stings of an accusing conscience. How much easier and more consoling would it be to renounce all inordinate attachments to created things, and to seek rest where alone it can be found, in the Sacred Heart of Jesus!

*

Christ, as we said, admitted human co-operation, in order to communicate to men the fruits of Redemption. There is, in this respect, a threefold apostolate, namely, that of the word, that of example, and that of desire;

and it is difficult to say which is most efficacious in extending the kingdom of Christ and promoting the salvation of souls.

*

The first, the apostolate of the word, is the original channel, by which a knowledge of God was diffused; and who can describe or measure the good which it has achieved? Count, if you can, the instructions, sermons, and addresses delivered by so many apostolic men, from the time that the Holy Ghost descended upon the Twelve down to the present day, during a period of nearly nineteen hundred years. But this sort of apostolate is not limited to the formal announcement of the word of God by the lawful ministers of the Gospel; it embraces every word spoken in the interest of heaven and of souls. What an immense harvest of apostolic labors all of us may thus store away!

*

The second is the apostolate of example. A holy life is a perpetual sermon. It may even be more efficacious than the most stirring exhortation; for the proverb says: "Words move, examples draw." The holy lives of apostolic men certainly impart to their words a wonderful force. Nay, more, all pious Christians thus become real missionaries. They preach, without words, to sinners as well as to the just, and so accomplish the precept of Christ: "Let your light so shine, that men may see your good works, and glorify your Father who is in heaven." Have you ever seriously reflected what rich stores of merit you can garner up by means of good example?

The third kind of apostolate is that of desire. It is the soul of the others, and does its own work, even when they are not in our power. We have a striking instance of it in St. Francis Xavier, whose desire was to convert the empire of China, to pass thence to Russia, abolish the schism there, and reconcile the empire to Holy Church; then to penetrate into Germany, and arrest the spread of Protestantism; and, at last, to repair to Rome and throw himself into the arms of St. Ignatius, his spiritual father in Christ. Who can tell how meritorious in the eyes of Christ was this ardent desire? He alone knows how many souls have been gained to His holy service by this mission of desire, carried on in the hearts of so many devoted missionaries. Not St. Francis alone, but all the true ministers of God's holy word, have felt, and still feel, this desire to work for His greater glory and the good of souls. What a burning flame glowed in the hearts of Sts. Peter and Paul, and of all their successors in the ministry! What a consuming fire must result from the united flames which burst forth from the hearts of all the Saints! Its effects may not, indeed, be noticed at present by any others than Jesus and His beloved Mother, but on the day of judgment they will be revealed to all men. Oh, what will then be the reward, not only of their works, but even of their ardent desires!

*

In this triple apostolate of the zealous servants of God we may behold a reflection of the Holy Trinity, whose greater glory of the propagation of Christ's kingdom upon earth. The mission of the word we may refer to the Father, who sent His eternal Word into the world in order to redeem it; that of example is emblematical of the Son, the model we must imitate in order to share in the merits of redemption. The mission of desire may be referred to the Holy Ghost, who, according to the language of the Scripture, "prays in our hearts with unspeakable sighs."

*

We must, moreover, remark, that this threefold mission is not confined to the consecrated successors of the Apostles, but extends, more or less, to all the faithful. St. Peter reminds the faithful that they are "a priestly people," and the Holy Ghost says, by the mouth of the Wise Man: "The Lord has trusted to thee thy brother." Who can calculate the good effected by unconsecrated missionaries in this threefold apostolate? And first in the apostolate of the word. Who can estimate all the good produced by the words and admonitions of pious fathers and mothers, of husbands and wives, and of the many fervent Christians, all trying in their own sphere to spread the true faith, to lead back the straying sheep to the fold, to enlighten infidels, who "sit in darkness and the shadow of death," to convert sinners; in fine, to encourage genuine piety, and the desire of perfection among the faithful themselves.

*

The mission of good example is still more extensive. Consider the examples of virtue given by one Saint—one who had not as yet entered upon the active duties of the apostolate. I mean St. Aloysius. How many souls were sanctified by the mere sight of this holy youth—this "Angel in human flesh," as the Church has called him? God alone knows. And since his holy death, how many more have been detached from an inordinate love of earthly things by the consideration of his angelic virtues! The persuasive example of this Saint has inspired many with the resolution to bid adieu, as he did, to the world with all its dangers, and to consecrate themselves, without reserve, to God. What are the lives of the Saints upon earth but a continued sermon? Though for ages they have slept in the tomb—their dust mingled with its mother earth, and their voices hushed forever—their glorious example is preaching still, and exhorting all to follow in their footsteps.

＊

But the most extensive and consoling apostolate of all is that of desire. It knows no limit of time or space, because our desires are independent of exterior circumstances, and wholly subject to our own control. Would to God we could look into the hearts of the Apostles, and of all apostolical laborers in the vineyard of the Lord! How greatly their desires surpassed their deeds! St. Francis Xavier used to call himself an idle man, because his heart, filled with a burning desire for the salvation of souls, embraced the whole world. Rejoice, pious souls, that God has so ordered things that in every place and condition you may co-operate in the glorious work of saving others.

THE WORD OF GOD.

THE channel by which the knowledge of God and of the Savior is communicated to man, is the word of God. "Going, therefore, teach all nations," Christ said to His Apostles. "Faith comes by hearing," as the Apostle affirms. No doubt the truth of God is independent of the means or the instrument by which it is announced. Yet God has been pleased to commit His truth, and the duty of spreading it, to frail men, and has left it in their power to do much, by their dispositions and their co-operation, toward making His laws known and accepted.

✻

The word of God is contained in Scripture and tradition. Both are distinguished by evident signs of Divine origin. Nowhere in all the world can a book be found which can be compared to the Holy Scriptures, and no tradition is so stamped with the seal of truthfulness and consistency as the Divine Tradition in the Church of God.

✻

The Holy Bible, written in prose, may, nevertheless, be called a great Epic, which sings the praise of Divine Providence in so sublime a strain that the greatest poets of ancient and modern times have never equaled it. Chateaubriand was right when he called the style of Holy Writ "at once the mirror and the despair of all mere human writers."

*

As the Bible is the most ancient of books, not to say anything of its sacred character, it has a right to be placed before all other books, not only in the Church, but also in every library. As it has stood the test of the severest criticism, it has a right to be held as the criterion, or standard, by which all theories and suppositions of science are to be judged. There is no opposition between science and revelation. There is only opposition between the plain statements of the word of God and the hasty, ever-shifting theories of some few sciolists, whose highest ambition is to prove that they are right and God is wrong.

*

The Holy Scriptures are only a part of God's word. Christ did not commit His teaching to writing. Not all that the Apostles wrote was inspired, nor has all that they wrote been preserved in writing. Yet all that Christ taught, all that the Apostles taught and wrote, was true, and it has all been preserved. This is the whole deposit of revelation, committed to the keeping of the Church. The inspired writings contain only a part of it. The Church jealously preserves and watches over the whole deposit. That which is not contained in the inspired writings, she keeps and hands down either in the writings of her Fathers and Councils and theologians, or by the ever-living voice of her teachers from generation to generation.

*

God is the most simple of all beings, and yet He is infinitely great and sublime. Should not this remind the preacher that simplicity is not incompatible with dignity and sublimity; but that, on the contrary, by allowing the argument to be seen under a less embarrassed form, it greatly enhances the merit of a sermon and imparts to it additional sublimity? Let the subject of a sermon, then, be sublime; its arguments plain and direct; its style like a mirror, whose principal beauty consists in its even and highly-polished surface.

*

If the preacher perceives that his hearers are not well enough instructed or cultivated to follow him, he should use a plain style and suppress some even of the strong arguments that he might advance in support of his subject. No matter how striking and forcible they are, what purpose can they possibly serve, if those to whom they are addressed can neither see their bearing nor understand their meaning? Weak eyes can not endure a strong light.

*

If we were to change a sword into a reaping-hook, that weapon would lose its beautiful shape, but, at the same time, it would become a very useful implement. The word of God is a sword. If there be question of nothing but defending Divine truth, it is well to use it as a sword. But, if it be our aim to instruct our hearers, and withdraw their hearts from sin, it is advisable to change it into a reaping-hook. For, in that case, we need not a straight weapon set with the keen edge of argument, but a useful implement employed by a practical application, to cut down the weeds of sin and evil habits.

*

Some adorn their discourses with all the charms of rhetoric. Their diction is polished and elegant, and every period symmetrically rounded off. Their sermons may be likened to the full armor of the knights of old. It is, no doubt, of service to those who are accustomed to it, but can only be a hindrance to others. David slew Goliath with a sling and a stone. So, for the majority of speakers, a strong, plain reason, wielded with force, and cast into the face of error or passion, is by far the most serviceable.

*

In addressing a congregation, our language must be like a mirror. This mirror must, first of all, be clear. We must speak only for the benefit of our hearers, for their temporal and eternal good; and we must make them feel that we do so. The slightest breath of selfishness would tarnish the clearness of the mirror. Secondly, it must be large enough to reflect the objects intended to be seen in it. To be plainly understood, some truths require more explanation than others. Finally, the mirror must have a suitable frame. In like manner, rhetorical ornaments, which are the frame of a sermon, may be used, but they should be adapted to the subject and the argument. Of what use would a gilded and most beautifully polished frame be, if it were to conceal a portion of the mirror? And of what use would be an elegant sermon, with rhetorical beauties, if it hide the meaning of the speaker, or prevent the whole truth from being plainly seen?

*

A convex mirror diminishes the size of objects, while a concave one, on the contrary, makes them larger. In like manner, a style too highly elevated diminishes the practical effect of Divine truths, while an unbecoming familiarity gives them an unnatural appearance. There is a golden mean, combining the advantages and avoiding the inconveniences of the two extremes.

*

To concentrate the sun's rays and kindle a fire at a certain point, the burning glass must be held at a certain fixed distance. So must heavenly truths be held to the hearts of men, to kindle therein the fire of Divine love. Elevation of thought and appropriate arguments exert their power upon the human heart. If the arguments are too feeble and shallow, the sermon will have no effect, but will leave the hearer as cold and unmoved as he was at the beginning.

*

To produce any good effect, a sermon should be carefully prepared beforehand, and at least the heads noted down in regular order. This preparatory labor enables the preacher to adopt the most convenient arrangement, and to express the most delicate shades of thought in such a manner as to move the hearts of those who listen to him. Let him not attempt to deliver a sermon without this. Otherwise his discourse will be wandering; and, if his efforts succeed, it will be by the merest chance.

*

The advantage of careful preparation may be illustrated by another comparison. Reasons are like a bundle of keys, which open locked doors. A lock-smith may have good reason to think, that one of the many keys in a bundle will open a certain door, but he can not feel sure before he has tried. If he has already done this, before using the keys, he will be spared a great deal of trouble. A similar remark holds true of the preparation of a sermon. We may be assured that in almost every case a negligent preacher says to himself, on descending from the pulpit: If I had that sermon to deliver again, I would do it better. If he had carefully prepared it, he would not have to reproach himself in this manner.

*

A well-prepared speaker is like a rider firmly seated in a saddle, his foot resting in the stirrups and his horse completely under his control. But a speaker unprepared is like an inexperienced rider, without a saddle. The horse becomes restive and heeds not the bit. So, by and by, he finds himself in the position of the person whose horse was running away with him, and who, when questioned by a bystander whither he was going in such a hurry, replied: " I don't know, ask my horse."

*

Do you think that it requires too much time and trouble to prepare your sermons in this manner? If so, you quite mistake. For, after such a preparation, a preacher can tranquilly employ in other occupations whatever time remains. Besides, he will be amply rewarded by the ease with which he can deliver his sermon; while the one who appears before a congregation without due reflection will find his task painful, and he will often be forced to wipe from his face the hot drops of agony. Besides, a written sermon may serve at another time, before different hearers, and thus spare him the fatigue of preparing anew.

*

Careless speakers will not be apt to feel the full force of these comparisons, because *sometimes* they succeed as well as if they had written their sermons, and perhaps even better. Granting this to be true, their *sometimes* is nothing by the side of their *many* failures; and, if through a spirit of levity they are not sensible of their error, their hearers certainly are. The sermons of such persons are like shallow rivers, full of sand-banks. They are interspersed with commonplace remarks and trite sayings, while the discourses of those who prepare, flow smoothly and without interruptions, like a clear, deep stream, and are listened to with unwearying delight. A new manner of illustrating and explaining will cause what has been often said before, to appear new and interesting. A river may always remain the same; and yet, if its banks are improved and embellished with villas and castles, another trip on its waters is perhaps more delightful than when made for the first time.

*

The beginning and end of a sermon, especially, must be prepared with great care; and the preacher must never allow himself to deviate from his pre-arranged plan. Thus, when we pour ink into a bottle, a large portion of it will be spilled unless we are very careful at the beginning and at the end. So, too, when we have filled a sack with grain, a great part of it will be wasted, if we neglect to tie it up securely. If, when a bottle is already filled, we continue to pour in more, the superfluity is wasted. If a vessel accidentally passes its stopping place, the disappointed navigator must look for another, with no certainty of finding one. The preacher is often in similar circumstances, when he draws toward the close of an unprepared discourse. He passes by many a favorable stopping place, and tries in vain to find another. A priest once remarked: "When I have prepared my sermon, I know, to the very minute, when I shall finish; but when I have not, then I have to say to myself: 'Parcat mihi Deus'—may God have mercy on me and on my hearers."

*

The water projected by a fountain is not intended to remain in the air. It must fall back into the basin. It is this circumstance, in particular that renders the appearance of a fountain so very beautiful and refreshing. In like manner, the words of the preacher must not remain upon the heights of interior contemplation, but must descend, by means of practical illustrations, to the common life and every-day wants of his hearers, in order to be heard with pleasure and fruit.

*

The main argument, which most convincingly proves a preacher's proposition, should, if possible, be made the point to which all the other arguments converge, like radii to their center. His proofs will thus leave a permanent impression, and the principal argument will remain in the memory, like a kernel, from which, even after years, the germ of moral fruits will spring up, though not a word of the sermon be remembered.

*

A high-flown, grandiloquent style places the thunders of the Divine word at so great a distance from us, that they sound as simple murmurings, while the lightning of God's judgments look like the harmless flashes of heat upon a summer evening.

*

If we wish to fill a bottle, we use a funnel through which we carefully pour the liquid into the vessel. From this we may learn how to act, when we wish to communicate religious instruction to uneducated persons. We should accommodate ourselves to their limited capacity, and, by slow degrees, introduce the knowledge of Divine things into their minds. If the speaker begins with abstract proofs, regardless of the intellectual caliber of his hearers, and then starts off into a strain of vague reasoning, he resembles a man who reverses the funnel and tries to put the mouth of it over the bottle. What such a preacher says will not be understood. It will, as it were, flow aside and never penetrate the intellect. His hearers will either feel uneasy, and perhaps ashamed of their incapacity, or they will perhaps pass many severe criticisms upon the speaker, who has so little tact to make his remarks clear and agreeable.

*

Rich cloth alone does not make a good coat. The stuff must be cut and fashioned into a garment by an experienced hand. In the very same way, good material is not sufficient for a good sermon. The orator must possess the talent and skill of so arranging and connecting his thoughts that they may suit his hearers.

*

Those who preach without regard to the disposition of their audience, are often too diffuse; they make the dress of their thoughts too large. Some, again, are too concise in their explanations; they clothe their thoughts in a garment altogether too small

*

Some acrobats attain to an astonishing degree of agility. They walk, with the greatest security, upon slender ropes placed at an immense height, and perform upon them as many feats as ordinary gymnasts do upon level ground. The intellect is capable of no less wonderful development, if it pursues a thorough training in logic. A power like this is invaluable to the orator; yet, while calling it into action, he must not forget that all who listen to him can not soar so high. In an audience there are always some who are wanting in intellectual culture, and for whose sake he must sometimes content himself with walking on level ground. Such persons would be but little benefited by a preacher who indulges in abstruse arguments. They might admire him, as the gazing crowd does an acrobat, but any attempt on their part to follow him would result in a complete failure.

*

The speaker should be plain, but not vulgar. There are various ways of walking on level ground, as you may easily see by comparing the gait of a polished gentleman with that of an uneducated rustic. A degree of elevation in thought and expression should, above all, characterize the sacred orator. It is due to the dignity of his mission, and of the subject on which he speaks; besides, it inspires his hearers with greater respect, and moves them to more serious reflection.

*

Even the most sublime truths must be communicated in simple language. The preacher who finds this impossible, shows that he does not himself understand them clearly; for whatever is clearly conceived, always has a corresponding clearness of expression.

*

To be effective, a sermon should not be like a glass lantern, which shows at once the light burning within. It should not be of such a nature that, from the very introduction, the audience can infer the gist of the whole discourse. Like the lantern of Gideon, it should rather be somewhat hidden at first, but presently allow a flood of light to stream upon the astonished audience. Then the trumpet sound of truth, together with the sword of eloquence, will frighten away error and the enemy of mankind, and the exultant heart will re-echo with the cry of victory.

*

A violent philippic delivered by the preacher is like a thunder-storm, accompanied by an unexpected hurricane and violent flashes of lightning, which make no distinction between the innocent and the guilty, or even, sometimes, strike the good and spare the criminal. Such a sermon, being wanting in the sweet virtue of charity, will either have no effect at all, or else a very injurious one.

*

On the other hand, a sermon, even though charged with the thunder of reproaches, if it is delivered with sweetness and moderation, may be compared to a storm announced by the lightning and accompanied by a refreshing shower. Such a discourse can not but fertilize the hearts of the audience.

*

Yes, the great art of the sacred orator lies in making every word that he utters sink deeply into the inmost recesses of every heart. Happy the preacher who knows how to preach in such a manner that every one present becomes his own preacher, applying the sermon to himself.

*

We speak of "impressing" a truth on the mind and heart of another. To do so successfully, we must prepare and soften them by convincing them that our only object is the eternal salvation of those whom we instruct.

*

To make this desired impression, it is by no means advisable to use cutting remarks and sarcasms. Such a course would probably displease our hearers, and entirely defeat our purpose. Let us rather use solid arguments, and show that we really feel the truth of our words, and they can not fail to persuade.

*

In explaining any truth to others, it should be our constant aim to place it in a clear light before their minds; for of what benefit is it to have a distinct conception of the matter in question, if we can not impart the same to others? They will remain in darkness.

*

It is very unpleasant for a preacher to see his listeners fall asleep during his sermon. Yet, could he penetrate the interior dispositions of many who listen to him with open eyes and apparent attention, he would behold them deeply buried in sleep. This sleep consists in a profound indifference to the great affair of salvation.

*

The speaker may sometimes notice persons about to leave at the beginning of his sermon. But, when they hear how interesting is the subject upon which he will address them, they are persuaded to remain; and, if he can increase the interest by a pleasing and eloquent style, they listen with delight until the close of the sermon. Such was the case with St. Augustine, when listening to the fervid words of St. Ambrose. "I heard him with pleasure," he says. "At first I used to exclaim, 'How beautifully he speaks!' but before long I added, 'And how truthfully!'"

*

St. Paul calls the word of God a "two-edged sword." One of the edges is the *truth* of the proposition, the other its *importance*. If a preacher has the ability to make his hearers understand how true and how important is the subject of his instruction, the word of God will no doubt pierce their hearts like a two-edged sword.

*

Imagine a book without stops, paragraphs, or chapters! What a wearisome task it would be to plod through such a volume, even if its contents were most interesting. It is no less annoying to listen to a sermon which has not been divided off into different points or heads. The speaker should pause at proper intervals, and allow his audience to observe the order and the connection of his reasons. Otherwise, it would be very tedious, indeed, to follow him through his delivery.

*

The eye soon wearies of a level landscape, unbroken by woods, or hills and valleys. It is very uninteresting to travel over such a country. In the same manner, a sermon which contains only plain, commonplace expressions, without any variety of style or elevation of thought, soon wearies the hearer. He would much prefer to listen to reproofs, though rather severe, or to arguments, though somewhat difficult to understand.

*

An old adage says: "Appetite comes while eating"—"L'appetit vient en mangeant." We should have to wait a long time, did we defer addressing a congregation until they manifest an eagerness to hear us. Let us, then, by a diligent preparation of the matter, make our discourses so savory that, though they feel not the pinchings of spiritual hunger, the very piquancy of the victuals set before them may sharpen their appetite, and so dispose them to give their famished souls the necessary sustenance.

*

A young cleric, after one of his first sermons, asked an aged preacher, who had been listening to him, how he liked the sermon. The old man answered: "Tolerably well; but when you grow older, experience will teach you to make your sermons plainer, louder, shorter." Or, as another experienced preacher expressed it: "Go to the pulpit boldly, speak distinctly, and leave soon." Notice especially the last advice: Leave soon.

*

A proverb says: "Brevity is the soul of wit." If the sermon contains points of general interest, it will suffer from vain verbosity, tending only to prolong it, without adding any new ideas. If it can advance no such claim, brevity is still more desirable.

*

Not to be tedious to the hearer, it is enough to be short, which can be done without much preparation; but to be short and interesting, requires much study before ascending the pulpit.

*

"Do not eat to entire satisfaction," is a good maxim to insure health. A speaker should guard against prolixity, never quite satiating his hearers but leaving them at the end of the discourse eager to hear still more. Thus he will always be heard with pleasure.

*

It is better for children to eat frequently and but little at a time. In like manner, it is preferable often to break to the people the bread of the Divine word, than to surfeit them by an excess of spiritual nourishment, at long intervals. Do not speak too much to them; but rather leave them under the impression that they have not heard enough. They will thus digest your instructions far better, and, as a necessary consequence, grow more rapidly in holiness of life.

A change in the order of the few letters of the alphabet gives us the countless multitude of words and phrases in our language. So, too, the different position of the seven notes of the scale gives us the infinite variety of musical compositions. In the same way, we may, with skill and study, present the truths of Faith under so many different aspects as to produce the effect of novelty, or at least to give the discourse the charm of variety.

*

As in every elegantly furnished drawing-room there is a mirror, which often forms its principal ornament, so, in every good sermon, there should be some striking example or argument, drawn from experience, and illustrative of the truth proposed. Therein the hearer may behold at once the likeness or the difference between himself and the model proposed by the Gospel.

*

Though a saloon should be very spacious and adorned in the most elegant style, yet if it is not furnished with a seat, no one will be disposed to remain in it for any length of time to admire it. So a sermon without practical applications, no matter how well elaborated, will become tiresome for the hearer.

*

Pictures add greatly to the embellishment of a room; but they must be placed in the proper light, and hung with taste upon the walls. What valuable paintings are to a room, well-chosen and appropriate illustrations are to a discourse. If these mental pictures are delineated by the vivid imagination and cultivated mind of the speaker himself, they will be original and of very great value. The same is true of examples drawn from the personal experience of the preacher. If not thoroughly original, they must at least be correct copies of a good artist; that is, of a reliable author.

*

In a well-furnished parlor there is some musical instrument, and generally the *piano-forte* is preferred, because it combines all the tones, and can even replace an orchestra. This should remind the preacher that tenderness and strength, sweetness and firmness, must be skillfully blended in his earnest efforts to move the heart, if he wishes efficaciously to influence the wills of those who listen to him.

*

Both the preacher and the confessor are fishermen. The former spreads his net, and, with powerful exertions, draws from the waves of perdition whole shoals of men at a time. The latter, angling for human hearts with hook and bait, does not catch so large a draught at once, but he labors with as great if not greater success. For it is easier to escape from the net than from the barbed hook.

*

We may likewise say that the preacher, having cast his net from the pulpit, draws it in again in the confessional, where he quickly perceives whether he has caught any fish, and of what kind they are; so that, aided by this experience, he is enabled to throw it out again with greater success.

*

How inexpressible his joy, when he catches a fish that preys upon others, because he then insures the safety of all those that would have become its victims.

*

Nothing is more liable to frustrate all the efforts of the fisherman than the presence of a sword-fish in the net. It would soon cut its way through, followed by the other prisoners. This destructive fish represents that class of listeners, who, by passing ironical or disparaging remarks on a sermon, destroy the effect produced on hearts better disposed to derive profit from the word of God. If they succeed in rendering the preacher unpopular, they offer sinners a plausible excuse for seeking to escape from his net, and plunging again into the deep waters of sin. Oh! how fearful an account will God exact from such person!

*

You lament that you can not preach so often as you would wish, or in those places and before those hearers that are to your liking. Beware, lest your apparent zeal be prompted by secret ambition. Look at Jesus, the model of evangelical laborers. For thirty years, His Divine eloquence was buried in the silence of His home at Nazareth. During His public life, it showed itself usually not in great cities, but in villages, in small hamlets, and before the lowly ones of earth. Study His spirit, and you will feel consoled.

*

Hot springs usually possess medicinal properties. The heart of the preacher must resemble one of these fountains, and continually pour out the warm stream of the Divine word. A sermon destitute of this internal heat may be sublime, but it will be utterly useless for healing the maladies of the soul.

*

"The wind bloweth where it listeth." It matters little who preaches a sermon, provided he is animated with zeal for the honor of God, and is filled with His Holy Spirit; for it is the breath of this Spirit that moves hearts.

*

The favor with which a speaker's remarks are received, depends, in a great measure, upon the love and esteem entertained for him by his hearers. That love is the key to their approbation. Another may deliver the same sermon, or even a better one, and be greeted only with half-suppressed yawns, or similar signs of weariness. Let it then, be the study of every priest to merit the affection of the people.

*

It is written of Christ, that "He began to do and teach." Mark the order. He first began to *do*, and then to *teach*. He recommends the same thing to His followers, when He declares "Whosoever shall do and teach, the same shall be called great in the kingdom of heaven." How profound is the knowledge of human nature displayed in this conduct of our Divine Model! Men like to listen to sermons illustrated by examples, which, if rightly chosen, are wonderfully persuasive. But the best illustration is the example of the preacher himself. It is hard to resist the influence of his words, if he is known to live comfortably to his theory, and to practice what he teaches others.

*

OUR LIFE FOR GOD.

THE Sacred Scriptures compare this life to divers objects, all expressive of some condition that is essential to a life truly meritorious and pleasing to God. Let us consider some of these comparisons. "The wise man," says Holy Writ, "buildeth his house upon a rock." This rock, this foundation, this corner-stone, is Jesus Christ, upon whom we build by a strong faith and an unswerving attachment to His holy Church. Our daily duties are so many different apartments in that house, and the resolutions which we make are the furniture with which they are supplied. The pious sighs, which elevate the heart to God, are steps leading to the upper story of the building. Confidence in God, prudence and discretion, are as hinges upon which the doors and windows turn. Self-contempt is the cellar, in which is preserved the delicious wine of spiritual consolation for the refreshment of humble souls devoted to prayer and solitude. Vigilance is the doorkeeper, who, after advising with discretion, decides upon admitting or excluding the visitors that present themselves. The heart is the fire-place, in which the flame of Divine love must always be kept alive. In fine, solicitude for eternal salvation is the roof which must cover the entire building.

Holy Writ compares life to a field or vineyard. Be careful to keep everything there in good order. The principal requisites for raising a good crop, are richness of soil, a fine situation, industry on the part of the laborers, and favorable weather. In the interior garden richness of soil is the good disposition of the soul. Our vocation to some particular state in life is typified by the quality of the grain for which the field is cultivated and destined. The seed cast on the field is the word of God. Continual effort to advance in Christian perfection is represented by the industry of the workmen.

*

Holy Writ also compares the life of man with a tree. The soil, in which it grows, is the heart. The root typifies our principles, resolutions, and practices; the trunk represents the anxiety which we feel for our salvation as the main affair of man. A pure intention in all that we do, gives to this spiritual tree its stately proportions and constant growth. Our various duties and obligations are the branches, the aspirations of our hope are the leaves, true humility the bark, and Divine grace the sap of the tree. And what are the delicate blossoms? The fervent desires and holy aspirations of the zealous Christian soul. The dew and rain that refresh them, when parched and withered by the summer heat of worldly trials and vexations, are the extraordinary consolations which the Almighty vouchsafes at times to the earnest soul. The sun, which imparts to the tree its health and vigor, and to the fruit its maturity and flavor, is our perfect conformity in all things to the will of God.

*

Again, Holy Writ compares this life to commerce and trade. In commerce, success depends upon the location of the store, the quality of the goods, the manner of dealing with customers, and skill in speculating. The proper location typifies each one's wealth; the goods sold represent the virtues which we practice; skill in speculating may well illustrate the discretion which we should use in the acquiring and increasing of our merits. Eagerness in availing ourselves of every opportunity of gain is the life of trade. It is no less essential for acquiring virtue and leading a holy life.

*

Holy Writ compares our life to a journey. Heaven is our home, toward which, during our present life, we should be ever journeying. Every one who wishes to travel well makes some preparation; and he does so with more or less care, in proportion to the dangers and difficulties of the road, and to the importance of the object for which he travels. How great, then, should be our solicitude in equipping ourselves for life's journey! The path is beset with dangers. The object at stake is heaven itself—a happy or unhappy eternity.

*

Holy Scripture compares this life with the profession of arms. The justice of a war depends upon its cause. Its ultimate success is due to a variety of circumstances, such as the position of the battle-field, the strength of the enemy, the skill of the commanding officers, the duration of the struggle, the quality of the weapons, etc. The glory which follows the victory is proportionate to the object intended. Since, then, the object of our spiritual combat is a heavenly crown, how great, how untiring, should be our efforts to gain the victory!

*

It must be evident to every Christian, that all these conditions of a successful contest have their counterparts in the spiritual warfare which we are daily waging against the enemies of our salvation. The object of this warfare is to reach the blessed destiny for which a loving God has created us. That destiny is to see with unclouded vision the God of life and light, and to dwell with all the happy inhabitants of heaven for eternity. The dangers of this spiritual warfare are the temptations which beset us day and night. Alas! how perilous is our situation! The three most terrible foes are the world, the flesh, and the devil. The commanding general is Lucifer, the chief of the fallen spirits, that traitor Angel who first broke peace in heaven. His allies and friends are our evil passions and inordinate inclinations, and the wicked principles and still more wicked example of the children of the world. What a terrible army! The motto inscribed on the banner which Satan unfurls, is: *Pride, Lust, Avarice.* The inducement he offers to make men enlist, is the transitory gratification of their criminal appetites. His officers are the demons who have acquired skill in this unholy warfare, in which they have taken part since the fall of the first man.

*

The leader of the children of God in the Church militant is Jesus Christ. The standard which He raises on high, and under which all who wish to save their souls must enlist, is the holy Cross, bearing the motto: *Deny thyself*. His invincible allies are the faithful Angels, headed by St. Michael. His officers are the Saints, who have so nobly vanquished the enemy in their different states of life. Mary, the heavenly Judith, watches and protects the children of God in this fearful combat. The struggle is terrible but short. The weapons used in this spiritual combat are the virtues practiced by us. That which gives them their edge and their strength is truth. Every one who uses them faithfully is certain of victory. The war-cry of the Christian soldier is that of the old Crusaders: *God wills it*.

*

Christ compares our labors for heaven to a banking business. We should endeavor to get the highest possible price of merit for our actions. The banking business, which is considered one of the most lucrative, is more or less extensive, in proportion to the number and amount of bills of exchange daily issued. The whole business is founded upon mutual confidence to accept the bill for the specified amount of money. Happy is he that, by purity of intention and an entire confidence in God, enters with Divine Providence into a business of exchange, receiving every day an abundance of new graces for good works performed. How great a treasure will he not put out on deposit, with the assurance of drawing it again in heaven!

*

While writing, we often have to dip the pen in the ink again, in order to make our characters legible. We must accustom ourselves, by a repeated renewal of our good intention, to dip the pen of our good will into the Sacred Heart of Jesus, that we may draw from it His precious Blood, and therewith record our good deeds in the Book of Life. If we neglect to unite our actions with the infinite merits of Christ, and to perform them with the intention which He had in all His actions, we resemble a person who writes without ever dipping his pen in ink, and who, of course, fails to make legible marks. Again, if we begin with that good intention, but neglect to renew it, we are like a writer who never thinks of dipping his pen in the ink a second time, after he has once begun to trace the first letters.

*

A person who wishes to fill a bottle with any valuable liquid, first rinses it carefully. Thus our hearts must be purified from the dust of earthly desires and the dregs of self-love, that they may be filled to overflowing with the love of God and of His holy Law.

*

St. Gregory calls Holy Scripture an epistle, written by God to mankind. Our life should be an epistle to God, informing Him that, by our actions, we have corresponded with His commands.

*

Unfortunately, however, the life of man seldom resembles an epistle written to God. One uses bad paper; that is to say, his heart is weak, and, like tissue paper, is unfit for writing. Another has what is called " a good heart," but the pen of his will is bad. A third mixes dust and sand with his ink; or, in other words, he has not a pure intention in performing his actions. A fourth, in fine, sits down at his desk, provided in the best style with everything necessary for writing; but, allowing the light of zeal to burn down, he is soon surrounded by utter darkness, and falls asleep.

*

St. Paul said that he labored more than the other Apostles, but he did not say that his labors were more fruitful than theirs. God does not look to the success; He rewards according to the amount of labor performed in His vineyard—" curam non curationem," writes St. Bernard to Pope Eugenius.

*

It is not every kind of suffering that leads to eternal life. Christ promised heaven positively to such only as suffer for Him and for justice sake.

*

What is necessary for salvation? First, to direct our care and attention to our last end, and then, without delay, to select the means best suited to make it a happy one. Let the dawning of each day witness in us a new increase of fervor for the acquisition of virtue and the imitation of the Saints. Let us not disregard the lessons of experience; let us resolve victoriously to overcome all obstacles, and to turn them to profit. These are the principal means to promote our growth in holiness, and lead us by degrees to the summit of perfection. But how few adopt them! On the contrary, the children of the world employ them most zealously in their way.

*

The children of the world have but one aim in view—to do their own wills, to be happy, rich, and honored. For this they live, for this they employ every sense of their bodies, every power of their souls. When the first beam of the morning sun falls upon their eyelids and announces the light of another day, their thoughts are not of God, who has preserved them from the thousand dangers of the night, but of what they must do to promote their life-long scheme of ambition. Indeed, in their way, they follow the maxim of the great Apostle: "Forgetting what is past, I stretch forward to the future." For these worshipers of the world, the four best things are, to be sheltered, fed, clothed, and amused; and the infallible means of attaining this fourfold object is *money*. Money, therefore, is their idol—the golden calf before which, in profound adoration, they bend the knee.

*

"Deny thyself" is, for our sanctification, the leading axiom taught by Christ Himself. Upon its application to our outward conduct depends the success of our efforts for perfection.

*

"Deny thyself." It is, in some sense, also the watchword of worldlings. Look at the great mass of the working classes. What self-denial they must practice, what privations they must suffer! And all this for a trifling gain.

*

"Deny thyself." It is the pass-word of the higher orders of society. Daily and hourly they must sacrifice to their position some favorite pleasure or inclination. None, indeed, are more the slaves of circumstances than those who dwell in the courts of kings. How many restraints human respect imposes upon them! How many humiliations wound their pride; how many wants their very abundance creates!

*

"Deny thyself." It is the only means of compassing even the joys of sense. What fatigue, what disgust, what sacrifices they impose upon those who seek after them! How readily even the voluptuary subscribes to the necessity of the axiom, "Deny thyself!"

*

Passion never finds what it seeks. On the contrary, it is punished with an insatiable longing; and, in the language of the Holy Ghost, "every sin is its own punishment." The proud man, who inordinately covets glory and distinction, very often finds only humiliation. The avaricious man is goaded on by an intense and insatiable desire of more; the lustful man is tortured by bodily disease; the contentious often lose by wrangling what they had much trouble to gain; the intemperate are surfeited with a loathing satiety. Think you that this sentence of heaven, already enforced against the sinner in this world, will be visited on him with less severity in the next?

*

How different is the lot of virtue, which not only finds what it seeks, but far more! It longs only to please God, and it is allowed to enjoy Him. It seeks only to do His will, and it is rewarded by a share in His bliss. It works not for wages, yet amasses an incomparable weight of glory.

*

The very language of Scripture seems to refer the sad carelessness of man in the work of salvation to want of attention. Hence the oft-repeated exclamations: Lo! See! Behold! which we find in the sacred text. Christ Himself exhorts us, in a still more emphatic manner. "He that has ears to hear," cries the Savior, "let him hear." He would intimate by these words that the truths of holy Faith are so great, that listening to them should be sufficient to make us live well. How, indeed, is it possible for beings, endowed with the use of reason, not to be awakened to a sense of duty by those Divine threats and promises? Yet even Solomon, though knowing and teaching those truths, did not persevere in their practice. What an example of human blindness and frailty! What a sad instance of the perils to which our eternal salvation is exposed!

*

If a good reader wishes to assist a bad one by reading with him, he must have patience, and not hurry on, nor even read in his ordinary manner. For else, instead of aiding his pupil, he will only confuse him. In the same manner, all who are intrusted with the precious charge of leading souls to God, must be patient and forbearing. Remember that perfection is a difficult lesson to learn, and virtue hard to acquire. Go on slowly, then; accommodate yourself to the weakness of your children in Christ, until, by His grace and your untiring instructions, they become confirmed in virtue.

*

What is virtue without love? Incense without fire, and therefore unable to diffuse the good odor of Christ.

*

Many are constantly forming new resolutions, but never put them into practice; others put them into practice, but without any fixed plan or design. These two classes of persons are, as it were, collecting materials for a building, and either making no use of them, or erecting the edifice at random.

*

The Christian who is always ready to make good resolutions, and yet remains negligent in their execution, resembles a man, who, at the approach of winter, is very industrious in cutting wood and preparing it for use, but who, when the snow-flakes fall and the cold frost penetrates into his dwelling, never uses the fuel.

A soul whose union with God is not perfected, but often interrupted by temporal cares and occupations, resembles a country with but one little spring of water, which frequently dries up. A soul, on the contrary, which lives in a sweet and permanent union with Him, may be compared to a lovely garden, in the center of which there is an inexhaustible fountain branching off into a great many little streams.

*

A sportsman, who beats the forest for a special kind of game, loses no time in chasing any other. Thus should we act in our endeavors to acquire a certain particular virtue. Wholly intent upon that object, we should direct toward it all our desires, affections, and resolutions.

*

Were a beggar to go from door to door, but not wait to receive the alms which the hand of charity is ready to reach out to him, we would most assuredly think him crazy. How many, in their inconstancy and levity, never take the time to carry their holy desires into effect. Such persons are like mendicants, who knock at the door of Divine mercy, but do not wait until the desired graces are granted.

*

A straight rod can be curved into a bow, and exercise a great projective power. First straighten your will, by a pure intention to serve God, to do His most holy will; you may bend it through fear and love; like a bow, it will serve to send off the shafts of determined resolution.

✱

The pious Christian considers himself bad, because he observes in his own heart an inclination to evil. The guilty sinner regards himself good, because he sometimes feels his heart moved by virtuous impulses. The one is deceived, but for his greater sanctification; the other is also deceived, but for his eternal reprobation.

✱

A convict, who has one hand and one foot chained, can indeed walk and labor; but how much fatigue does not the effort cost him! And, besides, how coarse and imperfect is not his work! In like manner, a soul, bowed down to the earth by the fetters of its many imperfections, and venial sins, can move a little in the service of God and perform some good works. But O, how slowly it advances, how soon it is fatigued! Far from aspiring to Christian perfection, it is satisfied with merely avoiding mortal sins.

✱

Garments must often be examined, and, if ever so slightly soiled or torn, they are brushed and mended. Indeed, we often brush them daily; for some fine dust will always settle within their folds, particularly when we are obliged to walk much through dusty streets. These garments may typify the conscience. Though, with God's grace, we can avoid great stains, yet are we liable to contract some dust in the daily walks of ordinary life. How shall we brush off that dust? By daily examination of conscience and by frequent confession.

*

Persons who try to effect a compromise between God and the world, who sometimes plunge into dissipation, and immediately after subject themselves again to the restraints of a penitent life, act like those who take honey in their mouths, and soon after replace it by wormwood. The honey loses its sweetness, and the wormwood tastes more bitter from the contrast. Ah! Christian soul, would it not be better to cease this trifling, and to live in the constant practice of self-denial?

*

God can easily change the very stones into children of Abraham. The devil, on the other hand, can transform those children of God again into stones, if they be so unfortunate as to listen to his suggestions. Experience shows, that hearts naturally soft and pliant as wax can, when turning away from God, become hard and unyielding as adamant; especially when they once have been good and zealous, and then go astray.

*

Few persons can write or work with the left hand, and fewer still can use both hands with equal dexterity. Scarcely a single artist can boast that skill. A Christian who, with perfect submission to the will of God, performs his duties no less under prosperous circumstances, no less in the time of dryness and desolation, than in the hour of heavenly consolation, is a writer or an artist who can use his left as well as his right hand. All the Saints possessed this wonderful art.

*

An artisan, whose wages are proportionate to the perfection of his handicraft, is all attention, especially as his work approaches completion. How much attention, then, should we bestow on our good works, for which we shall be rewarded according to our efforts! How carefully should we guard against any defect in the intention, calculated to mar their perfection! But, above all, how solicitously should we avoid, at the close, anything which might interfere with their perfect finish! Let us never forget the admonition of the Holy Ghost: "Unto the end corrupt not."

*

Much money, time, and labor are needed to grade and pave a turnpike. But, when the road is once finished, the fatigues of traveling are greatly diminished, while the money expended for it is soon returned by the toll-gate duties. So it is with a Christian life. It costs time and labor to prepare the road, to acquire the habit of virtue. But, when once we have gained this much upon ourselves, we are not exposed to meet so frequently with the obstacles of temptation and passion, which make the way to perfection almost impassable for so many. We run with ease in the way of God's commandments, and all the expenses incurred to acquire that case are more than compensated for by interior peace, and by that intimate union with God, which is a foretaste of heavenly joy.

*

Timid souls are afraid to make generous resolutions. Like small dealers, they do but a retail business, while courageous souls, like wholesale merchants, engage in a wholesale trade. The profits of the latter are more considerable in one week than those of the former in a month, or even a year.

*

St. Ignatius, having been asked to point out the shortest road to perfection, replied: "To hate what the world loves, and to love what the world hates."

*

Worldlings very often consider the men of God *eccentric*, while, in reality, they themselves are out of their true *center*, which is God.

*

The vain and the fashionable are fond of a rich and stylish apparel; "they love the purple and fine raiment." They are continually busied about their attire, and, in fact, seem to think of nothing but adding some new fringe or flower, that may set them off to still greater advantage. Is it so with the children of God? Far from it. Their constant aim is to divest themselves of something every day, to put off the garb of sin and the frippery of their many imperfections and earthly attachments, assured that God will clothe them in the magnificent garments of His graces, and that He will array them in the most precious robes of virtue.

*

The world often contradicts itself. It loves falsehood, and the punishment of falsehood is self-contradiction. This is nowhere so apparent as on the subject of death. Timid persons, who are fearful of danger, continually dwell upon it. Now, there is nothing which the children of the world fear more than death; nevertheless, they live in absolute forgetfulness of it. They know very well that they must die, but, practically, they do not believe it.

*

The selfish man apparently cares for no one but himself; and yet, he is the very person that wholly neglects himself. He is, indeed, always over-anxious about everything that belongs to him, but he never turns his thoughts seriously upon himself. Had he a well-ordered charity, he would not endure so much toil and fatigue, nor submit to such drudgery for the sake of so little gain; but, by laying up imperishable riches, he would prove to the world that he really consults his own interests.

*

A person suffering from chills may be clad in the warmest clothing, and yet be unable to drive away the sensation of cold. In the same manner, the exterior demeanor of the sinner may be good and moral, while, in the depths of his wicked heart, he feels the chills of worldliness and the want of the warmth of true virtue.

*

A book, which is not bound and protected by a good cover, can not be used for any length of time without being torn and spoiled. Virtues, not secured by firm and deeply-rooted principles of religion, will soon suffer from intercourse with others. The best cover to preserve those leaves upon which we write the record of our lives, is contempt for human respect, and fidelity in the exercise of prayer and union with God.

*

Considering the lightness of a single sheet of paper, who would ever imagine that several like it, bound together, could make a heavy book? We may say the same of a slender wisp of straw. How light it is! And yet, when many such are packed together, how great is the weight! This illustrates an important truth; numbers of venial sins, and even imperfections, when taken together, may cause a heavy weight of guilt.

*

St. Teresa was right in saying, that it is far less dangerous to have many imperfections, than to have but one deeply-rooted, besetting passion. Let us illustrate this by a comparison. If a vessel is exteriorly coated with dirt, it may easily be cleansed by merely plunging it into water. But if a deep stain has penetrated it in some spot, it is a very hard task to purify it, so as to make it fit for use.

*

How slowly drag the feet of the culprit, as he approaches the place of his doom! But the sinner is hurried on, by unrelenting time, to the judgment seat of condemnation; and yet he delights in the rapidity with which he moves. A "fast life" is his glory. He enjoys himself and carefully shuns every appearance of a discomfort, which would only be transitory. He never once bestows a thought upon his coming perdition. O, what a deception! Yes, truly, the greatest fools are they who believe that the Gospel is wisdom, yet live according to the maxims of the world.

*

Cold glass sweats when exposed to a damp atmosphere. There are persons, who are very cool and indifferent about mortifying themselves; and yet, when they listen to religious instruction, they are easily moved to tears. But, alas! those tears have no more power of softening the hard stone of the heart, than the drops, which trickle down the cold surface of the glass, have of melting it away.

*

How foolish would he be, who would refuse a present of some precious wine, because he would be obliged to furnish a barrel to contain it! Far more foolish are those, who can not persuade themselves to practice acts of self-denial, which would secure to them a rich supply of graces from heaven. Their niggardliness puts an end to the favors of divine liberality.

*

In order to crystalize certain liquid substances, we let them evaporate, by exposing them to the influence of heat. If our daily life is kept under the influence of Divine love, our attachment to earthly things will soon diminish. The evaporation which then takes place is the result of serious reflection on the words of the Wise Man, "vanitas vanitatum," all is vanity, except to serve God, to know His most holy will, and to live accordingly. Thus our life acquires the desired consistency, and the crystal of real virtue is formed.

MODELS OF PERFECTION—THE SAINTS.

How tame and unattractive would be the appearance of a city that could show no churches, with their towering steeples and lofty spires! What those spires and steeples do for the beauty of an earthly city, the Saints do for the grandeur of the heavenly city. Their lives, sanctified by the practice of the most sublime virtues, are as the spires and domes and turrets on the wonderful cathedrals of the heavenly Jerusalem.

※

The virtuous examples of the Saints are like the bells in church towers. With what harmony and sublimity they ring forth their peals of jubilee upon each returning festival!

※

Christ compared a holy man with a man of great learning. The servants of God are indeed very learned, for what is so difficult to acquire as a knowledge of the science of the Saints? Before completing their course, they must pass through many trials and examinations.

The different virtues are so many propositions to be proved, and their arguments are sustained against wily, quibbling opponents, whose sophistries are well calculated to mislead. The best method to adopt in such a dispute is that which is called *in forma*. In this case, it consists in leading a well-regulated life, and never slackening in the practice of virtue. "Keep order, and order will keep you."

*

Most men wish to be considered masters in their respective callings, and nevertheless few merit that distinction; not because they neglect what, in their opinion, is great and important, but what they deem trifling and insignificant. How few, alas! are always watchful to detect and amend small faults! Sad, indeed, is this negligence when carried into the spiritual life.

*

The labor of the artisan does not convert baser materials into gold or jewels. He that works in the precious metals is entitled to the name and pay of a goldsmith; while, with much greater fatigue, the common blacksmith earns comparatively small wages. In the same manner, our reward in heaven will depend much on the object for which we labor. The more closely it bears upon the great work of God, namely, the salvation of souls, the more precious is the substance in which we labor, and the greater will be our recompense.

*

He that would seek to imitate the Saints in their sublime and heroic virtues, before purifying his conscience from inclinations to sin and imperfections, would pursue the wrong course, and would behave like a man who would try to leap to the height of a mountain on the other side of a wide ravine, in place of crossing a bridge and ascending the mount slowly, thus avoiding the danger of falling down a precipice.

*

One who is ignorant of geography and history has no claim to be classed among scientific men. So, also, one who has never studied the geography of his own heart, with all its moral proclivities, and has not carefully reviewed the history of his life, can not hope to be ranked among the Saints.

*

We compare ourselves to the Saints, and they appear very great to us. They compared themselves to Christ, of whom it is said in Scripture: "He hath exulted as a giant to run his way." In their own eyes, the Saints were very lowly.

*

The examples left us by the Saints are always to be admired, but frequently they can not be imitated. However much they exceed our strength, they may at least move us to do with joy, resoluteness, and fervor what we can. They are like the towering heights of the Alpine mountains, cheering and inspiring to view, though difficult to scale. The mere consideration of heroic deeds elevates the mind and encourages us to clamber at least as far as we can.

*

How often do we hear from the lips of the lukewarm such expressions as the following: "I do not aim at becoming a Saint; I am content with being a good Christian." Did the Saints aspire to anything else than to be good Christians?

*

The Church calls the day of a Saint's death his birth-day. It is, indeed, the dawning of a new life for the happy soul escaped from "this body of death." The birthday of a child is hailed with festive celebrations, especially if born to a noble inheritance. What felicitations, then, should greet the Saints when they close their eyes to the world and its vanities, to take possession of their thrones in the kingdom of heaven.

*

"The depths were not as yet, and I was already conceived." The abyss of guilt was not yet opened by the fall of man, when Mary, in the depths of Divine Providence, was already destined to be the dawn and the evening-glow of Redemption. Conceived without stain of sin, she was the dawn whence issued the Sun of Justice; and when that Sun was sinking on the Cross, Mary, at its foot, appeared as the evening glow, that no human being, looking upon that scene, should ever despair.

*

THE ANGELS.

THE words of St. Paul regarding heaven: "Eye hath not seen, nor ear heard, neither hath it entered into the heart of man, what things God hath prepared for them that love Him," may be understood in reference to the holy Angels. No imagination can picture even a shadow of the beauty and bliss of the heavenly creation, and especially the glory and happiness of an Angel.

What is the splendor of the sun compared with the light of glory which surrounds every Angel? Were one of those heavenly spirits to show himself visibly, the sun would at once disappear, just as do the stars when the sun begins to diffuse his light over the earth.

On the other hand, because of the frightful hideousness of a fallen Angel, we may say with truth: No eye has ever seen, no ear ever heard and no heart ever conceived the ugliness of a devil and the torments he suffers.

Some day, and that not long hence, you will resemble one or the other of these Angels.

*

"Who is like God?" This was the battle-cry which rang through heaven when, sword in hand, the faithful Angels attacked the rebellious spirits and hurled them down to the abyss of hell. By calling to mind God, reflecting who He is, and remembering His promises and threats, you will be victorious over every temptation.

*

There are nine choirs of Angels, and their different qualities beautifully indicate the various stages of progress in the way of Christian perfection.

The spirits of the lowest choir are those whom we designate by the name of Angels simply. They reflect God's providence by leading every rational being to a happy destiny, that is to last for all eternity. It is from this choir that the Guardian Angels are taken. The first requisite in order to advance in the way of Christian perfection, is identical with that which is needed for making the first step to attain salvation, namely, an intimate conviction of the eternal truth: The end of man is to serve God. This ought to be placed before the mind in all its grandeur and gravity.

*

The spirits of the second choir are the Archangels. They are the representatives of the succors given us by God in the mighty battles which we must fight against all the enemies of our salvation. Self-denial is the second condition by which to advance on the way of Christian perfection; and in proportion as we exercise the spirit of abnegation, of interior and exterior mortification, we shall advance in perfection.

The Angels of the third choir are the heavenly Principalities. They typify the authority of God as the source of all prerogatives conferred upon creatures. The third condition to be complied with, in order to advance in perfection, consists in despising the world and its honors, in flying from even the shadow of vanity. Even in the exercise of penance, vanity may lie hidden. Progress in perfection is incompatible with vanity and human respect.

*

The Angels of the fourth choir are the heavenly Powers. They are the reflection of God's omnipotence, operating through all created powers. The fourth requisite for progress in perfection is, amid sufferings and tribulations, to surmount all obstacles that are opposed to the practice of virtue. Patience is here the watchword.

*

The Angels of the fifth choir are called the heavenly Virtues. They represent God's omnipotence in the order of grace. The fifth requisite of progress is, with Divine grace for our ally, to battle with and overcome all interior trials. These are often more violent and powerful than those from without.

*

The Angels of the sixth choir are the heavenly Dominations They symbolize the majesty of God as the ruler of the world. The sixth requisite for advancement in perfection is to be animated with zeal for the extension of the kingdom of God on earth. We manifest this zeal in practicing the corporal and spiritual works of mercy with heroic fortitude.

*

The Angels of the seventh choir are the heavenly Thrones. They are types of God's immutability and eternal tranquillity. The seventh requisite for advancing in perfection consists in the constant, quiet fulfillment of our good resolutions. We must free ourselves of all inconstancy and vain anxiety, exhibiting, even in our countenances, the internal calm that arises from our trust in God.

*

The Angels of the eighth choir are the Cherubim. They are symbols of God's infinite intelligence and omniscience. The eighth requisite to make progress in perfection is an increase of supernatural light to ascertain the most holy will of God, and of grace to act conformably with it, being indifferent to everything else, even to the success of what we do to serve God.

*

The Angels of the ninth choir are the Seraphim. They live as by the breath of God's infinite love; they seem to be the very flame of love. The ninth and last requisite to advance in the way of Christian perfection is this burning love of God above all things; loving nothing, except in Him and for His sake; so that to us may be applied the words of St. Paul: "In Him we live, and move, and have our being." This is the very summit of perfection.

✱

Let us often think of the holy Angels, and invoke the assistance of the different choirs to practice those virtues of which they are the exemplars, and on which depends our spiritual progress.

✱

The Angels are by nature spiritual beings, that is, not possessed of carnal bodies. If we succeed in completely subjecting the body, with all its carnal desires, to our reason and will, under the law of God, we shall become, through virtue on earth, what the Angels are by nature in heaven.

THE WAY OF PERFECTION.

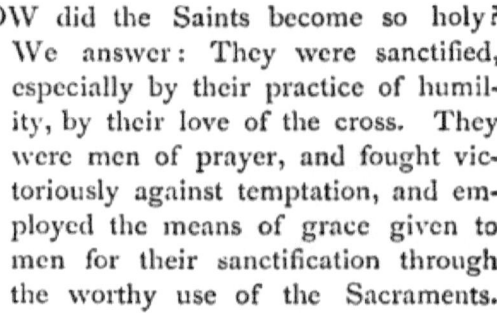OW did the Saints become so holy? We answer: They were sanctified, especially by their practice of humility, by their love of the cross. They were men of prayer, and fought victoriously against temptation, and employed the means of grace given to men for their sanctification through the worthy use of the Sacraments. We have already had occasion to direct attention to the necessity, beauty, and efficacy of these virtues, and to the means of acquiring them. We will add some further reflections on them, because of their extreme importance in the Way of Perfection.

*

As a vessel can not be filled anew, unless we have previously emptied it of its former contents, so also the heart can not receive the gifts of God, unless a thorough knowledge of our own nothingness has freed it from self-love, by which it is naturally filled in consequence of the first sin of man, which made human nature turn away from God to itself.

*

"Prayer," says the catechism, "is a raising of the heart to God." By a law of spiritual attraction, whenever the heart is lifted up to God, God in turn descends into the depths of the heart of the humble.

According to the comparison of Christ Himself, St. John the Baptist was as a shining lantern in the house of Israel. His virtue was protected by self-abnegation, self-contempt, self-abasement. How many, by selfishness, self-esteem, and self-love, fail to keep their light closed up in a lantern, but allow their candle to melt away, and are soon buried in the deepest night!

*

The obscurity which surrounds true humility, by no means lessens the enlightening power of good example. On the contrary, it increases it, as the gloom of night increases the brightness of a burning lamp.

*

Often, when we think that humiliations degrade us in the eyes of others, they do quite the reverse, especially if it is evident that we have been unfairly dealt with, and that we bear the injuries heaped upon us with meekness and patience.

*

How beautiful the eulogium pronounced upon a Saint: "Vir fuit major omni laude, quod nullum voluit cum meruerit omnem!" He was a man above all praise, because, though deserving of all praise, he wished for none.

*

In truth, to wish for no praise merits all praise, because he that refuses to take any praise for himself, gives it all to God.

"Occultare occultationem, hoc magnum est"—to hide the desire of remaining hidden, or, in other words, to conceal the love of being unknown, that is great! A person thus disposed does not seek to appear humble, but contemptible.

*

Swindling is never more dangerous than when committed by prominent members of society. In like manner, self-esteem and vainglory are never more hurtful, than when entertained by those who have been favored with extraordinary gifts of nature and grace.

*

It is easier to find a hat that will protect us from the sun's heat, than one that will shelter us from the heavy rain. In like manner, it is easier to meet with that humility, which is capable of bearing the withering sunshine of praise, than with that, which is requisite to withstand the drenching showers of contempt.

*

Many act in a very humble and unassuming manner to gain a reputation for sanctity. Out upon such latent pride, which apes genuine humility!

*

Christ restored sight to the blind man in the Gospel, by the application of dust mixed with spittle. Both of these ingredients are emblems of contempt for transitory things. You may therefore infer, that no salve has more virtue for the cure of those who are spiritually blind, than a contempt of the world.

*

As God permits the faithful Christian to have some imperfections for his humiliation, so the devil leaves the sinner some virtues to make him still more arrogant. The former, by a knowledge of his weakness, is incited to make new efforts for God and his own salvation. The latter by the light of his apparent goodness, is led to indulge a false security. How terribly he will be undeceived at the hour of death, when it will be too late, too late!

*

To prevent writing from being blurred, we sprinkle sand over it or press it against blotting paper. To preserve our good works free from the stains of self-love and vainglory, we should employ, as sand, the remembrance of that death, which every moment draws nearer—we should meditate upon the shortness of life, which, before another hour has passed, may be over for us. This " *memento mori* " is an excellent means of preserving, pure and unsullied, the record of our lives and of keeping its pages free from the stains of vanity. The blotting paper is an emblem of the acts of humility, prompted by the knowledge of our own unworthiness and of the infinite merits of God.

*

Who would not endure the most painful afflictions, sufferings, and tortures for *one day*, if he were certain that by so doing he would secure perfect bodily happiness for the remainder of his life? Would he not say: After all, it is only for *one day?* And for heaven we are not disposed to suffer willingly, though we know that every day may be our last, and that if our life should last even a million of years, nevertheless, in comparison with approaching eternity, its duration is not as long as the twinkling of an eye.

*

The Apostle affirms that the sufferings of this world can not be compared to the joys, by which they will be rewarded throughout a happy eternity. We may say, with equal truth, that the sinful pleasures of the passions bear no comparison with the torments that rack the sinful soul even in this world. What, then, shall we say of the torments that await the reprobate in the home of endless woe?

*

Divine vengeance never shows itself under a more dreadful form, than when it surrenders the sinner to the cravings of his passions and allows him to find the means of indulging them. The criminal gratification of the unhappy man tends but to increase the weight of that anchor, which will one day drag him to perdition and fasten him to the lowest depths of the unfathomable gulf. On the other hand, God never bestows a greater blessing on His faithful children than when He permits them to meet with oppositions and trials, to draw them nearer to Him, and to prepare for them a place of glory in the highest regions of everlasting bliss.

*

In the preparation of medicines, apothecaries make use of the filtering-cloth, to separate the purer and finer portions from the coarser ingredients. For the soul the best filtering-cloths are the searching interior trials of the heart and mind.

※

Christ says to every one, who aspires to the better gifts: "If any man will come after me, let him deny himself, take up his cross daily, and follow me." He does not use the words, "drag his cross," because they might seem to sanction a slothfulness, wholly unworthy of His disciples. How much better is it to shoulder the cross resolutely, as did the patient Lamb of God, than to draw it behind us, as do so many indifferent Christians! Our Savior proved His love for us by the cross; let us also prove our love for Him by the cross.

※

A piece of metal receives its form and its value, as coin, from the stamp which it bears. It loses nothing by the impression of the stamp, and it gains very much. Contradictions and persecutions are like a stamp for our virtue. They impress on it the mark of genuine merit and of a heavenly reward.

※

A person who is going to carry a heavy load, places upon his shoulders a pad of wool or some other soft substance in order to lessen the pressure. Meekness and humility in our conduct are the wool of the Lamb of

God, which will lighten, to a remarkable degree, the heavy cross of tribulation laid upon us by an all-wise Providence.

*

By being mixed with sugar, the most bitter substance becomes not only palatable, but even savory. Certain fruits, which have a disagreeable, acid taste, make, if put up with sugar, a most exquisite jelly, with just enough native tartness to give a relish to the preparation. In like manner, trials, though themselves bitter to poor human nature, may be so far sweetened by a perfect resignation to the holy will of God, as to become the favorite aliment of our souls.

*

But we must be careful to sweeten fruits in time; otherwise the sugar will not be able to mix with them before we wish to use them. Some persons accept their trials with very bad grace, and make no acts of resignation, until there is no longer any means of escape. Better, far better is it, to make them beforehand; for then no sufferings will be able to embitter our lives. We will experience an incomparable sweetness in serving God, and will constantly grow in merit.

*

Some spices must be crushed before they exhale their perfume. Might not one suppose that this would destroy them entirely? Yet the very reverse is the case. This may serve to show that troubles may apparently crush a man, while in reality they are sent by the hand of the Almighty to draw forth all the hidden sweetness of his virtue.

*

"Blessed is the man who suffers temptations, because when once he is proved by them, he will receive the crown of eternal life." The sufferings caused by temptations are the most painful and the most dangerous. For many, they are the occasion of their departing from God, and from a virtuous life in the service of God. But, on the other side, they have been and are for many, as they were for St. Paul, the occasion of purifying their virtues and of increasing their merits for a happy eternity.

*

Moses, praying with arms outstretched toward heaven, gained a glorious victory for Israel. The two arms used by the Christian in his struggles, are the two reflections: I have but one soul; shall I save or lose it? There is but one eternity; will it be a happy or a wretched one? So long as these thoughts seriously occupy our minds, we need not fear for the final result of our spiritual combat.

*

How beautiful this sentence of St. Augustine: "Lectio inquirit, meditatio invenit; oratio pulsat, contemplatio degustat!" Reading seeks, meditation finds; prayer asks, contemplation tastes.

*

"In every oblation thou shalt offer salt." Mark that the Holy Ghost directs the use of *salt*, not of *sugar*. Salt imparts a savor to victuals, and stands, in this passage of Scripture, for the conditions necessary to make our sacrifices pleasing to God. Be not, therefore, alarmed or annoyed if you feel not that sensible devotion which is so sweet and consoling. What God requires, and what is always in your power, is discretion and prudence, which should always accompany your actions, and preserve you from any excess.

*

The tender feeling, which is commonly termed *sensible* devotion, is all but sensible in one respect, while it is far too sensible in another. Persons who revel in its sweets are often too tender in regard to trials and adversity. They take offense at everything, and let others feel it too. Their devotion is sensitive rather than solid. They are prone to inconstancy, and, by their mawkish sentimentality, often disgust those whose sterner virtue has been proved on Calvary.

*

We speak of the *unction* of devotion. Yes, devotion is a healing unguent for the many wounds made by our daily imperfections. It anoints the heart, and makes it impervious to the stream of troubles which constantly flows over it. It softens the soul, that it may readily yield to the impressions of grace. It soothes the bruises of affliction. It assuages, especially, the pain of the many burnings and scaldings, from which we are certain to suffer when we expose ourselves unwarily to the fire of passion.

*

The Rosary! What a beautiful form of prayer it is, and how dear to the hearts of Mary's loving children! But how often do we say it with so many distractions, that instead of a wreath of beautiful roses, we offer to the Immaculate Mother a crown of thorns!

*

How foolish would you consider a person who, though very thirsty, would leave a fountain, gushing with a limpid stream, from a vain desire of seeing whether, at some other fountain, he may not find water enough to cool his parching tongue! Quite as foolish would he be who, when engaged in mental prayer, would quit a point in which he finds refreshment, with the view of trying whether another point is capable of affecting the heart at all.

*

A person who wishes to get an audience from a king or an emperor, makes the most careful preparation before entering into the presence of that august personage. Not only does he bestow particular attention on his dress, but he studies the very language which he will use. How earnestly, then, should we try to array our hearts in the pure robe of innocence, and to adorn our souls with the choicest virtues, before approaching God in prayer!

How recollected we should be when about to enter into His holy presence! With what reverence and devotion should we be penetrated!

*

No human language can be learned without studying it; nor can the language of prayer, by means of which we hold converse with God. Ah! how few become perfect in it!

*

There are persons with whom we find it difficult to obtain an interview. They are "engaged," or they are "not at home." Even our Lord finds it difficult to speak to them; they are too much occupied with other things to listen to the voice of God; or they are not at home, their thoughts wandering constantly among the distracting occupations of a worldly life.

*

Between solid and mere sensible devotion, the same difference exists as between oil and grease. When heated, they are both equally liquid; but oil remains so even when cooled down, while grease soon becomes thick again. So unreal devotion cools into tepidity and languor when the warmth of sudden fervor has passed away.

*

A similar contrast is remarked in every smelting furnace. In the fiery caldron the slags can scarcely be distinguished from the metal. But as soon as both flow out and harden by exposure to the air, there is no longer any resemblance between them; the metal alone is pure and solid.

*

How consoling it is to revisit our native land, endeared to us by the sweet recollections of childhood! Even a stay of a few days refreshes and invigorates us. Such is the effect produced upon the soul when we perform the *Spiritual Exercises* of St. Ignatius. When we performed them for the first time we were, so to say, born to life and light. Whenever we repeat them, we breathe once more the air of our native land, and feel strengthened to resume, with new fervor, the thorny path up to the mountain of perfection.

*

Moses, who held the tables of the law in his hand, was the same that conversed with God as intimately as a friend is wont to converse with a friend. When he left the sanctuary after that sacred converse, his face shone with a radiant light. This serves to show us that we shall never obey the law as we ought unless we love to hold constant intercourse with God.

*

The prayer of the tepid and distracted soul is but too often a lie, according to the expression of our Lord: "These people honor me with their lips, but their heart is far from me." The aspirations of the fervent Christian, on the contrary, are true, because his lips speak the sentiments of his heart. Such a person can pray with confidence, because He, who searches the secrets of the heart, is a witness to his sincerity. "O God!" may he exclaim, "I love Thee with my whole heart, with my whole soul, with all my strength; and Thou, the Eternal Truth, knowest it."

*

Some pray with so many distractions that they merit the reproach of St. Chrysostom: "You do not understand yourselves; how, then, can you expect God to understand you and give you what you want?" Their prayer is no prayer. Others direct all their attention to the subject of their petition, but do not elevate their hearts to God. They ask, but do not pray.

*

The greatest and most learned saints often confessed, with St. Thomas Aquinas, that they derived far more light from prayer than from study. We may all say the same, for prayer disposes us to live according to our knowledge. The student, whose deep researches are not aided by prayer, may be compared to a man who examines a painting by the feeble glimmer of a lamp; while the one, whose efforts are guided by faith, hope, charity, and prayer, is like the man who beholds the painting in the clear light of the noontide.

*

Generally speaking, those learned men, who derive their knowledge from study alone, resemble canals, which derive their water from other sources. They are but the conveyers of other people's ideas; while the man of prayer draws his thoughts from the depths of his communings with God. This imparts originality to all his views, even on the tritest and most hackneyed subjects.

*

St. Augustine makes this beautiful remark on the phrase *Deo Gratias*—thanks be to God: "Quid melius ut animo geramus et ore promamus et calamo exprimamus quam Deo Gratias? Hoc nec dici brevius nec audiri latius nec intel.igi altius potest." What could the mind think, the lips utter, or the pen write, better than *Thanks be to God?* We can say nothing briefer, hear nothing more comprehensive, think of nothing grander, do nothing worthier.

*

Let us pray in this way, entirely united with the most holy Will of God, and God will also do our will, and more than we ever could wish for our own good.

*

The Niagara Falls present a magnificent picture of human life in its struggles with temptations and the impetuosity of passion. For miles and miles before the cataract forms, floods of water begin to hurry along with impetuous velocity, dashing furiously over the rocks which they meet along their course, and which seem eager to bar their progress. At last they reach the precipice, and, with reckless fury, precipitate themselves into the foaming depths below. Then comes a reaction. The turbulent waters, as if terror-stricken at their own frantic haste, pause a moment and seem to long for rest and peace. But only for a moment! The bed of the stream suddenly descends, and once more all is tumult, noise, and confusion, while the waters dash onward to the *whirlpool*, an immense basin inclosed between deep and rocky banks, towering a hundred feet above. The maddened current is stopped by a perpendicular wall of rock, and forced to cut a passage, by which it discharges itself into Lake Ontario. What a wild contest seems to be raging in the hurrying floods! And how the interest of the view is increased and animated, when logs, floating down the cataract, are raised aloft by the whirling tide and seem almost like living beings engaged in mortal combat— now appearing, now vanishing from the scene, till, by some unexpected stroke, they are hurried into the channel, and are calmly and quietly borne along to their final destination in the lake.

*

In the midst of the tumult of conflicting passions, the sinner, molested and tormented by the contradictions and persecutions of others, and of his own temper and lascivious desires, plunges into the stream of muddy waters, until God, by a wonderful effect of Divine mercy, places some unexpected obstacle in the way of his passions, and almost forces the prodigal to return, by a sincere conversion, to the peace and quiet of home. But disappointed desire will not be so easily deprived of its prey. For a time the sinner struggles in the whirlpool of inveterate habits and evil inclinations, until Divine Providence, by a singular concurrence of circumstances, vouchsafes to assist him with extraordinary means of salvation. He receives the grace to hear a sermon, which touches his heart, to meet with a virtuous friend, to be united in marriage to a virtuous person to witness the death of an acquaintance, as did St. Margaret of Cortona, to read a pious book, as did St. Austin, or to assist at a mission. Then, by seeking for perfect reconciliation with God in the Sacrament of penance, he conquers the tempter and begins to move onward without further disturbance, to his last resting-place, the ocean of a happy eternity.

*

What is powder? Only dust; and yet, what power in it for good, if rightly used? There is another dust, no less powerful, if we would only direct our thoughts toward it during life. Our days, perchance, are bright with the unclouded ray of joy, and death, with careless kindness, seems to pass us by. But, may we not learn a different lesson in the silent graveyard? Go to that quiet city of the dead, take a handful of its dust, and try to realize the doom that awaits you. As surely as the sun now shines, and the summer breeze bends the waving grass upon the graves, or scatters the rose leaves from the bush which affection has planted over the last resting-place of loved ones, so surely shall we one day take up our abode in the silent tomb. O! what a powerful aid against temptation might we not find in such a meditation!

*

Prayer and union with God will pour the waters of pious meditation in copious showers upon our hearts. Good resolutions, formed before the moment of temptation arrives, may be compared to the efforts of the firemen to have all things in readiness before the alarm is sounded. This should admonish us that every motive likely to strengthen our resolutions ought to be called into requisition. Regard for our honor, and even human respect, though but imperfect motives, ought to be summoned to our aid. Quickness, calm, perseverance, and an abundance of water, are the most important requisites for subduing a fire. In the moral order, a calm promptitude at the first sign of danger, perseverance in resisting the temptation, and fervent prayer, are requisite to subdue our passions.

*

It may happen that a nail, even though it has a good head, gives way and bends, but it is not on that account utterly useless. It can be straightened and used again. It may also happen that, in consequence of unforeseen difficulties, our good will and strong resolutions are at first ineffectual, but we should not lose courage on that account. We should endeavor to amend the fault committed, and cheerfully begin anew. Upon second trial, we often act with more energy, charity, and prudence, and thus succeed.

*

The moment that a person endeavors to increase his height, by raising himself on his toes, he begins to stagger, and is unable to withstand a sudden shock. In the moral order, if we seek to elevate ourselves above the reach of temptation, through pride, we lose our safeguard against temptation, and are in great danger of being prostrated at the first attack.

*

The threads of a good net are so close together that a fish, once caught, can not possibly escape. What benefit, then, is it for the poor captive to dart about in its prison, and to look through the many openings upon the scenes amid which it formerly sported? The devil tries to catch souls in the net of temptation, leaving to them many openings of a vain self-confidence, through which they expect some future day to make their escape. But they will be sadly disappointed, and too late will discover that they are indeed captives.

*

We are seized with astonishment and overwhelmed with horror when we read that the heathens sacrificed human beings, and even their own children, to idols. But why do we not experience the same feelings when we consider how infidels, and even persons who call themselves Christians, sacrifice human beings upon the altar of their evil desires, by perverting them and killing their souls, not only for time, but for eternity? They deliberately cast them into the blazing fire of the Moloch of their passions, and finally into the abyss of everlasting fire and torment in hell. Oh, cruelty, far more pitiless than that of heathen barbarism!

*

Though on the road to perfection we are liable to encounter numerous obstacles, it is altogether our own fault if we run against them. They are like stumps, which a little care and experience enable the driver to avoid. If, then, you stumble, blame not the Providence of God, but your own imprudence, which impels you headlong, regardless of the impediments besetting your path.

If the devil has no ally in the fortress of the heart, all is safe. That fortress can never be taken, unless some passion, playing the part of Judas, treacherously surrenders it to the foe.

*

"The devil," as St. Peter tells us, "goes about like a roaring lion, seeking whom he may devour." This wicked spirit is ever on the watch for those souls who fly from his seductive temptations. But, unfortunately, of the majority it may be said that they run after him. He has only to open his mouth and devour them.

*

No matter how many temptations we may have, and how grievous they may be, with God's help we can always resist, and, if we will it, we shall certainly overcome them. The devil has many a cunning snare with which to catch and ruin souls. The best means to defeat his crafty designs is to be very truthful and sincere with our superiors and spiritual directors.

MEANS OF PERFECTION—THE SACRAMENTS.

"BLESSED are those who have not seen and have believed." How beautifully these words are exemplified in every one of the Sacraments! The eye sees nothing but the simplest acts; and yet, how important they are when viewed by the light of Faith! The water flows upon the brow of the neophyte, and, at that instant, streams of grace pour into his soul. From a slave of Satan he becomes an adopted child of God. A throne is erected in heaven and a radiant crown prepared for the future heir to celestial glory. The Bishop signs the forehead with chrism and pronounces a few mysterious words. Instantly the Holy Ghost takes possession of the soul as of His temple, and adorns the heart of the confirmed with His seven gifts. The priest takes bread and wine into his hands. Often he celebrates in a poor log chapel, upon an altar destitute of ornaments, and robed in vestments of the poorest kind. He utters the simple words of consecration, and lo! Jesus descends from heaven, attended by myriads of Angels, who adore Him under the sacred species. O, how beautiful is that host, resplendent with the glory of God Himself, in comparison with which the lustre of the sun, the moon, and the stars is but darkness! From the host Jesus continually sends up to His heavenly Father the incense of Divine adoration, thanksgiving, praise, and prayer. What a magnificent spectacle for the Angels, and those pious souls who daily contemplate it! How simple is the act of absolution, and yet, what a miracle of Divine love! The galling chains of sin are broken, the slave of hell becomes a child of God. How consoling is it to behold a soul fortified, by the simple anointing of the body, for the last fatal combat, and then entering upon her heavenly inheritance! Similar remarks are applicable to the other Sacraments, which relate to the state of man on earth. Holy Orders give him powers, which even the angelic choirs do not share, and elevate him to the dignity of "Vicar of God." The Sacrament of matrimony is an emblem of the union contracted by the Christian soul with God, and destined to be continued for all eternity. Yes, thrice blessed are they that believe, because they see with the eyes of Faith!

*

In the eyes of human pride, it looks humiliating for the man of learning and experience to submit to the advice of his confessor and spiritual adviser. But besides the certain assurance that Divine Wisdom itself guides mankind, by the authority of the legitimate ministers and superiors of the Church, an axiom dictated by mere human prudence declares that "no one is a good judge in his own cause," and another that a physician when sick should call in a fellow-physician to prescribe for him. Hence, when we go to confession, we act in conformity with the teachings of common sense, while, at the same time, we obey the precept of our Divine Savior.

Why go to confession? We sin again, if not in serious matters at least in minor points. And why bathe ourselves? We must do so again on the morrow. Why dress the hair? It will be deranged again. Why weed our gardens? The weeds will soon spring up again. Why eat? Before long we shall be hungry again. No one would consider such questions reasonable. What, then, shall we say of the question: Why do we go to confession?

✻

St. Peter compares the relapsing sinner with a dog coming back to his vomit. Dogs also like to conceal a piece of meat in the ground, but, after a while, they will come back to make use of it. So the sinner going to confession, if he is not really resolved to give up his bad habits, tries to conceal, under the dust of an illusory contrition, the object of his passions; but soon after confession he returns to these hidden pieces to feast on them again.

✻

Smugglers apparently submit to the law; yet, when they have eluded the vigilance of the officer on duty, they chuckle over their success, and consider that fortune has favored them in a special manner. So it is with a certain class of penitents. According to all appearances they confess sincerely; but, at the same time, they congratulate themselves, if their sins are not seen in their true light by the confessor.

✻

When a door is locked with a number of locks, it is not sufficient to open one, for, in that case, it still remains closed. The same thing holds true of the forgiveness of sins. In order that the priest's absolution may open the door of the heart to sanctifying grace, it is not sufficient to confess only a certain number or kind of sins. All the keys must be submitted to the vicar of Christ, the Confessor, that he may open the door to Divine grace.

*

Broken pieces of porcelain, properly cemented together, often adhere all the more firmly. A person who has had the misfortune to fall into sin, may prepare from the dust of true contrition and the tears of penance a cement, that will enable him to persevere, with greater fidelity, in his good resolutions.

*

What is meant by that garment, that ring, those shoes, mentioned by Christ in the parable of the Prodigal Son? The garment is sanctifying grace, the ring is the pledge of fidelity, the shoes are our resolutions to lead a holy life. And what is that banquet prepared for the returning penitent? It is Holy Communion. And those sweet strains of music? They are the union of all our faculties in the service of God; the harmony of the heart and intellect, of the will, memory, and imagination in praise of God.

*

The Sacraments.

Even in nature there are facts calculated to convince scrupulous persons that there may be impressions and convictions which are positively erroneous, notwithstanding an apparent evidence to the contrary. For instance, if you stand in a valley when bells are rung at a certain place, the sound will seem to you to proceed from quite a different direction. But a person standing upon the hill above can easily discern whence the echo comes. The scrupulous person, agitated by various impressions, is like the person in the valley, and ought to look up to the person on the hill, the Confessor, for direction.

*

Blessed is the eye which sheds tears of true repentance! It shall forever contemplate what here no eye has ever seen. Blessed is the ear which listens to the consoling words of absolution! It shall one day hear what no ear has ever heard below. Blessed is the heart which has been wounded with the sword of true contrition! It shall forever feel the joy, which, on this earth, no heart has ever experienced.

THE MOST HOLY EUCHARIST.

KING ASSUERUS, desirous to show the world the greatness of his empire and the richness of his treasures, invited the principal inhabitants of his dominions to a festival, which lasted one hundred and eighty days. In the New Testament, Christ has instituted the Blessed Sacrament, and invited the people of the whole world to a Divine banquet, which has lasted over eighteen hundred years, and which will last to the end of time. Which of the two is the greater banquet?

✱

The banquet of Assuerus was given in a garden. The banquet of Christ is celebrated in the paradise of the Church. For the former, tables were prepared; for the latter, innumerable altars are erected. Courtiers waited on the guests at the tables of Assuerus; Angels throng around the altars of Christ, to minister to the devout Christian. The former are the great ones of earth, the latter are the Ministers of the Most High. There the wine was of the best quality; here the drink is Divine. What a heavenly banquet!

✱

"There is no people that hath its gods so near to it as our God is to our petitions." Thus spoke Moses under the Judaic dispensation. He did not know what was to come, and how much nearer God was yet to draw to the children of the New Covenant. Among the Hebrews there was o ly one temple; there was one tabernacle, to which only the High-priest had access. Among us there are as many temples as there are churches, as many tabernacles as there are altars; and every priest is privileged to approach them. The tabernacle of old held only the tables of the law, and a little manna of the desert; our tabernacles contain the Giver Himself of the law, and of the manna, which only prefigured Him.

*

How useful is the bread-tree! But it will not grow in every climate. In the paradise of the Church, there is a bread-tree—the Holy Eucharist—growing eternal life, as Christ Himself solemnly declares: "He that shall eat of this bread shall have eternal life;" and this tree bears its fruit with equal perfection in every climate and in every season.

*

If the astonishment of Elizabeth, when visited by the Mother of God, was so great that she exclaimed, "Whence is this to me, that the Mother of my Lord and God should come to me?" what ought to be your feelings when Jesus visits you in Holy Communion? And this happiness you may often enjoy. Should not your heart continually entone the Canticle, "Magnificat anima mea Dominum?"

If Christ had deigned to enter into the hearts of those only whose consciences were **never stained** with the guilt of mortal sin, but always remained as pure as that of St. John on the night of the Passion, even then He would have shown us wonderful condescension. But what an excess of **love and mercy, that** He should unite Himself to those **who often crucified** Him in their own hearts! Only think that **He did not** refuse to give Himself even to Judas, who was about to betray Him! What an astonishing prodigy of love!

*

We might well praise God for His love and desire of being with us in the Blessed Sacrament, even if He had given to no one but the Holy Father, His Vicar on earth, the power of changing bread and wine into his Body and Blood, and if the consecrated species had been allowed to remain only in one Church in the Eternal City. What infinite praise, then, should be given to Him, who, like a good shepherd, is always with his flock in the Blessed Sacrament!

*

When Jacob received the blessing of primogeniture, his appearance was that of Esau, but the voice and the person were his own. The sacramental species likewise seems to be only bread and wine, but the voice which speaks to our hearts, and the Being who enters them, are truly Divine. The fervent Christian hears that voice with delight, and feels the presence of his Lord. In the Blessed Sacrament, Christ gives to the devout soul, together with His blessing, the right to eternal happiness.

When David was gathering materials for the future temple, he explained his anxiety in these words: "The work I undertake is great, because I am preparing a dwelling-place, not for man, but for God Himself." How great, then, should be our care and solicitude to prepare a worthy habitation for our Lord, who comes to us at the moment of Holy Communion! Should we not heap up the precious treasures of virtue, that we may adorn our hearts with them?

*

A legend tells us, that Christ Himself, accompanied by His holy Angels, came to bless the Church of Einsiedlen, in Switzerland. Hence the commemoration of that mysterious ceremony, called "The Angels' Consecration." When Christ, attended by the heavenly court, enters the heart of the child, prepared for the first time for Holy Communion, He also consecrates a living temple to the honor of his heavenly Father.

*

The priest, when saying mass, washes the tips of his fingers, to indicate how pure and free from every imperfection should be the heart which is preparing to receive the Holy of Holies in the Blessed Sacrament.

*

When Christ first distributed Holy Communion to the Twelve, there was one who received unworthily. Have we not good grounds to fear that among those who approach the Holy Table at Easter only, there may often be found a Judas?

What was the astonishment of the Jews on beholding Christ eat with sinners! Think, then, what should be ours, since we know that Jesus not only eats with sinners, but gives Himself to them as nourishment? For in a greater or less degree we are all sinners. "Non solum cum peccatoribus manducare vis, sed Te ipsum ab illis manducari jubes!" exclaimed St. Jerome, when the Holy Viaticum was given to him on his death-bed. "O res mirabilis!" sings the Church, "manducat Dominum, pauper servus et humilis!"

*

Mephiboseth, the son of Jonathan, though himself a prince, hearing that David had invited him always to eat at the royal table, exclaimed, in the humility of his heart, that he was wholly unworthy of such a favor. Oh! what a deep sense of our unworthiness should we not have on approaching the Holy Table, when we consider that the King of Heaven has invited us to partake of His banquet of love!

*

The Sacramental species is like the border of Christ's garment. Let us approach it with a faith as lively as that of the sick woman in the Gospel; and no doubt we shall feel, as she did, the healing power of its touch. We shall be cured of the infirmities of our daily imperfections, and freed from all attachment to the joys of this world.

*

Were there no Blessed Sacrament, what joy should we experience on hearing the Guardian Angel awaken us with the words: "Rise, Jesus is coming to thee this morning!" Oh! with what happiness would your heart be filled, with what impatience would you await the coming of the Divine Guest! Do you feel thus on the morning of your Holy Communion? Surely you ought to be equally happy.

*

If the Angels were capable of envy, they would be tempted when they see the children of men receive the Lord in Holy Communion, and behold the immense treasures of grace imparted to them. Scripture relates that when a banquet was given to the Prodigal, upon his return to his father's house, the son who had always remained with his parents, was angry at the honors heaped upon one whom he considered unworthy of them. This is a type of that holy envy, which even the Angels might experience, when they behold the banquet given to the sons of men, once lost but now found again.

*

When the Son of God became man for our salvation, He descended to earth without leaving heaven; and when He had accomplished His mission He returned to heaven without wholly quitting the earth. Now, as ever, He dwells among us in the Most Blessed Sacrament of the Altar. O, how strong are the ties of love which detain Him a prisoner in the Tabernacle

*

By Holy Communion, Christ, the Word made flesh, seems to make all men, who receive Him worthily, sharers in the great mystery of the Incarnation. For His Divinity being inseparably united to His Humanity, not only His flesh and blood, but His very Godhead, are incorporated with us. O, what an unspeakable honor to human nature!

※

No leaven whatever is mixed with the Sacramental bread. This ought to teach you that when going to Holy Communion not the slightest feeling of aversion, enmity, or ill-will should sour your feelings toward your neighbor.

※

The Apostle advises us to bear with us, at all times and in all places, "the good odor of Christ." This fragrant odor should be especially perceptible on the day of Communion, when Christ Himself has entered our heart. Our tongues should diffuse this odor, because they have touched Jesus, and our very breath should exhale the perfume of His presence. All who approach us should feel that we have been penetrated with the fragrance of His Divine virtues.

※

If, in the morning, a person puts a strong aromatic spice into his mouth, its odor will remain so long as nothing else is taken. The Most Holy Eucharist is a heavenly spice. It is that Body which Mary Magdalen anointed with precious spikenard; it is that Body embalmed with spices by Joseph of Arimathea and Nicodemus on the day of its deposition in the Sepulchre; it is that Body which was overshadowed by the Holy Ghost and enriched with Divine virtues. Indeed, Holy Communion should impart to all our thoughts, desires, and affections, no less than to our words and actions a celestial perfume, delightful to every one who approaches us.

✻

Perfumes placed among articles of clothing serve as a protection against moths, which would insensibly destroy the texture, while at the same time they impart a delicious fragrance, which the clothes exhale as if it belonged to them. The Blessed Sacrament, worthily received, is celestial perfume for our hearts. While preserving us from the many imperfections which would otherwise feed upon our good actions themselves, it likewise imbues us so deeply with the good odor of Christ, that virtue seems to be the natural offspring of our soul.

✻

When an earthly king enters a city, the question is not how well his subjects desire to receive him, but how they actually do receive him. But the King of heaven is pleased to accept the good will for the deed. A longing desire to receive Him, and an effort to prepare the little tabernacle of our heart in a becoming manner, are the most certain means of drawing His blessings upon us, when He so far stoops to our lowliness as to enter into our bosom.

✻

Christ advises you to take the lowest seat when you are invited to a banquet. If you do so from a sense of humility, you will be the nearest to Him, who calls

Himself "the last of men." Approach Him, especially at the banquet of Holy Communion, with this sense of humility, as the unworthiest of all.

*

"Let us rise and go hence," said Jesus to His disciples after giving them Communion. "Let us go and die with Him," was the exclamation of His followers. Readiness, zeal to advance with alacrity and courage in the path of piety—these should be the feelings produced in us by Holy Communion. Let us prove its efficacy, not only by sweet aspirations of devotion, but by heroic acts of virtue.

*

As soon as the sun's rays touched the manna, it melted away. As soon as the rays of mere worldly thoughts and desires touch the mind, the efficacy of Holy Communion, that heavenly manna, is gone. Remain, therefore, after Communion, in the quiet of meditation, and spend a considerable time in fervent thanksgiving.

*

As the palate discovered in the manna every variety of taste, so the heart finds in the Holy Eucharist every kind of grace. The poor, the persecuted, the suffering, the tempted, the happy, the fervent Christian, who hungers after Divine love and thirsts after holiness—each one tastes in Communion what he most desires, Jesus, the fountain of life and grace.

*

If Jesus is the true tree of life, every Communion is a new tree planted in the garden of the heart, to bring forth the fruits of everlasting life. Oh, what an Eden of happiness there must be in the hearts of those who often communicate worthily!

*

The reciprocal relation between the different states or branches, if we may so call them, of Christ's Church, is called "the Communion of Saints." There is an exchange of good offices and suffrages and love between earth and heaven, and that exchange can not take place till after the act of Divine consecration, by which the Saints are completely transformed unto the likeness of God.

*

If, according to the words of Christ, "the eyes which behold Him are blessed," how infinitely blessed must be the tongue which receives Him, and the lips which are moistened with His Blood! How favored the heart which He makes His abode! How honored the body with which He unites His own most precious Body and Soul in Holy Communion!

*

Esther, desirous to avert the doom hanging over her race, did not urge her request until Assuerus was seated at table, thinking that he would then be more disposed to grant it, and she was not disappointed. If you only knew how anxious Jesus is to grant your petitions, when we partake of the holy banquet of Communion, your prayers would long since have been heard. Haman, representing your predominant passion, would have been put to death, and you would be happy and secure against his designs.

*

After having partaken of our meals, we usually spend some time in conversing with our friends. After having tasted of the Divine banquet, we should remain with Jesus, and converse with Him as long as possible.

*

To reap an abundant harvest of spiritual fruit during Mass, you should assist at that Holy Sacrifice, spiritually arrayed in garments similar to those worn by the priest at the altar. The alb is emblematical of a good intention, and the girdle of the heartfelt reverence with which we must assist at the Sacrifice. The maniple denotes contrition; the stole crossed upon the breast, our love for Jesus crucified. The chasuble is an indicative of our efforts to make progress in perfection. The chalice is an emblem of hope and confidence in Divine Providence. The bread and wine denote our desire of daily offering to the Lord something which might prove an obstacle to our advancement in virtue. Ah, how sad it is that the vestments in the sacristy of the heart are often as poor and mean as those in the sacristy of the humblest little country chapel!

*

Christ instituted the Blessed Sacrament as a commemoration of His Passion. Alas! how often He is really crucified again by the unworthy reception of His precious Body and Blood!

Happy the priest to whom it is permitted to say Mass every day! Thrice happy the one, who, on Christmas, celebrates thrice! Infinitely happy the one to whom that power has been given, of which the Church sings: "Quibus datum est ut offerant et sumant ipsi et dent ceteris libamen hoc dulce et suave!"

*

Happy, especially, the priest who, with the power of consecrating, carries with him his Lord and Savior! We may apply to him the words of the Angel to Mary: "The Lord is with thee;" and his flock may hail his approach with the welcome strain: "Blessed is he who cometh in the name of the Lord, and who bringeth with him the God of heaven Himself." That was a solemn "fiat" by which God created the world. Yet how infinitely more solemn was the "est" by which Christ consecrated the Holy Eucharist, and by which daily and hourly the stupendous miracle of transubstantiation is renewed upon our altars!

*

By the power of that creative "fiat" the sun shone forth in the firmament of the visible heavens. In virtue of this mightier "est," the Sun of Grace illumines the firmament of the Holy Church.

*

St. Paul says: "Whoso approacheth God, must believe that He recompenseth every good." This is especially true of Holy Communion, by which the Lord deigns to come to us. A living faith in His real presence, united with great confidence in His infinite goodness, is the best preparation for Holy Communion.

*

The prophets had a longing desire for the coming of Christ, the promised Messiah. But if they had known how replete with grace His advent was to be, and what blessings He was to bestow upon the devout members of the Church by His real presence in the Blessed Sacrament, and especially by giving Himself to them in Holy Communion, how great would not have been their anxiety to participate in the advantages of the New Covenant!

*

One day, while preparing for the holy Table, St. Gertrude implored the Blessed Virgin and all the Saints to infuse into her soul the zeal and love which filled their own. Hereupon Christ appeared to her, assuring her that her request was granted, and she would really receive Him in her heart, adorned with the jewels of the desire of all the Saints in heaven for Holy Communion.

*

Saints have sometimes seen Angels adorning, with fragrant flowers, the altar upon which Mass was to be celebrated. Those heavenly spirits are much more anxious still to beautify the heart, which Jesus is about to honor by His presence.

*

The Angels bring us a variety of gifts from heaven, but the priest, by consecration, brings us the Giver of all gifts. The Angels rejoice at the reconciliation of a sinner with God; priests, by their absolution, bring about that reconciliation. What a sublime dignity is the priesthood, superior even to that of the Angels! The Angels, though intrusted with the salvation of souls, are continually absorbed in the contemplation of the Divine Essence. So priests, too, should be zealous in promoting, by day and by night, the salvation of souls; but, at the same time, never forget God, for whose love they are endeavoring to save souls created to His image.

*

Christ said that He had not whereon to lay His head. Christians can never make this complaint. We have whereon to lay our heads in sweet repose, when tired and exhausted by the vexations of the world. Behold the Disciple whom Jesus loved. See him at the Last Supper, resting his head upon the bosom of the Savior. "But," you may say, "I am not St. John, and Jesus is no longer upon earth." Be not discouraged; the same place of repose is still on earth. It is the Sacred Heart of Jesus, ever present in the Blessed Sacrament. When, by a worthy Communion, He has entered into your bosom, what can prevent you from reposing upon His Heart? He invites you to do so, when He says: "Come to me, all you that labor and are burdened, and I will refresh you."

*

Blessed be the earth, which bears the grain used in making Hosts for consecration! Blessed be every drop of dew and rain, which moistens it! Blessed be the first ray of the sun which fosters it! Blessed be the air which refreshes it! Blessed be every sunbeam which ripens it! Blessed, thrice blessed, be all that aids in making it the element of the Holy Eucharist!

*

Blessed be the earth which yields the grapes used in making wine for consecration! Blessed be the stem, the fruit, the refreshing rain, the ripening sun, and all that contributes to prepare this other element of the Holy Eucharist! *Cant.* v. 2.

*

Blessed also be the tree which furnished the wood of which the tabernacle is made, or the stone and marble of which is formed this small dwelling-place in which Jesus Christ lives on earth among men until the end of time! Then all who belonged to Him on earth will be forever united with Him in heaven, where our own heart will be the permanent tabernacle of the Sacred Heart of Jesus through all eternity. Amen.

THE STATE OF PERFECTION.

THE religious life may be compared to the garden of Paradise, in which, as Holy Scripture testifies, God placed all that was pleasing to the eye and delightful to the taste. For all that can be charming to the soul desirous to serve God, is found in the religious state. The four streams which water this paradise and fertilize it, are the vows, the rules, the constitutions, the daily occupations. The tree of life in the midst of the garden is the Blessed Sacrament, always present under the same roof. The Cherub keeping guard at the entrance is fidelity to the duties of the religious profession. There is also a tree of the knowledge of good and evil, but it no longer bears forbidden fruit; on the contrary, the greatest blessing of the religious consists in knowing, by the vows, the rules, and the word of the Superior, how to distinguish good from evil, and in all things to accomplish the holy will of God.

Adam, by his fall, sundered the bonds which united the human race with God. He evidently offended against the spirit of the three religious vows, because he sinned by disobedience, by an inordinate desire of possession, and by a longing for sensual delights. But, through the merits of the Redeemer, sin has given us an occasion to render ourselves especially pleasing in the sight of God, by the observance of the three religious vows. We can thus attain a higher degree of perfection than was granted to man, in the state of original justice, because we thus live an angelic life even before participating in the joys of heaven.

*

The children of the world wonder how souls, binding themselves by religious vows, and renouncing the pleasures of the senses, can be joyous. Is it not rather surprising that beings, created according to God's image and for the possession of heavenly bliss, should seek happiness in the vain and trifling pleasures of the earth? Happy the man who, on entering a religious Order, bids farewell to everything, so as to verify the declaration that "nothing of the world remained in him save a contempt for it!"

*

Without order, there is no beauty, no power, no permanent success. Without order, there is no real comfort, no useful employment of time, no silence, no solid virtue, no perfection. The very name of a religious family or community, living together under a rule, approved by the Holy Church, seems to indicate as much. For such a family is called an *Order*. Should not this convince us of the great value and importance of order?

*

The religious Order, known under the name of the *Society of Jesus*, was established on the anniversary of the Assumption of the Blessed Virgin Mary. The day on which commemoration is made of our Blessed Lady's entrance into the Society of Jesus in heaven, St. Ignatius and his companions chose for the establishment of their Society. On that day, in a little chapel on the Mount of Martyrs, near Paris, they consecrated themselves to the service of religion. Could the infant Order have selected a more appropriate day or place?

*

It is worth notice that certain privileged classes, which princes wish to honor with special marks of distinction, are called *Orders*. The honor attached to membership in such a body is especially great, when conferred on only a few, and as a reward for extraordinary services, rendered by the subject to his sovereign or the state. He that is called to a religious life enjoys a similar distinction, all the more honorable in proportion to the limited number of those that follow a religious vocation, and to the merits of the Order whose insignia he wears.

*

How consoling it is for a person, who has passed through his noviciate and makes his profession in an Order of his choice, to reflect that Christ, surrounded by the members of the Order, who are now in glory, invests him, as a new Knight of the Cross, with the insignia of His special favor and distinction!

*

The essential part, the very life of every religious Order or community, consists in the three vows, which are called the Evangelical Counsels. These are typified, and their influence in the sanctification of our lives is shadowed forth in many passages of Holy Scripture, as, for instance, in the offering of the three Magi, the first offering made by the Gentiles to Christ. Gold, the purest and most precious of metals, points to the vow of Obedience, by which the intellect, the noblest power of the soul, is consecrated to the service of God. As gold communicates its own splendor and value to articles comparatively common, so obedience imparts to our most ordinary actions the splendor and value of true virtue.

✻

Frankincense points to the sacrifice of all sensual pleasures, through chastity, which causes man to forget that he has a body, leading him to direct all his thoughts and desires toward heaven, and to long for God alone, in whom he expects to find perfect happiness.

✻

Myrrh points to the sacrifice which the will makes, through poverty, of all the goods of this world. Of our own free will we renounce the possession of all things, and proclaim our readiness to drain the cup of poverty to the very dregs. Oh, what royal gifts! By bestowing them we earn the right of dwelling forever with Christ, the King of kings.

✻

Sacrifice is the highest act of Divine worship. But no sacrifice is so complete as that wherein the victim is *self*. Such is the sacrifice made by the religious, when he binds himself by vows.

By the vow of poverty, man sacrifices to God the whole exterior world, renouncing the possession of all things whatsoever, so that he is no longer master of anything but himself. But, by the vow of chastity, he sacrifices his body also, so that, in some sense, it is no longer his. His will, however, still remains his own, and, by indulging it, he still exercises the authority of a master. This he likewise surrenders, by the vow of obedience, and so immolates himself as a perfect holocaust to the service of God.

*

In the world, a hero is decked with the crown of victory when he has subdued new countries. In heaven, the Christian who despises every earthly good, for God's sake, and, by the vow of poverty, entirely defeats his mortal enemy, covetousness, will be crowned with the never-fading laurels of victory.

*

In the world, the soldier gains renown when he stands undaunted in the midst of his enemies, and cuts his way through their inclosing ranks. In heaven, great glory awaits him, who, by the vow of chastity, gains a complete mastery over his own body, and, while still clothed with rebellious flesh, lives as if he had shaken it off, together with all its lusts and cravings.

*

Lastly, in the world, he is called great who governs millions and makes laws according to his own pleasure. In heaven, he is looked upon as truly noble, who, by holy obedience, freely submits his own will to that of his Superiors and regards them as the representatives of Christ. Such a man understands the art of governing himself, which is avowedly far more difficult than that of dictating to others?

*

Every master claims the right to command and exacts obedience from his servants, whether they approve of his orders or not. What reason, then, have the children of the world to condemn the practice of blind obedience in the service of Him, who is the Master of all, the Lord of Lords!

*

Military discipline, in particular, is excessively strict. It exacts from soldiers the most punctual and unhesitating obedience. The slightest breach of discipline is severely punished, and in time of war sometimes subjects the offender to death. Why, then, condemn docility to the laws of God, and particularly the obedience of religious to their Superiors? The members of religious Orders are the soldiers of the militant Church. Why, then, should they not be allowed to follow the maxims of obedience and subordination?

*

By blind obedience the religious saves time, and the price of time, as St. Chrysostome observes, is even God Himself; because, by employing it well, we gain heaven, the essential source of whose joy is God. When, therefore, the religious are in doubt regarding any matter, they may spare themselves the trouble of examining; holy obedience will decide for them.

*

In the savings-bank of Divine Providence, obedience places the capital of all our talents and virtue, so as to draw the highest interest of merit. For, as Scripture says, obedience is better than sacrifice. Yet, we know, that sacrifice is by nature the noblest act of Divine worship. How anxious we should be to make heavy deposits in that bank!

*

Holy obedience is the most accurate time-piece that we can find to regulate our actions in such a manner as not to lose a moment of time. It not only points out the hour, but tells us what particular duty we must then perform. The rules and constitutions of religious Orders are the wheels and the machinery of that clock. The authority of the Superior is the weight which causes the pendulum to move in an orderly manner, neither too quickly nor too slowly, but steadily and constantly.

*

One mode of catching birds is to place a net upon the ground and decoy them with grain. The net is then quickly drawn, and the unsuspecting victims are in the power of their captor. Suppose a man should see a few birds in the net, and, eager to secure them, should draw it, regardless of the advice of another, who, standing on a higher spot, and seeing a great number of birds flocking to the net, beckons to his comrade to wait. Would you not consider that man very foolish? By his eagerness to secure a few, he frightens the rest away, and thus loses much more than he gains. The religious who does not blindly follow the behests of obedience is no less foolish. He pursues what to him seems the better way of acting, because he does not see the immense treasures of graces and spiritual favors which Divine Providence has in store for him. "Vir obediens loquetur victorias" —the obedient man shall speak of victories.

*

It is of no consequence whether a ruler is made of wood or of gold. All that is necessary is to hold it steady. The will of the Superior in a religious house should be like a ruler for those under his authority. Use this ruler as a guide for your actions, be careful not to change its direction, and all will be well.

*

Though a person should keep this ruler steady, if he pays no attention to its direction, his lines may still be crooked. In the same manner, the commands of the Superior are of no spiritual advantage if they are interpreted by inferiors according to their own personal whims and caprices.

*

If we modify the orders of superiors according to our own views, we act as school-boys who take their teacher's ruler and pare it down in order to improve it. Instead of attaining their end, they of course succeed only in making it more crooked. The commands of the Superior give those under his charge a degree of security which they could never have attained by themselves. This is confirmed by the very construction of the word. For *command* is derived from the Latin *mandare*, which is composed of two others, *manum* and *dare*, meaning to extend the hand and assist another. God, through the command of the Superior, extends His hand to the obedient religious to lead him in the way of salvation and perfection.

✱

Glass is not of itself a mirror. It becomes one when coated with quicksilver. Man, left to his own judgment, has a very indistinct view of the manner in which he should act, or rather of the correctness of his actions. But, by the union of his judgment and will with those of his Superior, he can more clearly distinguish right from wrong, particularly in the mysterious ways by which Divine Providence sometimes guides souls to the sublime heights of perfection.

✱

In a religious Order, the will of the inferior is a mirror in which the will of the Superior is to be reflected. Unfortunately, the image is often distorted. For, owing to human weakness or malice, the subject often presents a concave or a convex, instead of a plane surface.

✱

Owing to the elasticity of ivory, a billiard ball, when touched by the cue, readily moves in the direction intended by the player. This may serve to illustrate what should be the disposition of religious under the guidance of Divine Providence. Were they always to conform with perfect readiness to the will of God, and willingly yield to the impulse given them, how surely would they reach their final destination!

*

Happy will be the lot of him who possesses this spirit of conformity, and who always moves under the direction of the Superior; but woe, eternal woe, to him who allows himself to be borne hither and thither by his own wayward fancy! In a religious community, the Superior indicates to those under his charge the way in which they must walk. But he does not expect them to go on in it blindly, at the risk of falling into every pit and striking against every obstacle. He could never sanction such rashness, because he knows too well the injunction of St. Paul: "Rationabile obsequium vestrum"—let your obedience be reasonable. Enter, then, blindly upon the way pointed out by obedience, but walk in it cautiously.

*

To do everything in the most perfect manner—this was the wonderful vow of St. Teresa. Every fervent child of Holy Church should conform his life to the spirit of this vow, and always strive to advance in the path of virtue. Ever since the Lord uttered His omnipotent *fiat*, every power of nature, every creature of God, urged on by the immutable law of nature, strives to reach its own state of perfection. All labor to perform their duties with the utmost fidelity. In the motion of the sun, and of all the heavenly constellations, we may see a most beautiful example of this wonderful fidelity, this desire to abide in the service of God, and the performance of His holy will. What a constant lesson for us, who are endowed with immortal souls and reasoning powers! Let us try at all times to perform the most holy will of God, and never grow weary in our endeavors to attain perfection. May this glance at the universe increase in each one of us this earnest desire, and may every one of the *Views* proposed for our consideration contribute to the same end.

*

And now, dear reader, we conclude this gallery of our Photographic Views. We hope you understand their meaning and their bearing. They are so many little stars, shining in the firmament of truth; they are so many cells of the spiritual hive, in which the mind can store away for future use the honey gathered from the blossoms of moral reflections. They are so many sheaves, taken from the field of truth; they are so many pearls, fished up from the vast ocean of thought. We might have continued them to greater length, but we are mindful of the poet's admonition to be moderate:

"Est modus in rebus, sunt certi denique fines."

We trust that the views we have presented in this volume will have made upon the reflecting reader this impression: That moral and revealed truths are not isolated, not disjointed and standing apart, but are connected with all other truths in the visible and invisible world. He that loves God rejoices that everything speaks to his heart of Him whom he loves above all things else, and in whom he will one day see everything as it is in its Divine prototype, when he will behold God, the eternal truth, no longer reflected " as in a mirror, but face to face," in His own Divine Essence. Amen.

www.ingramcontent.com/pod-product-compliance
Lightning Source LLC
Chambersburg PA
CBHW022334230426

43664CB00040B/630